CHINA
and
TAIWAN

CHINA and TAIWAN

Cross-Strait Relations Under Chen Shui-bian

Sheng Lijun

ZED BOOKS, London & New York

INSTITUTE OF SOUTHEAST ASIAN STUDIES, Singapore

Cover photograph: President Chen Shui-bian delivering his inaugural speech, "Taiwan Stands Up: Advancing to an Uplifting Era" (*Courtesy of the Department of Information and Cultural Affairs, Ministry of Foreign Affairs, Taiwan.*)

First published in Singapore in 2002 by
Institute of Southeast Asian Studies
30 Heng Mui Keng Terrace, Pasir Panjang, Singapore 119614

E-mail: publish@iseas.edu.sg
Website: http://www.iseas.edu.sg/pub.html

First published in North America and Europe in 2002 as a copublication by
Zed Books Ltd
7 Cynthia Street, London N1 9JF, UK, and
Room 400, 175 Fifth Avenue, New York, NY 10010, USA.

Distributed in the USA exclusively by Palgrave, a division of St Martin's Press, LLC, 175 Fifth Avenue, New York, 10010, USA.

Zed ISBN 1 84277 318 6 (cased)
Zed ISBN 1 84277 319 4 (limp)

A catalogue record for this book is available from the British Library.
Library of Congress Cataloging-in-Publication Data has been applied for.

ISEAS Library Cataloguing-in-Publication Data

Sheng, Lijun.
   China and Taiwan: Cross-strait relations under Chen Shui-bian.
   1. Taiwan—Foreign relations—China.
   2. China—Foreign relations—Taiwan.
   3. Chinese reunification question, 1949–
   4. Chen, Shui-bian, 1951–
   5. Taiwan—Politics and government—1988–
   I. Title.
DS799.63 C5S54   2002   sls2002010878

ISBN 981-230-110-0 (soft cover)
ISBN 981-230-097-X (hard cover)

Typeset by International Typesetters Pte. Ltd.
Printed in Singapore by Seng Lee Press Pte. Ltd.

Contents

1

Introduction

Since his election on 18 March 2000, Taiwan's new President Chen Shui-bian has surprised many people by his flexibility in handling the tension across the Taiwan Strait. He has not adopted the provocative style of his predecessor Lee Teng-hui, and as he himself often did before becoming President. Instead, he repeatedly appealed for improved relations with Beijing. Taking his cue from the historic reconciliation between North Korean leader Kim Jong Il and his South Korean counterpart Kim Dae Jung in their summit in Pyongyang in mid-June 2000, Chen invited Chinese President Jiang Zemin for a summit "to shake hands and reconcile in creating a historic moment". He said, "If North and South Korea can, why can't the two sides of the [Taiwan] strait?" For inspiration, he even placed in his study a picture of the Korean leaders shaking hands at their summit.[1]

Though it is too early to say what will become of the two Koreas, their dramatic summit, after fifty years of military confrontation, with reunification as their jointly declared target, is historic enough. However, a cross-strait summit along the lines of the Korean summit is unlikely to take place soon. There are several reasons for this.

The first and foremost reason is that, as the former head of Taiwan's Mainland Affairs Council (MAC), Chang King-yuh, has noted, "[T]he two Koreas do not have a problem of whether there is one Korea or whether they are Korean".[2] Both the Koreas strongly and consistently embrace the notion of one nation, one people, and eventual reunification.

Chen and the ruling Democratic Progressive Party (DPP) have so far refused to accept the notion of one China, even if they could interpret this "one China" as the Republic of China (ROC) instead of the People's Republic of China (PRC). Chen insists that "the summit should not be limited by preconditions"[3] — that is, Beijing's insistence on the "one China" principle.

While the two Koreas firmly recognize each other as being part of one nation, Chen, the DPP, and many people in Taiwan do not consider themselves as belonging to the same nation as the Chinese on the mainland, though they recognize, as Chen said in his presidential inauguration speech, that "[T]he people across the Taiwan Strait share the same ancestral, cultural, and historical background".[4] Chen has not accepted China's demand to say he is "*zhongguoren*" [Chinese].[5]

During Lee Teng-hui's twelve years in power, the percentage of people in Taiwan who considered themselves as solely Chinese dropped from 48.5 per cent in January 1993 to 13.1 per cent in mid-1999. Those who considered themselves Taiwanese rather than Chinese increased from 16.7 per cent to 44.8 per cent for the same period. Those who said that they were both Taiwanese and Chinese increased from 32.7 per cent to 39.9 per cent.[6]

The leaders of the Koreas accepted reunification as their common target for the summit, and declared in their joint declaration "to work for the reunification in this direction in the future".[7] On the other hand, Chen only listed reunification as one of many options, and insisted that there should be "no pre-set direction" for cross-strait talks.

Secondly, Kim Dae Jung, a world-renowned advocate of democracy, did not set democracy against reunification. When asked whether North Korea's Stalinist-style authoritarianism was any problem to reunification, he replied that pushing for reunification "is not conditional, but a compulsory and absolute responsibility".[8]

In Taiwan, in his twelve years in office, Lee set democratization against reunification (listing democracy in China as one precondition for reunification talks), used indigenization against national identification with "one China", and exploited cross-strait tensions for internal politics.

The concern of the South Koreans over democracy may manifest itself later on, but it did not stop them from agreeing to reunification and to the historic summit in that direction. On the contrary, an opinion poll conducted in 2000 demonstrated that 76.6 per cent of the people in Taiwan insisted that there should be no talks on unification until the mainland started the process of democratization.[9]

Thirdly, the two Koreas are more or less equal to each other both geographically and in population size while China dwarfs Taiwan. Taiwan does not enjoy the same international recognition and protection by the U.S. military as does South Korea. However, China currently does not have a clear edge over Taiwan militarily, much less in terms of its internal social and political cohesion.

Fourthly, the two Koreas have used a top-down approach with high-level contacts first. Taiwan and China have used a bottom-up approach, with more than a decade of business, tourist, and cultural exchanges. However, as demonstrated below, Beijing could only take the bottom-up approach since Taipei had rejected its proposal for a top-down approach.

With these differences, a cross-strait summit for reunification will not come about easily. This research focuses on the latest developments in cross-strait relations, that is, from Lee Teng-hui's announcement in July 1999 of the "two states" theory to a year after Chen Shui-bian's election as Taiwan's new President. The first part of the study shows how Lee's "two states" theory came about, and its impact on Beijing. The second part focuses on Chen Shui-bian's election and his mainland policy. The third part discusses the reorientation in China's Taiwan policy.

In the 18 March 2000 presidential election, the Kuomintang (KMT) government was defeated by the pro-independence DPP for the first time after fifty-five years in power in Taiwan. With Chen Shui-bian's election, many people in Beijing questioned the feasibility of their existing Taiwan policy:

- whether the "peaceful reunification strategy" would still work?
- whether the United States merely wants to maintain cross-strait stability; or promote Taiwan's final independence; or use Taiwan not only to slow China's rise but also to eventually dismember China?
- whether China should continue to follow Deng Xiaoping's policy of keeping a low profile and avoiding conflict if this policy cannot stop the determined push from both Taiwan and the United States?
- whether China's modernization would be better served by solving the Taiwan problem now or later?
- whether force can eventually be avoided in solving the Taiwan problem? If not, would it cost more to use it now or later?

Though once a radical advocate of independence for Taiwan, Chen, after the election, has not taken the provocative style of his predecessor, Lee Teng-hui. The reasons include the fact that, unlike Lee, he has not yet consolidated his control at home beyond challenge. Secondly, he is different from Lee in a number of important aspects, such as his strategic assessment of mainland China.

After the Tiananmen incident of 1989 and the Soviet collapse in 1991, the world expected a follow-up collapse of the Beijing government. With such a strategic misperception, London moved away from the co-operation of the 1980s to confrontation with Beijing on Hong Kong's hand-over back to China, and Washington brushed China off and began to read Japan as its future strategic challenge. Following China's surprising rise, however, Washington, from the second half of 1993, turned around to view China as a future strategic rival, and hence formulated the U.S. China policy of engagement and containment. London, for its own interests, began to soften its confrontation with Beijing, after realizing that the Beijing government's collapse was not imminent, at least not before Hong Kong's hand-over in 1997.[10]

However, Lee Teng-hui was persistent in his belief that Beijing would collapse soon. In fact, he stated this several times in 1996 and told Taiwanese businessmen not to invest heavily in China. Hence, his China policy of *jieji yongren* (go slow and be patient).[11]

This perception accounted heavily for Lee's highly provocative stance towards Beijing. If one perceives otherwise, one will then have to be very cautious. Should Taiwan become an independent state in future, it would have to avoid tensions with its giant next-door neighbour, not as a favour to China but for its own interests. If Chen, on the other hand, perceives that Beijing is not likely to collapse, no matter how much he favours Taiwan's independence, his strategic choices would certainly be different from those of Lee.

In contrast to Lee's provocative style, Chen has been very careful in his words and made many conciliatory remarks. Lee Teng-hui, based on the perception mentioned earlier, did not try to stabilize cross-strait relations but instead launched one big wave after another in cross-strait relations. He believed that the controversy generated would benefit Taipei in the end. "The more controversy, the better".[12] On the contrary, Chen Shui-bian wants to stabilize cross-strait relations. Lee did not want to negotiate with Beijing on a binding cross-strait framework because he believed, as expressed in his book *Taiwan de Zhuzhang* [Taiwan's Viewpoint], that China would disintegrate.[13] He was strongly against the American proposal to have an "interim agreement" for cross-strait stability. However, Chen is keen to have such a binding framework and, on his own initiative, raised the proposal of an "interim agreement" with Washington.[14] He even proposed to Beijing, in his 2001 New Year speech, to consider a gradual integration across the strait.

The future of cross-strait relations depends on at least two factors. First, how will Chen elaborate and concretize his currently broad and abstract cross-strait proposal of "integration"? Secondly, will the ruling DPP toe Chen's policy line? Not to stay on these two courses would invalidate Chen's good intentions and cause Beijing to interpret his overtures as a tactic to buy time and a cover-up for his independence pursuit.

Taipei, under both Lee and Chen, has failed to come to the negotiation table with Beijing, but for different reasons. Before 2000, Beijing was willing to negotiate but Lee refused. Now, Chen is willing but Beijing has refused for its own reasons, as will be discussed. When either side resists, an outsider, such as Washington, cannot do much to push them to the negotiation table.

In this study, the term "China", after 1949, refers to the PRC whereas the term "Taiwan" refers to the ROC in Taiwan, or the islands it occupies. Thus, the term "Taiwanese" refers, when describing people, to all the people in Taiwan, including mainlander Taiwanese. The *pinyin* system of transliteration is used for Chinese names and words, whereas the Wades-Giles transliteration is used for those in Taiwan. Newspapers cited in the book, if they are the website edition, do not carry page numbers.

I would like to express my gratitude to the Institute of Southeast Asian Studies, where I am a Senior Fellow, for funding this research project and the provision of research facilities and assistance.

Notes

1. John Pomfret, "Taiwan's President Calls for Summit with China", *Washington Post*, 20 June 2000; and "China Cold to President Chen's Call for Summit", Reuters Newsline, 20 June 2000.

2. Ibid.

3. Pomfret, op. cit.

4. See Chen's presidential inauguration speech on 20 May 2000 in the Appendix.

5. For the difference between calling himself *zhongguoren* (Chinese) and *huaren* (also Chinese), please see the discussion in the section "How Does China Read Chen Shui-bian?".

6. The 1993 figure is obtained from the Mainland Affairs Council (MAC), quoted in Julian J. Kuo, *Minjindang Zhuanxing Zhi Tong* [The DPP's Ordeal of Transformation] (Taiwan: Commonwealth Publishing, 1998), p. 123. The mid-1999 poll was commissioned by the MAC and conducted by the China Credit Information Service. See "Highest Percentage Ever Consider Themselves Taiwanese", Central News Agency (Taipei), 3 September 1999.

7. See the text of "North-South Joint Declaration" in the *Straits Times* (Singapore), 16 June 2000.

8. *Yazhou Zhoukan* [The Asia Week] (Hong Kong), 19–25 June 2000, pp. 6 and 7.

9. MAC News Briefing, no. 0178 (Mainland Affairs Council, Taipei, 29 May 2000), p. 2.

10. Though there was still tension over democracy between Chris Pattern, the British Governor of Hong Kong, and Beijing, even after 1995, this did not mean that London still held its previously wrong assessment of the stability of the Beijing government. This was largely because democratization, once started, would self-generate some momentum, like a ball rolling down the hill, and would not stop immediately.

11. *Chung Kuo Shih Pao* [China Times] (Taipei), 14 August 1996.

12. Jason Blatt, "Taipei 'to Face Beijing Force' ", *South China Morning Post* (Hong Kong), 11 August 1999.

13. See Lee Teng-hui, *Taiwan de Zhuzhang* [Taiwan's Viewpoint] (Taipei: Yuanliu Publishing House, 1999), p. 241. The title for the English version of the book is *With the People Always in My Heart*. In the book, he hopes to see China divided into seven autonomous regions: Taiwan, Tibet, Xinjiang, Mongolia, north-eastern China, southern China, and northern China.

14. Monique Chu, "Chen Sees Benefit in 'Interim Agreement' ", *Taipei Times*, 16 February 2001. See also *Ming Ri Bao* [Tomorrow Times] (Taipei), 25 February 2001.

2

Background

During the Mao Zedong era, China had two distinct policies towards Taiwan. From 1949 to the early 1950s, Mao was determined to liberate Taiwan through force. From the early 1950s to the late 1970s, China, though still mainly basing its Taiwan policy on liberation through force, started to propose negotiations with Taiwan. However, Taiwan dismissed these initiatives as propaganda. Nevertheless, the two sides did try to contact each other very cautiously through secret channels, and worked out some tentative proposals and arrangements for reunification, which were similar to the "one country, two systems" formula presently proposed by China. This process, however, ceased when the Cultural Revolution began in China in 1966.

From the late 1970s, when the Deng Xiaoping era started, Beijing no longer talked about liberating Taiwan through force. It formed a new policy for "peaceful reunification". Subsequently, it launched a series of peaceful initiatives towards Taiwan. In January 1979, the Standing Committee of China's National People's Congress (NPC) sent "A Message to Compatriots in Taiwan".[1] On 30 September 1981, Ye Jianying, chairman of the Standing Committee of the NPC, announced a nine-point proposal for solving the Taiwan issue.[2]

These various statements were more conciliatory and offered more specific concessions to Taiwan than was the case previously. Apart from the proposed "three direct links and four exchanges"[3] to be established before political negotiations would take place, Beijing also guaranteed in these statements that, after reunification, the present economic and social system, the armed forces, economic and cultural relations with foreign countries, and the way of life, would remain unchanged. It also appealed for an end to the military confrontation across the Taiwan Strait. On the same day that "A Message to Compatriots in Taiwan" was issued, China's Defence Ministry announced the end of the two-decade-long symbolic bombardment of Kinmen Island and other offshore islands. Beijing also began to reduce its troop concentrations in Fujian province facing Taiwan.

It called for reunification talks with Taipei and promised that after reunification Taiwan could enjoy a high level of autonomy.

Beijing's initiatives towards Taiwan came in a blast of publicity. The weeks following Ye's announcement saw dozens of gestures, ranging from suggestions that Taiwan jurists establish ties with the mainland to offers that Chiang Kai-shek's remains might be brought back from Taiwan to the family tombs in his native town, Fenghua. China also took specific unilateral actions to encourage trade, such as ending customs duties on goods from Taiwan, strongly urging businessmen in Taiwan to co-operate economically with China.[4] It also promised that Taiwan could retain its intelligence, administrative, and legal systems. In the new Constitution of 1982, it added a special provision; Provision 31 stipulates that it allows the setting up of a special administrative region, for which a special new law would be passed. This was targeted at both Taiwan and Hong Kong.[5]

On 26 June 1983, Deng proposed to "have talks on an equal footing and the third co-operation between the two parties [the Chinese Communist Party (CCP) and the KMT]. [We] will not raise it as talks between the central government and a local government". He also noted that after reunification, the two different systems could be practised on the mainland and Taiwan.[6] On 22 February 1984, Deng officially announced the "one country, two systems" formula for reunification.[7]

Taiwan successfully absorbed the shock of the normalization of China–U.S. relations in the late 1970s, and China's subsequent initiatives and pressure. This, in part, was due to international support from some major powers, especially the United States through its Taiwan Relations Act and continued arms sales, and partly to Taiwan's strong tenacity and determination to survive.

In the mid-1980s, there was a thaw in cross-strait relations, which developed fast, but mainly in one-way unofficial economic relations: tens of thousands of Taiwanese businessmen went to invest in and trade with mainland China, but not the reverse, because of the ban by the Taiwan Government on investment and goods from mainland China.

At the same time, the two sides also took steps to increase their overall contacts. Beijing pushed vigorously for formal political contacts and earlier talks on reunification. Taiwan also agreed to negotiate cross-strait affairs involving what it called "common power" (*gong quan li*), not officially but through a semi-official organization, the Strait Exchange Foundation (SEF), established in February 1991. Beijing accepted this informal arrangement and set up its own counterpart, the Association for Relations across the Taiwan Strait (ARATS), in the hope that this process would lead to talks on reunification.

In September 1990, Taiwan set up the National Unification Council (NUC) as an advisory body to the President. In January 1991, Taiwan's Executive Yuan set up the Mainland Affairs Council (MAC) to make overall plans for handling mainland affairs. On 23 February 1991 and in March 1991 respectively, Taiwan's

NUC and the Executive Yuan adopted the "Guidelines for National Unification". On 30 April 1991, Taiwan announced that "the period of mobilisation for the suppression of Communist rebellion" would be terminated on 1 May and the "temporary provisions" of the Constitution in force during the "mobilisation" period would be annulled simultaneously. In other words, Taiwan would no longer treat the CCP as a rebellious organization. In July 1992, the Executive Yuan passed the "Regulations on Relations between People in the Taiwan area and on the Mainland".

The ARATS and the SEF had several informal meetings in 1992 and early 1993, which led to a groundbreaking meeting in Singapore in April 1993 between Taiwan's Koo Chen-fu, chairman of the SEF, and his mainland counterpart, Wang Daohan of the ARATS, called the "Wang-Koo meeting". At the meeting, Koo and Wang signed the "Cross-Strait Agreement on the Use and Inspection of Affidavits", the "Cross-Strait Agreement on Matters Related to Inquiry by Registered Letters and Relevant Compensation", the "Agreement on the System for Connection and Talks between the Two Sides", and the "Joint Agreement of the Wang-Koo Meeting".

Since then, the two sides have conducted fifteen rounds of negotiations (as of 1995). The second round of the Wang-Koo meeting was scheduled on 20 July 1995. The SEF vice-chairman, Chiao Jen-ho, had already held preparatory talks with his ARATS counterpart Tang Shubei in early 1995.

On 22 May 1995, to the surprise of many, the United States, reversing a sixteen-year ban on U.S. visits by high-ranking ROC officials, suddenly granted a visa to President Lee Teng-hui for a six-day "private" visit to his alma mater, Cornell University. This prompted a crisis in both China–U.S. relations and cross-strait relations. China suspended the Wang-Koo meeting and held military exercises and conducted "missile tests", from July 1995 to March 1996, near Taiwan Island, as a strong warning.

The tension across the Taiwan Strait began to decline from late 1996. In October 1998, Koo Chen-fu finally made his tour of China. During his visit, the two sides reached a four-point consensus, among which was a planned return visit to Taiwan the next year by ARATS chairman, Wang Daohan.[8] Though no significant progress was made from the visit, the two sides still went ahead to prepare for Wang's return visit.

After several rounds of negotiation between Li Yafei, deputy secretary of the ARATS, and his SEF counterpart Jan Jih-horng, Wang Daohan announced in late June 1999 that he would pay a return visit to Taiwan in the following October. China hoped that there would be no restrictions on the topics for discussion. To prepare for Wang's visit, it planned to hold a forum in late August on mainland China–Taiwan ties and would invite senior Taiwanese statesmen responsible for handling contacts with the mainland. The two sides agreed to a visit by Taiwanese legal experts to China, and a visit by a Chinese agricultural delegation to Taiwan in August. Jan suggested building detention centres in Xiamen for those mainland Chinese who were caught illegally entering Taiwan. Li said that China was willing to co-operate, but would not be able to take full responsibility for the problem.[9] China hoped that a hotline would be set up between the two sides after Wang's visit, which would be of a "higher status" than routine communications between the ARATS and the SEF. It also asked for discussion of closer co-operation on economic issues, such as on agriculture, and listing political matters in the coming Wang-Koo talks.[10]

Suddenly came Lee Teng-hui's announcement of the "two states" theory, which, as discussed in the following chapter, plunged cross-strait relations to another low.

Notes

1. The Standing Committee of the National People's Congress of the PRC, "A Message to Compatriots in Taiwan", *Beijing Review* 22, no. 1 (5 January 1979): 17.
2. They are: 1) unfettered movement, trade, and communications between Taiwan and the PRC; 2) autonomy for Taiwan and the retention of Taiwan's own armed forces; 3) a role for Taiwan officials in the PRC's national political system; 4) retention of Taiwan's capitalist economy; 5) financial aid for Taiwan from the central government when in need; 6) freedom for people from Taiwan to settle on the Chinese mainland; 7) a profitable role for Taiwanese capitalists in China's economic modernization; 8) talks between the KMT and the CCP for reunification; and 9) the welcoming of proposals from the masses on how reunification should be accomplished. See *Beijing Review* 24, no. 40 (5 October 1981): 10–11.
3. The "three direct links" referred to direct trade, transportation, and postal services between the mainland and Taiwan; the "four exchanges" referred to the establishment of exchanges between relatives and tourists, academic groups, cultural groups, and sports representatives.
4. See Kenneth S. Chern, "The Impact of the Taiwan Issue on Sino-American Relations, 1980–82", in *China in Readjustment*, edited by Leung Chi-keung and Steve S.K. Chin (Hong Kong: University of Hong Kong Press, 1983), p. 381.
5. For the new constitution, see *Renmin Ribao* [People's Daily] (Beijing), 6 December 1982.
6. Deng Xiaoping, "Zhongguo Dalu He Taiwan Heping Tongyi De Shexiang" [An Idea for the Peaceful Reunification of the Chinese Mainland and Taiwan], in *Jianshe You Zhongguo Tese De Shehui Zhuyi* [Build Socialism with Chinese Characteristics] (Beijing: People's Press, 1987), pp. 17–19; and "Yige Zhongguo Shi Wuke Zhengbian De Shishi" [One China is an Indisputable Fact], *Renmin Ribao*, 12 August 1999.
7. The "one country, two systems" formula was originally meant for reunification with Taiwan rather than Hong Kong, but was later also applied for Hong Kong. Xu Jiatun, *Xu Jiatun Xianggan Huiyilu* [Years in Hong Kong] (Taipei: Lien Ho Pao Publishing House, 1994), p. 324.

8. The four points are: 1) holding dialogues on various topics, including political and economic issues; 2) increasing cross-strait exchanges at all levels; 3) giving greater concern to functional issues, such as providing help in cases involving the personal safety and loss of property of each other's residents in each other's territory; and 4) a return visit to Taiwan the next year by Wang Daohan.

9. Tara Suilen Duffy, "Taiwan, China Seek to Restart Talks", Associated Press Newsline, 28 June 1999.

10. Willy Wo-Lap Lam, "Post-Talks Hope for Cross-Strait Hotline", *South China Morning Post*, 15 February 1999.

3

Lee Teng-hui and the "Two States" Theory

The "Two States" Theory

In an interview with a German radio station, Deutche Welle, on 9 July 1999, Lee Teng-hui, to the surprise of many, for the first time openly defined the relations between mainland China and Taiwan as "between two countries (*guojia*), at least special relations between two countries". With this definition, he abandoned Taiwan's previous position of China and Taiwan being "two equal political entities", which, according to him, were actually equal to "two countries". He also noted that there was no need for Taiwan to declare independence again since it (ROC) had always been an independent country since 1912.[1]

Taiwan's Foreign Minister Hu Chih-chiang, SEF chairman, Koo Chen-fu, the MAC chairman, Su Chi, and other high officials immediately confirmed this as the government position. Koo changed his previous position (that he had held in his meeting with Wang Daohan in October 1998) and publicly called cross-strait ties country-to-country (*guojia*) relations. The MAC was thus instructed to replace its previous reference of "two equal political entities" to that of "two countries (*guojia*)" in its future government documents, and to completely drop the reference to "one country".[2] On 12 July, MAC Chairman Su Chi claimed that from then on Taiwan would drop references to the idea of "one China".[3] Later, the MAC, under pressure, came out with an English version of Lee's such theory of "two countries". It was translated into "two states of one nation", avoiding the use of the sensitive word "countries" (*guojia* in Chinese can be translated into either country, or state, or nation).[4] On 22 July, it changed it to "special state-to-state" relations.[5]

The Presidential Office and a central KMT meeting disclosed that the "two states" concept was the product of a year-long study by the Select Group on

Strengthening the Sovereignty Status of the Republic of China, which was headed by the secretary-general of the Presidential Office, Huang Kun-huei.[6] Therefore, the "two states" theory was not a personal view or a slip of the tongue, but a set government policy. Taiwan confirmed this as a fundamental policy change, to be followed by a series of changes in state policy and law, such as the State Security Law, Regulations Governing Cross-Strait Relations, and the Nationality Law.[7]

Lee was expected to raise correspondingly new political, economic, and social policies before leaving office. He was also expected to push ahead with constitutional amendments to give the "two states" theory a firm legal foundation. This was expected to take place together with a major overhaul of the constitutional and legal framework, covering all aspects of law, ranging from the definitions of state and institutions to territories and people. All government decrees, notices, memoranda, and propaganda materials, including Internet websites, would be revised to reflect Taiwan's new status. Government ministries were told to draw up a full list of documents that needed amendment.[8]

On 14 July, following a meeting of the standing members of the KMT Central Committee, Taiwan announced that it would launch a major diplomatic offensive to promote its "two states" policy to the international community. The initiatives included sending the chairman of the Council for Economic Planning and Development, Chiang Pin-kung, to attend the Asia-Pacific Economic Co-operation (APEC) meeting in New Zealand in September 1999, where he would explain the "new principle" to regional leaders at the gathering. It would ask its allies in the United Nations to help explain its "two states" concept whenever they addressed the United Nations General Assembly. In addition, it would ask them to co-sponsor a motion that would allow Taiwan to join the United Nations on this new basis. Previously, its bid to re-enter the world body was made by asking for a repeal of U.N. Resolution No 2758 of 1971, which gave the China seat to the PRC. Taipei would now ask for permission to join the United Nations as a new and separate state, using the German model to support its motion. It would also instruct all its foreign representative offices to explain to their host governments the applicability of the German model, which was embodied in the "Grundlagenuertrag", or Fundamental Treaty of 1972, between the two Germanies.[9]

Beijing's Responses

As expected, Taiwan's new initiative provoked China's fury. Wang Daohan warned that the "two states" policy had removed the basis for further dialogue between the ARATS and the SEF. He demanded an explanation from Taiwan. Otherwise, he might be compelled to cancel his planned visit to Taiwan in

October 1999.[10] China demanded a retraction of the "two states" statement and a return to the "one China" position. It claimed that Lee had taken an "extremely dangerous step" towards splitting China, and warned him against playing with fire. It reaffirmed that it had never renounced the use of force to prevent Taiwan's independence and warned Taiwan not to underestimate Beijing's determination and capability to uphold the nation's sovereignty, dignity, and territorial integrity. It warned that Lee had taken "the people of Taiwan, as well as his foreign patrons, hostage down his road of destruction and into his suicidal, separatist adventures".[11]

Newspapers, mostly in Hong Kong, quoted unspecified Chinese sources, saying that China was considering a military response. The exercises conducted by the People's Liberation Army (PLA), though small-sized and far away from Taiwan, were reported to be warnings. Chinese newspapers carried many editorials and articles denouncing Lee's "two states" theory. Chinese military specialists and scholars, in their personal capacities, issued stern warnings, also mainly through the media in Hong Kong. For example, Hong Kong's *Wen Wei Po* quoted a senior researcher at the PLA's Academy of Military Science, Yan Zhao, as saying that military conflict in the Taiwan Strait could erupt at any moment. He also said that Beijing would not stop using force even if the United States intervened.[12]

One Step Back, Two Steps Forward

Under mounting pressure from both Beijing and Washington, Lee Teng-hui began to tone down his advocacy of the "two states" theory. He blamed the media for "misquoting" him. The Presidential Office explained that what Lee had said was "special state-to-state relations" and not a "two states" theory. On 26 and 27 July, Lee said: "As a matter of fact, I did not mention a 'two states theory' in the interview with the German radio. ... I realise my idea would be better understood if the queries the German reporters raised could be read carefully". He said that the media coined the "two states theory".[13]

It was a play of words. The crux of the matter here was not who coined the term "two states" theory (Lee did not use the term himself in the interview), but the international media's description of what he had said as the "two states" theory was not wrong. He had not been "misquoted" either, since Koo Chen-fu, Su Chi, and other Taiwan high officials changed their previous position on Taiwan–China relations following Lee's interview.

Lee insisted that this state-to-state relations was a special one. The term "special" referred to the emotional ties between the people of Taiwan and China ("[They] have special feelings towards each other.").[14] However, he did not specify how "special" it was. In other words, this special emotion could also mean hatred, or what was popularly expressed in Taiwan as "*bei qing*" [the mentality of being victimized (by the mainlanders)]. This could imply hatred and revenge instead of love. Koo's clarification on 30 July, and the MAC's statement on 1 August did not succeed in making things better.[15]

Such ambiguity and self-contradiction could also be found in Lee's explanation that he had no plan to declare independence. In the 9 July interview, he had said, as quoted above, that there was no need for Taiwan to declare independence again since it (the ROC) had always been an independent country since 1912. That said, Lee's "concession" that he had no plan to declare independence were empty words. At the same time, the MAC insisted: "The two sides of the Taiwan Strait have been divided into two states and China's sovereignty and territory have been cut apart."[16] This was a refutation of the Chinese insistence that a country's administration could be cut apart but not its sovereignty.

China and Taiwan also differed in their usage of the term "independence". When Lee said that he would not declare Taiwan's independence, in essence, he meant that he would not declare a Republic of Taiwan (ROT). However, to China, the term "independence" meant a split with China, whether in the name of the ROT, or the ROC. To declare the ROC and the PRC as two separate and independent sovereignty states was to split China and therefore declare Taiwan's independence, especially as the DPP had declared Taiwan's independence in the name of the ROC, instead of the ROT.

Lee assured Washington that Taiwan's mainland policy remained "intact". Yet in the same interview of 9 July, Lee also said: "Since we made our constitutional reforms in 1991, we have redefined cross (Taiwan) Strait relations as state-to-state". In other words, if cross-strait contact since 1991 was already what Lee described as "state-to-state", then Taiwan's mainland policy was indeed "intact". However, it was not the case to China and many other countries that had been told that cross-strait dealings should be placed on a state-to-state basis only after July 1999.

Lee said that he made the "two states" claim so that Taiwan would be treated as China's equal in future talks on unification.[17] In the past, Taiwan had insisted on "two equal *political* entities". Now, this equality had changed to *sovereign* equality, not even in the sense of two central governments representing one state, but in two separate states. It called this a necessary step to prepare Taiwan for talks on unification, and offered to agree to China's demand of holding some form of political dialogue, if China accepted Taiwan's new status.[18] Presidential deputy secretary-general, Lin Pi-chao, said:

> We have made preparations to push for the political dialogue and drafted several proposals based on Taiwan's new status declared by President Lee Teng-hui. We are willing to adopt a more positive attitude at the negotiation table if their reaction is practical and rational. We definitely would not want to see a backward step in

cross-strait relations, and we hope Wang Daohan would visit Taiwan as scheduled.[19]

Taiwan knew only too well that Beijing would never accept the "two states" theory in exchange for political dialogue, for the political dialogue was about having one state, not two.

It made another "concession" by claiming to return the 1992 consensus between the ARATS and the SEF. The consensus, it said, was that "*yi ge zhong guo, ge zi biao shu*" [one China but free interpretations], and both sides agreed to disagree. Since one side allowed the other the right of free interpretation, Taiwan, accordingly, had the right to interpret the "one China" principle as saying that "one China" was something in the future. There was no "one China" at present but two states.[20] It also cited Jiang Zemin's eight-point proposal of 1995, which had said that both sides could come together to talk about anything. It claimed that this meant that it could talk in this way.

Beijing was annoyed. It accused Taiwan of distorting Jiang's words. When Jiang said that both sides could discuss about anything, it was within the framework of "one China", which was clearly stated at the very beginning of Jiang's eight-point proposal. It also claimed that it had never agreed to "free interpretation" or "agreed to disagree" on "one China", but only said that it would not discuss the political content of the "one China" policy in talks on pragmatic matters.[21]

Beijing and Taipei reached a vocal consensus regarding the "one China" policy in a meeting between the ARATS and the SEF in March 1992, and reaffirmed it in the first round of the Wang-Koo meeting in 1993, namely, that the two sides should adhere to the "one China" principle. This principle was then explained in three sentences: (1) There is only one China in this world; (2) Taiwan is part of China. However, the two sides had different versions for the third sentence. For Beijing, it read that "the PRC is the sole legitimate government of China", while for Taipei it was the ROC. Taipei later claimed that the "two sides agreed to disagree on one China", and "*yi ge zhong guo, ge zi biao shu*" [one China but free interpretations]. Beijing denied that it had allowed any "free interpretations" of the "one China" principle and that it had never "agreed to disagree". It said that in 1992, the ARATS had made clear its position to the SEF: "The one China principle should be adhered to. So long as this position is claimed in talks on practical matters, [we] *may not discuss the political content of this one China*."[22] On 16 November 1992, in talks on practical matters, the ARATS and the SEF expressed their consensus on the "one China" principle, verbally. The ARATS said: "Both sides of the Taiwan Strait adhere to the one China principle, seeking national reunification. But the political content of the one China will not be involved in their talks on practical matters".[23] The SEF said: "In the process of both sides of the Strait making common efforts at seeking national unification, although *both sides adhere to the one China principle*, they have a different understanding of what is this one China".[24] Thus, China now insisted there was only consensus by the two sides on the "one China" principle. As for its content, the two sides did not discuss this. How could there be a consensus, as Taiwan claimed, when "both sides agreed to disagree on one China".[25]

With these "explanations",[26] Taiwan's claim that it had not abandoned the "one China" policy and sought eventual unification with China did not appease the latter. As U.S. Secretary of State Madeleine Albright said in late July, these explanations "thus far don't quite do it".[27]

Taiwan resisted this pressure. Lee insisted that Taiwan and China must deal with each other on a "state-to-state" basis. Though the theory had not been codified into the state Constitution, it had, by the end of August, been enshrined, by way of a KMT resolution, in the party charter. Thus, it has become a formal document. At the same time, as another "concession", the KMT reaffirmed Lee's assurance that Taiwan had no plan to codify it into the Constitution. However, in early September, Taiwan's National Assembly voted to extend its four-year term by another 25 months. The reason given by its Speaker, Su Nan-cheng, on 6 September was that it planned to "suspend" or "temporarily freeze" the present Constitution and would instead draft a "basic law" to "reflect its current constitutional reality". According to him, the extension was necessary "to provide sufficient time and space for a major constitutional revision".[28] In other words, Taiwan could claim to be faithful in keeping its words (as it promised U.S. special envoy Richard Bush in July) of not revising the Constitution to encompass the "two states" theory. However, it was going to "suspend" and "freeze" the Constitution (it had never made the promise not to do so) and draft a new basic law to "reflect its current constitutional reality", that is, "special state-to-state relations" with China.

Changes in Taiwan's Unification Position

Contrary to Lee's claim that the "two states" theory represented no change in Taiwan's mainland policy, the change is obvious and significant. Taiwan under both Chiang Kai-shek and Chiang Ching-kuo had held a consistent position that both mainland China and Taiwan are Chinese territory and there is only one China, and this China is the ROC, not the PRC. This position began to change when Lee stepped into office in 1988.

In the late 1980s, Lee Teng-hui said: "One China is the supreme principle". On 23 February 1988, shortly after he assumed office as President, he insisted on the "one China policy, not two Chinas policy".[29] In 1990, Lee raised the notion of "one China, two governments". He said: "One country, two governments. This is a fact".[30] In its "Guidelines for National Unification" of February 1991, Taiwan held that "there is only one China", but for the first time, it used the notion of "one China, two equal political entities". After 1991, Taiwan began to emphasize that "Taiwan and the mainland are both parts of China" and the PRC "is *not equivalent* to China" (instead, the PRC *is not* China, as acknowledged before). It would now no longer compete with Beijing for the "right to represent China" in the international arena. Rather, it began to emphasize that the two parts of China should have the right to participate alongside each other in the international community as equals prior to unification.[31]

By 1993, Taiwan's position on sovereignty had changed to that of one China but administered by the ROC and the PRC in two different parts. It insisted that Taipei had "exclusive sovereignty" over the island of Taiwan, the Penghu Islands in the Taiwan Strait, and Kinmen and Matsu Islands off the Fujian coast.[32] At the Seattle APEC meeting in November 1993, Taiwan raised, through its then Economic Minister, Chiang Pin-kung, the notion of a "transitional 'two Chinas' policy heading toward unification".

In 1994, more changes took place. Taiwan's 1994 White Paper on cross-strait relations pointed out: "The two sides should be fully aware that each has jurisdiction over its respective territory and that they should coexist as two *legal* entities in the international arena".[33] Hereafter, the emphasis shifted to "coexistence of two equal international legal entities", or "the ROC in Taiwan and the PRC in China", as stated by Lee on his visit to the United States in 1995. Instead of "two equal entities" or "two equal political entities", Taiwan, this time, used the expression of "two *legal* entities in the international arena" or "two equal international *legal* entities". Here, the very word "legal" strongly implies "sovereignty", that is, two equal sovereign entities. Taiwan asked China to drop its old-fashioned thinking of "one China", which, it said, was only a cultural concept, and suggested that sovereignty could be shared by both the ROC and the PRC in the United Nations as equals.

After 1994, Taiwan only talked about "two equal political entities" across the strait without mentioning "one China". In past years, Taiwan had claimed that the ROC had always been an independent sovereign state. However, in November 1997, in two separate interviews with the *Washington Post* and *The Times* of London, Lee Teng-hui declared Taiwan as "an independent, sovereign country, just like Britain or France".[34] Under pressure, Lee then accused the journalist of having misquoted him, and the Taiwan government explained that "Taiwan", as used by Lee, was meant to be the ROC. In February 1999, at a lunch in his hometown of Sanchih in Taiwan, Lee said: "It can be said for sure that Taiwan is an independent state. Taiwan is Taiwan. This is a clear matter". He said that the message would be conveyed to Beijing when the two sides resumed high-level negotiations.[35] Here, Lee gave a big hint of the coming "two states" position. On 9 July, he formally raised the "two states" theory and, for the first time, Taiwan defined its relations with the Chinese mainland as one between two states, though a "special one". This was a big leap. The phrase "two equal political entities", as was its previous position, would at most mean two equal or even two central governments, but still within one state. Even the phrase, "the independent and sovereign ROC" was, according to the ROC's current constitution, to encompass the Chinese mainland. Taiwan's constitutional reform in the early 1990s only temporarily limited the ROC's jurisdiction to Taiwan proper, Penghu, Kinmen, Matsu, and other islands around it. The revised constitution itself did not state that the jurisdiction of the Chinese mainland had been given to the PRC. It has never split the ROC's sovereignty between the ROC in Taiwan and the PRC. In other words, it has never withdrawn its sovereignty (only jurisdiction) from the Chinese mainland. Hence, Lee's "two states" theory was a big step forward, and, as a matter of fact, a violation of the ROC's state constitution.

To Kill Two Birds with One Stone

Lee's motivation for choosing this time to bring up the "two states" theory has been subject to various interpretations. In my view, Lee wanted to kill two birds with one stone: he wanted to influence the forthcoming presidential election on the one hand. On the other, he wanted to initiate a confrontation between China and the United States and pull the United States into the hot water on Taiwan's side.

Lee wanted to lay further groundwork for what in his mind was the future of Taiwan before his presidential term expired. Lee explained in August 1999: "I will no longer be the president at this time next year. ... But I realise my redefinition of statehood might allow the successor to handle the issue easier".[36] He wanted to cut his successor into shape. In other words, after the "two states" position had been formally accepted by the KMT, as it was in late August, it would be difficult for the KMT candidate, Lien Chan, to challenge it. It would also undercut the presidential candidate, Soong Chu-yu, who did not agree with Lee's mainland policy.

Back in October 1996, Wang Daohan had told this writer in an interview: "Lee Teng-hui does not trust Soong Chu-yu and Lien Chan because of their mainland background." Later, it turned out that Lee dumped Soong. As for Lien Chan, even if he had won the presidential election, he would still be under Lee's strong influence. Without Lee's support, he could not win the presidential election (in fact, Lee failed to give Lien strong support at the critical moment of the 2000 presidential election). With Lee still acting as the KMT chairman after leaving office as President in 2000, and the "two states" theory being formally incorporated into the KMT party charter, Lien would not have much room to manoeuvre. As Taiwan's *China Times Express* put it, "He [Lee] does not trust the political line of his successor, so he's simply taking it upon himself to force the situation to a point of no return".[37]

Secondly, while his controversial remarks prompted a flurry of angry protests and threats from Beijing, Lee continued to mock the PLA. In a meeting at the Presidential Office on 10 August 1999, he said that the controversy would benefit Taipei in the end. "The more controversy, the better. Only this way will everyone pay attention to the key of the Republic of China's existence. When the whole world knows the Republic of China's difficult situation, afterwards it will be easier to do things".[38]

The following may reveal Lee's strategy. Lee is not an "IBM" (international big mouth) as some Taiwanese have called him. This was shown in his extremely cautious style, both before he succeeded Chiang Ching-kuo in early 1988 and before he established his sure control of the KMT in late 1993. Only after 1994 did Lee frequently ridicule Chinese leaders, such as publicly calling them a group of "hooligans" and "bandits" in 1994; mocking the PRC as the "son" while calling the ROC the "father" in 1995; saying that China "is stupid" though "big" in 1997; making highly controversial statements in his conversation with Japanese writer Ryotaro Shiba in May 1994, in his speech at Cornell in June 1995, in his book *Taiwan de Zhuzhang* [Taiwan's Viewpoint] in May 1999, and in his "two states theory" in early July 1999.

All this should not be dismissed as merely Lee's personal style or "a slip of the tongue". He did all this in a calculated manner, to put Taiwan constantly in the international limelight so that Taiwan would not be forgotten by the world. In this perspective, though winning over one or two small diplomatic allies from China did not tilt the diplomatic balance (given that Taiwan had fewer than thirty such small diplomatic allies), its importance lay in the international media coverage that Taiwan wanted, in order to remind the world of its existence and its plight. The same was true for Taiwan's strenuous efforts in sending its leaders and high officials abroad for visits, almost for any reason. It believed that this would eventually win it more international sympathy, which was vital for its survival as a sovereign state. International silence kills. This explains why Taiwan has been expending so much effort and money on these small countries and on its "pragmatic diplomacy". This would also explain why, as soon as the Taiwan issue had calmed down, Lee (or Taiwan) would most likely make another major international splash. This was Lee's strategy for Taiwan: with constant international splashes, it would attain international attention, and more and more international sympathy.

This international sympathy, at present, contributes to Taiwan's security. However, it will not be enough in the future when China's continued rise further tilts the balance of power across the Strait. Taiwan feels that time is not on its side. This reality invites another speculation on Lee's motives: Lee was actually exploiting current American sympathy and worsening China–U.S. relations to secure U.S. military commitments to his cause.

Lee must have known that the Chinese had become very irritable and emotional after the U.S. bombing of the Chinese embassy in Belgrade on 8 May 1999, and over the persistent U.S. refusal to allow China's earlier entry into the World Trade Organization (WTO). The Americans were also agitated over the nation-wide anti-American student demonstrations in China after the bombing and Beijing's increasingly hawkish position. Various political forces inside the United States, with the 2000 presidential election in mind, were exploiting the alleged Chinese nuclear spying case, human rights record, and so forth to orchestrate political pressure against Clinton's China policy. Antagonism between the two countries suddenly escalated. Never had the prospect of a large-scale China–U.S. confrontation become so imminent since their *rapprochement* in 1972.

Why, then, did Lee choose *this time* to raise his long-prepared and highly provocative "two states" theory? There is no other convincing explanation except that he meant to incite Beijing into making the expected angry response, which was stronger than its military exercises in March 1996. Why? If Beijing could not control its emotions or the tremendous domestic pressure to use force, the United States would then have to get involved militarily, especially as the time neared to the U.S. presidential election. No American statesmen could be seen to tolerate a Chinese military response against a democratic Taiwan. Should a military clash occur between China and the United States, China–U.S. relations would worsen irreconcilably. Taiwan would become another Kosovo or South Korea, in the sense of a guaranteed U.S. military commitment. Taiwan's status as a full-fledged independent sovereign state would likely be secured. Without this, Taiwan's current security is only built on shifting sand under the heavy shadow of a rising China. Even if the United States did not position its troops in Taiwan as it has done in South Korea, or make such a firm military commitment as it had done in the case of Kosovo, U.S.–China relations would become too rigid for China to play around.

Changes in China's Perception of Taiwan[39]

Lee's constant efforts in his cause have led to a fundamental change in China's perception of Taiwan's real intention on reunification and, consequently, doubts about the latter's previous "peaceful reunification strategy", tempting it to form a new Taiwan strategy. This section discusses the evolution of China's perceptions of Taiwan, in order to lay the basis for discussion, in the rest of this study, of the reorientation of China's Taiwan polices.

When Chiang Kai-shek and Chiang Ching-kuo were in power in Taiwan from 1949 to 1987, Beijing never suspected them of seeking Taiwan's independence. Mao Zedong knew his old rival too well to be disturbed by the thought of Chiang Kai-shek seeking Taiwan's independence. He only considered Chiang's resistance to be "because he is unwilling to confess being defeated" or a "matter of face", not out of any intention to seek Taiwan's independence. On the contrary, the two Chiangs suppressed those who advocated independence no less harshly than they did the communists in Taiwan. They often resisted strenuously what they suspected as U.S. efforts to permanently split Taiwan from China. As a matter of fact, in private talks, and occasionally in the official press, many Chinese officials and scholars highly respected the two Chiangs as national heroes, but not as ideological comrades, as far as reunification and maintaining China's territorial integrity were concerned. They were considered as highly patriotic, and their close alliance with the United States against Beijing stemmed from the need for survival and their ideological commitment against communism, but never against reunification.

It is now widely known that in the 1950s and 1960s, Chiang Kai-shek had tried to maintain secret channels of communication with Beijing for negotiation, and on several instances he had sent his own men for secret discussions with leaders in Beijing on reunification. So far it is uncertain how many times the two sides had contacted each other for reunification talks. However, there is no doubt that the two sides did have such contacts, which was confirmed in December 1995 by Qiao Shi, then chairman of the Standing Committee of China's National People's Congress.[40] Interviews by this writer in China and the latest Chinese official publications also confirm this point; at least, the secret channel by Hong Kong-based correspondent Cao Juren is not in doubt.

Cao had close personal ties with both CCP and KMT leaders, either before or after he left the mainland and settled in Hong Kong. From 1956 to 1965, Cao made trips between the two sides, which finally resulted in six mutually-agreed conditions for reunification in 1965, namely:

- Chiang Kai-shek would return to the mainland with his subordinates and settle in any province of China except Zhejiang Province. He would remain as the top leader of the Kuomintang.
- Chiang Ching-kuo would be the governor of Taiwan Province. Taiwan would retain what it had had for twenty years except to give up its rights over diplomatic and military affairs, and agreed to Beijing's request that tillers would have their own land. This agreement would be renegotiated after twenty years.
- Taiwan would not receive any aid from the United States. If there were financial difficulties, Beijing would provide the same amount of financial aid as the United States used to provide.
- Taiwan's naval and air forces would be reorganized under Beijing's control. Its infantry will also be reorganized and reduced to four divisions, with one division stationed in the Kinmen and Xiamen region and three divisions in Taiwan.

- Xiamen and Kinmen would be merged as one free city, standing between Beijing and Taipei as a buffer and liaison zone. The commander of the army division in this area would also be the mayor of the city. The commander would have the rank of lieutenant-general and should be acceptable to Beijing politically.
- The official ranks and salaries of all civil officials and military officers in Taiwan would remain the same and the living standards of the people in Taiwan would only go up and would not be allowed to go down.

Based on these six conditions, Chiang agreed to negotiate in 1965.[41]

In fact, other secret channels also facilitated this breakthrough in 1965. For example, in October 1958, Zhang Shizhao, who enjoyed intimate personal relations with top leaders in both Beijing and Taipei, went to Hong Kong to convey two proposals from Beijing to Chiang through the KMT's connections in Hong Kong. The first was the minimum request, that is, though the two sides may avoid negotiation temporarily, they should start to build some initial contacts, such as direct post and telecommunications, direct flights, and sea transportation links either officially or through private organizations. The second proposal was that Taiwan would have its own government, armed forces, and party organizations, which would be assisted financially by Beijing, provided that Taiwan agreed to be part of the PRC.[42]

As Taiwan did not respond to these two proposals, in another secret meeting with "special guests" from Taiwan in 1960, Mao and Premier Zhou Enlai put forward a plan, *yi gang si mu* (one principle and four points), for negotiation with Chiang on reunification. The principle was that Taiwan must return to China. The four points were:

- After Taiwan's return, Chiang would retain all the rights over the organization of key local government and military personnel, except diplomatic rights which would be handed over to the central government in Beijing.
- The central government would provide financial support in case of budget shortfalls for the armed forces, the government, and the economy in Taiwan.
- Social reform in Taiwan would not be carried out immediately, but would wait for the right conditions with respect to Chiang's view, and after consultations with Chiang.
- Each side would refrain from any behaviour that would be harmful to the unity of the other side.[43]

All the above proposals were actually embryonic forms of the "one country, two systems" formula which Deng later publicly enunciated in the early 1980s.

Owing to the Cultural Revolution, contacts between the two sides ceased. Given the disasters taking place in China, Chiang was understandably unwilling to continue the process. In any case, Beijing was totally preoccupied with its internal chaos to give proper attention to such a matter.

The process resumed when Deng assumed power in China in the late 1970s. From then on, Beijing launched wave after wave of initiatives towards Taiwan for a peaceful reunification.

This effort started to gain favourable responses from Chiang Ching-kuo in the 1980s, as claimed by Qiao Shi in a conversation with Professor Wang Chi of Georgetown University in the United States. In that conversation, Qiao Shi also disclosed that Beijing and Taipei had discussed ways to reunify when Chiang Ching-kuo was still alive.[44]

According to other Chinese sources, Chiang Ching-kuo and Beijing kept secret and informal channels for contacts for several years in the 1980s. In 1987, Chiang finally took an important formal step to negotiate on reunification. However, this process ceased almost as soon as it started. One reason is that Chiang Ching-kuo died early the very next year. Secondly, according to Chinese sources, the Americans intervened in the process: Washington sent officials from the Central Intelligence Agency (CIA) to Taiwan to investigate the reported secret contact between Beijing and Taipei and had talks with Chiang Ching-kuo. After the CIA officials left, Chiang said to the people around, "We are still a colony." The American show of "concern", if not succeeding in terminating the process, must have made Chiang more cautious about proceeding.[45]

This story from the Chinese side should not be dismissed as groundless, especially when such a high-ranking leader as Chairman Qiao Shi confirmed on one official occasion that such contacts had been made. Though the details remain vague, it is clear from information from other sources,[46] that Chiang did make an effort to contact Beijing. Secondly, he did not enjoy good relations with Washington, and was on constant guard against the Americans supporting the local pro-independence groups, or other power groups trying to weaken or overthrow him. Thirdly, the Americans had intervened during the power transition period in Taiwan politics from the late 1980s to the early 1990s by supporting Lee Teng-hui in one way or another.

At the same time, when Chiang Ching-kuo was trying to make contact with Beijing, he adopted several measures which led to a thaw in cross-strait relations. One was to allow people in Taiwan to go to the mainland to visit their relatives there, although via Hong Kong. Partly for this reason, Beijing had a high opinion of Chiang, viewing him as doing his bit to prevent Taiwan's independence.

After Chiang Ching-kuo's death in January 1988, Beijing pinned its hopes on Lee Teng-hui to continue the process, as reflected in the two telegraphs to Taiwan by the then CCP General Secretary Zhao Ziyang. The first one was sent on 14 January 1988, addressing the KMT Central Committee. While expressing condolences on Chiang's death, Zhao hoped that "the new Taiwanese leader ... would carry further the recent favourable developments in the cross-strait relations".[47] The second was sent on 8 July 1988, addressing Lee directly. While conveying congratulations to Lee on assuming the chairmanship of the KMT at its 13th National Congress, Zhao reaffirmed his hope that Lee would continue efforts at reunification.[48]

In mid-1991, an anxious Beijing made an open appeal for such negotiations by issuing a three-point "7 June Talk". The statement was a milestone in the evolution of China's Taiwan policy. It was issued in the name of the Office for Taiwan Affairs of the Central Committee of the CCP. The main points were:

- An earlier authorization of relevant departments and organizations for three direct links for cross-strait exchanges;
- Talks would be initiated between the CCP and the KMT for a formal termination of cross-strait hostility, leading to gradual reunification. Under the "one China" principle, other issues could also be discussed. People from other parties and circles in Taiwan could also be invited for the discussion; and
- The CCP welcomed visits by KMT leaders or persons authorized by the KMT Central Committee. The CCP was also willing to visit Taiwan if invited.[49]

Taiwan did not respond to the appeal of the "7 June Talk" until two years later, at the first Wang-Koo meeting in Singapore. At a dinner, Tang Shubei, vice-chairman and secretary-general of the Association for Relations across the Taiwan Strait (ARATS) asked why Taiwan had let the chance of negotiations pass, by not responding to the "7 June Talk". His counterpart from the Strait Exchange Foundation (SEF), Qiu Jinyi (in Chinese *pinyin*) replied that the proposed negotiations were on a party-to-party basis (that is, between the CCP and the KMT, instead of government-to-government). Therefore, it could not be accepted. Consequently, Taiwan decided not to respond.[50]

However, by the end of 1991, Beijing was feeling uneasy about Taiwan's position on reunification. Chinese President Yang Shangkun changed the wording in an internal document from "placing our hope on the government of Taiwan and placing our hope on the people in Taiwan", into "placing our hope on the government of Taiwan but more hope on the people in Taiwan". Clearly, Beijing now harboured suspicions about the "government of Taiwan".

According to Xu Jiatun,[51] in a personal conversation between Deng Xiaoping, then premier Zhao Ziyang, and himself in the mid-1980s, the three had considered that the reason for Chiang Ching-kuo's refusal to agree with Deng's "one country, two systems" proposal was because of "loss of face" — because the ROC government would be relegated to a local government after reunification. From late 1989, Beijing began to feel uneasy about Lee's stand on reunification.[52]

The uneasiness, at that stage, was due to the fact that, firstly, Chinese leaders did not know Lee as well as they had known the two Chiangs. Secondly, Lee is a native born Taiwanese (though his ancestral home is in China's Yongding, in Fujian Province), and he has never lived on the mainland. Consequently, he would not have strong personal feelings towards the mainland as did the two Chiangs. Thirdly, Lee was not enthusiastic and eager for the reunification talks mainly because of his anti-communist ideology. Fourthly, some even thought that Lee could not afford the political price to pursue the reunification issue too far because he was still weak compared with other veteran KMT leaders. Though they were not sure of what Lee would do once he consolidated his position in the KMT, they warned against a premature judgement of Lee at that time.

Based on this perception, Beijing did not try to influence the internal transitional politics of Taiwan in the early 1990s in the belief that there was no fundamental difference between Lee and Hao Paocun, or other veteran KMT leaders who were engaged in a fierce power struggle with Lee for the KMT leadership. Both Lee and Hao were anti-communist, possessing similar attitudes towards reunification under the "one country two systems" formula. It was purely a power struggle, not a struggle between those who were for Taiwan's independence and those who were for Taiwan's reunification. Now, Beijing came to take the view that Lee was against reunification not because of his anti-communist ideology like Hao, or internal politics, but because of his other personal beliefs. This makes Lee different from Hao.

In the informal meetings between the ARATS and the SEF in 1992, especially the one in August, Taiwan's insistence on "*yi ge zhong guo, ge zi biao shu*" [one China but free interpretations] made China suspicious of Lee's real intentions on reunification. Whereas its previous uneasiness about Lee was largely because of a lack of personal information, contact, and therefore understanding, now it felt that it had, through these informal meetings, sounded Taiwan out on its true position on reunification. This marked a significant milestone in China's perception.

Before an SEF negotiation team went to Beijing on 7–11 April 1993 to finalize the details for the forthcoming first meeting between Wang Daohan and Koo Chen-fu, the Taiwan government, through the Mainland Affairs Council (MAC), announced on 3 April a five-point instruction (actually five No's) to limit the function of the negotiation team, namely: (1) no political issues were to be involved; (2) no contact or meetings with mainland government high officials; (3) no discussion on direct two-way investment; (4) no discussion on what the SEF was not authorized to do; and (5) no formal signature of any agreements.[53] In the early morning of 11 April, when the SEF team had finished its negotiations with the mainland side and was ready for a farewell meeting with their host Wang Daohan, the MAC telephoned the team at their hotel, ordering it to withdraw one agreement, which had already been agreed upon and duly recorded in the meeting's minutes — that is, that the Wang–Koo meeting should be regularized and held once a year. The MAC even stated that if China did not agree to this, Taiwan would rather cancel the forthcoming Wang–Koo meeting.[54]

Annoyed as he was, Wang Daohan still accepted this sudden change of mind and attended the first round of the Wang–Koo meeting in Singapore on 27 April 1993, where, in order to make it a success, he finessed political issues to concentrate on practical matters. Despite the public celebration of the great success of the Wang–Koo meeting on the surface, Chinese leaders felt, but were not certain, that something was amiss with the Taiwanese leaders. While China claimed the meeting as a step of historical importance, heading towards reunification, Taiwan also claimed it as a step of historical importance, but in its illustration to the world of Taiwan and China being two equals and China as being, as a matter of fact, divided and separately administrated.[55] It seems that the shadow of darkness over the Taiwan Strait was looming larger.

By late 1993, Beijing had noted that the tendency towards independence in Taiwan had accelerated alarmingly with many independence organizations mushrooming and many Taiwanese independence figures returning from overseas. The government also for the first time tolerated them when they actively advocated Taiwan's independence. Some Chinese strategists suspected Lee of even protecting and encouraging this independence trend. However, it seemed that this time, Chinese leaders did not reach a consensus and conclusion about Lee as it had after Lee's trip to the United States in 1995. Jiang Zemin still sent a telegram to congratulate Lee on his retention of the chairmanship of the KMT at its 14th National Congress on 19 August 1993.[56] One reason for this was that, to use the expression of some Chinese scholars, "by this time Lee's true colour was still hidden underground". While encouraging this independence tendency under the guise of "democratization", Lee also pushed for the first round of the Wang–Koo meeting in 1993, which Beijing eagerly viewed as a breakthrough in cross-strait relations. However, on hindsight, Lee's push for the Wang–Koo meeting was a well-designed tactic to mislead Beijing into the belief that Lee was interested in reunification, and that the increasing tendency towards independence in Taiwan was not something that Lee agreed to but something he was not able to stop. Lee's tactics worked well, at least in making Beijing hesitate to put its weight behind Hao in the power struggle between Lee and Hao for the KMT's leadership in 1993.

Another factor that accounted for Beijing's high expectations of Lee was the secret round of communications between Lee and Chinese leaders. Before his death in early 1988, Chiang Ching-kuo had agreed to send a five-man group to visit the mainland for secret talks on reunification. After Lee came to power in 1988, although he did not send the five-man group, he agreed to a secret channel between Beijing and Taipei. Nan Huai-chin, a respected senior historian and philosopher in Hong Kong, arranged for the secret meetings between the two sides in Hong Kong. Beijing first sent Jia Yibin, a member of the Standing Committee of the Chinese People's Political Consultative Conference to see Nan on 31 January 1988, with a request to meet Lee. On 21 April 1989, together with Yang Side, director of China's Taiwan Affairs Office and the representative of then Chinese President Yang Shangkun, Jia went to see Nan again in Hong Kong. Yang asked Nan to convey Beijing's sincere wishes for cross-strait talks to Lee Teng-hui through Nan's former students Su Chi-cheng and Cheng Shu-min, who were both Lee's confidants.

Nan went to Taiwan and met Lee in 1990. In December 1990, Su Chi-cheng, Lee's secretarial chief, met secretly with Yang Side in Hong Kong. These secret meetings continued the following year in Hong Kong, Beijing, Shanghai and Zhuhai between Su Chi-cheng and Cheng Shu-min and officials from Beijing, including Wang Daohan, Yang Side, and Xu Mingzhen. In August 1992, Xu Mingzhen visited Taiwan with the excuse of visiting his relatives there. Thereafter, he made several more visits to Taiwan.

In these secret communications, to show his "sincerity", Lee once told emissaries from Beijing that if Beijing did not like the KMT he would work to cripple it. If it did not like Hao Paocun, he would make efforts to "pull him down". It seemed that Beijing was somewhat taken in by Lee, partly because of his secret communications and partly because, as some people speculated, Lee had once joined the Communist Party in Taiwan.[57]

However, Lee was only successful this time, when he used the first round of the Wang–Koo meeting of 1993 and these "secret communications" to obtain Beijing's support. He faced resounding failure when he tried it for the second time — he tried to use the second round of the Wang–Koo meeting in July 1995 to persuade Beijing about his "pragmatic diplomacy", such as his U.S. trip, his potential trips to other countries, and Taiwan's bid for United Nations membership. Lee thought that Beijing, eagerly looking forward to another breakthrough in cross-strait relations through the Wang–Koo meeting, would likely be more accommodating. However, Taiwan was wrong this time.

By this time Beijing had come to realize that Lee wanted the second round of the Wang–Koo meeting, not so much because he wanted a breakthrough in cross-strait relations but to use it as a bargaining chip for Beijing's acquiescence to his "pragmatic diplomacy". Beijing was not willing to pay such a high price for the second round of the Wang-Koo meeting which, in its view, would be beneficial not merely to China but also to Taiwan, especially when the second round was expected to solve some pressing technical issues, such as protecting Taiwanese investments in the mainland and Taiwanese business interests in Hong Kong before Hong Kong's return to China in July 1997. What is more, Taiwan's independence was not a subject Beijing would agree to exchange for, once it perceived Lee's hidden agenda for Taiwan's independence, either as the ROC, or the Republic of Taiwan (ROT).

It should be pointed out that despite suspicions about Lee, Beijing, for a long time, was unwilling to accept that Lee was totally for Taiwan's independence, and expected to see an accommodating Lee on the reunification issue, even when there had been apparent evidence to the contrary after 1993. By August 1993, with Beijing standing idle, the so-called "main-streamers" under Lee finally tipped the balance of power in the KMT. Despite the main-streamers under Lee having successfully removed most of the KMT leaders who had advocated reunification, Beijing still had hope in Lee, regarding him as the person with whom Beijing was prepared to negotiate on reunification.

This point was confirmed by this writer's interviews with the ARATS chairman, Wang Daohan, in October 1996. Asked whether at the first Wang–Koo meeting in 1993 China had foreseen cross-strait relations retrogressing so much, Wang said that China had never expected cross-strait relations to proceed smoothly. However, at that time it only expected that threats to rock the boat would come from the international community — that is, the United States or Japan — but not from Lee.

From 1994, Beijing began to realize that it could not rely on Lee to pursue reunification. With a firm control over the KMT, a confident Lee seemed to care less about Beijing's reactions. Many incidents happened that shocked Beijing into reconsidering Lee's true stand on reunification. His "pragmatic diplomacy", such as the bid for U.N. membership for Taiwan, became intensified. On most of his visits overseas he pushed for his "pragmatic diplomacy", such as during his vacation leave to the Philippines, Indonesia, and Thailand in 1994; his visits to the United Arab Emirates and Jordan in 1995; and his visits to several African and Latin American countries in 1994.

The confident Lee became more outspoken about his personal stand on reunification and more unconstrained in his verbal attacks on Beijing. By calling Beijing leaders "a group of bandits and hooligans" in a Presidential Office press release, at the Lake Incident of 1994, Lee greatly hurt the feelings of the leaders in Beijing.[58] Even more so in May 1995, he mocked the PRC as the "son" while calling the ROC the "father".[59] Chinese strategists told this author that after reading the report on Lee's derogatory father-and-son analogy, Qiao Shi wrote in a report: "*ci ren tai xiao zhang*" [This man is too arrogant].

However, the two most significant events that proved to be turning points in Beijing's perception of Lee were Lee's conversation with Japanese writer Ryotaro Shiba in May 1994; and Lee's speech at Cornell University, in the United States, in 1995.

Lee's conversation with Japanese writer Ryotaro Shiba shocked many people in Beijing who had previously placed hopes on Lee regarding the reunification issue. In the conversation, Lee strongly and clearly expressed his determination to lead Taiwan away from mainland China, his preference for Japanese culture to Chinese culture, and his unwillingness to see a strong and unified China ("a

Chinese empire", to use his own terminology) in future. Many people in Beijing came to consider this as his true voice. Secret communications between Lee and Beijing continued, but, by this time, Beijing felt that Lee was not keeping his promises and was tilting towards Washington.[60]

However, no fundamental policy change took place regarding Lee. The main reasons included, first, that some people doubted that Lee, despite his personal inclination towards independence, had the determination to take drastic steps to push for Taiwan's independence. If not, the drift towards independence, though still annoying to Beijing, would likely be slow and manageable, and, therefore, it was not worthy of a dramatic reaction for the time being. Secondly, some were unwilling to admit their wrong assessment of Lee earlier, either because of the political implications to their positions or because this was almost equal to a complete denial of all the work they had done in past years. They warned of the danger of a premature final judgement about Lee. At least, what Lee had done so far did not demand a fundamental change to China's Taiwan policy. Thirdly, some believed that what Lee had done was because of the political and social situation in Taiwan. Any other politician who was in Lee's position would have done the same if he wanted to survive politically, although these people considered that what Lee had said was going a little too far.

There were also other differences of view, and therefore no consensus was reached to push for a major policy change like that following Lee's U.S. visit in 1995. For example, some People's Liberation Army (PLA) think-tanks and other élite think-tanks warned in 1994 that Lee and Washington would soon go further and faster in their co-operation to reach Lee's first target in his "pragmatic diplomacy" — that is, Lee's visit to the United States. However, the Ministry of Foreign Affairs considered this unlikely even before the United States' announcement of the visa decision for Lee's visit in May 1995.

Nevertheless, Chinese President Jiang Zemin still made the eight-point proposal on 30 January 1995, calling for a termination of hostilities across the Strait and the first meeting of leaders of both sides. Why did Beijing still make such a proposal despite its suspicions of Lee? First, China's Taiwan Affairs Group had started from June 1993 to prepare a new guideline for reunification soon after the first Wang–Koo meeting in April 1993. The guideline was completed in November 1993, before the APEC meeting in Bogor, Indonesia. As Beijing was then disturbed by the fact that most of those KMT leaders who had advocated reunification had been phased out and the KMT was dominated by "main-streamers" who opposed reunification, and also because cross-strait relations were seriously strained following the Lake incident and Lee's interview with Japanese writer Ryotaro Shiba in 1994, it chose not to announce the proposal in 1994 while studying the new situation in Taiwan's politics. By the time it was announced in early 1995, Beijing did not have *very high* expectations of Lee. It mainly wanted to put a stop to deteriorating cross-strait relations.

Secondly, announcing the proposal would keep the initiative with Beijing. It thought that even if the eight-point proposal failed to generate the best results, it would likely serve to slow down the pace of Taiwan's drift towards independence. Thirdly, some Chinese leaders still had a lingering hope in Lee and wanted to put him under "further observation". One of China's top Taiwan specialists, Li Jiaquan, noted that even at that time Beijing still maintained the approach of "curing the sickness to save the patient" on Lee because it still considered it as, to use another popular Chinese political expression, "a contradiction among the people (or ourselves)" instead of "a contradiction between people (or ourselves) and the enemy".[61]

In fact, Beijing listed three possible responses from Taiwan regarding Jiang's eight-point proposal: warm; lukewarm; and cold. Beijing thought that the first was not possible and the last they would not like to see. It hoped for the second one, but what Beijing got was worse than the worst scenario. Lee's six-point response in April 1995, to use a Chinese expression, was simply "shadowboxing" (that is, lacking substantial measures for a major breakthrough in cross-strait relations) the essential part in Jiang's eight-point proposal. It was followed by Lee's visit to the United States. The visit was given high publicity and treated as a *de facto* state visit. In his public speech at Cornell University, Lee strongly advocated "popular sovereignty" and the "ROC in Taiwan" and declared that he would "challenge the impossible". Taiwan's subsequent actions included an intensified bid for a U.N. seat, its Premier's visit to Europe three days after Lee returned home, its Deputy Premier's planned visit to Canada, and Lee's instruction to "make full use of the excellent situation" following his visit to "go all out" to expand Taiwan's international space. All these sent such a strong message to Beijing that Lee not only personally favoured Taiwan's independence but also had the determination to "go all out" instead of "bit by bit".

At first, Beijing suspected Washington of trying to sabotage the improvement of cross-strait relations by driving such a wedge through granting Lee, on 22 May 1995, the visa for his U.S. tour. Thus, before Lee's speech at Cornell University, Beijing made sharp responses only to the United States but not to Taiwan. However, it was at the same time quietly waiting for Lee's response. Articles that were published later in Chinese newspapers criticizing Lee had actually been prepared from early June 1995 but were not allowed to be published because Beijing wanted to watch Lee's behaviour and speech in the United States first. Lee's speech at Cornell University and his behaviour in the United States were quickly conveyed to the anxiously waiting Chinese leaders, who made the final judgement on Lee after studying every word of his Cornell speech. Then came the decision to make a strong response to stop Lee in his tracks. The die had thus been cast. Strongly critical articles were then allowed to appear in all major newspapers in China. As one Chinese saying goes, "once the water is spread to the ground, it is difficult to take it back".

In contrast to the earlier belief that international forces were the threat to China's reunification, now Beijing saw the threat as coming from Lee himself, who was pushing for Taiwan's independence out of both ideology and his personal feelings and beliefs. And he had the determination to go far to "challenge the impossible (Lee's own words)". In Beijing's view, Lee's push, either intentionally or unintentionally, had helped "international forces" to contain China.

Beijing's anger at the "Chinese helping foreigners to contain China" was aggravated by a feeling of having been fooled, or having played into the hands of Lee, and the memory of Lee's derogatory remarks about the Beijing leadership. All this added strong sentiments into the popular resentment against Lee, the internal political strife and policy debates regarding Taiwan and the U.S. intention that followed Lee's U.S. visit. It would have been surprising if China did not react strongly towards Taiwan.

The enlarged meeting of the CCP Central Committee in Beidaihe in July 1995 passed the decision to hold military exercises. It was at first decided to hold just one exercise to get an idea of Lee's response. As it turned out, Lee took an uncompromising stance. Beijing, therefore, decided to maintain the pressure by holding more military exercises.

China Ponders

The perception change, as discussed above, brought about a policy change, as witnessed since 1995. China abandoned its hope on Lee. However, before Lee announced the "two states" theory, China still had some expectation of a somewhat "gentle" Taiwan, as was the writer's impression during an interview with Wang Daohan in mid-June 1999, only three weeks before Lee's "two states" theory was announced. Wang enunciated three scenarios for his October visit to Taiwan: as a big sensation like *Huanzhu Gege*;[62] being humiliated and coming back with a bleeding nose; and somewhere in between. He said the first scenario was very difficult to achieve, but he would make an effort to achieve the third one. This author's impression from interviews with him and other Chinese Taiwan specialists was that China seemed to still believe that many Taiwanese did not have an accurate picture of China's Taiwan policy because of Lee's influence. Once these people got the picture, the situation would improve. For this purpose, it was better for Wang to visit Taiwan to tell the people there in person and in detail about China's Taiwan policy so as to correct any misunderstanding.

The wide support in Taiwan for Lee's "two states" theory may have caused Beijing to have second thoughts about this expectation and the rationale for its "peaceful reunification" strategy. Was there still a basis for a strategy that emphasized the "two trusts", namely, trust in the Taiwan government, and trust in the people of Taiwan (regarding their intention for reunification)?

A Deteriorating Political Environment for Reunification

China gave up hope on Lee Teng-hui after his visit to the United States in June 1995. However, it did not completely give up on the KMT. This was shown in its reception of Koo Chen-fu on his visit to China in October 1998, and Wang Daohan's planned Taiwan visit in October 1999. It was aware that Koo would not bring many concessions when he visited in October. The tour was mainly to meet the pressure from both the United States and China to resume cross-strait contacts, and to show the Taiwan people that the KMT was more capable (relative to the DPP) in handling cross-strait relations, in preparation for the coming legislative, mayoral and city council elections in December 1998.

Why did China agree to Koo's visit when there was no prospect of substantial concessions? One factor may have been its concern about Taiwan's forthcoming legislative, mayoral, and city council elections in December 1998. Some Chinese analysts believed that the KMT could lose its majority in Parliament to the DPP. No matter how much China distrusted Lee, it still preferred the KMT to be in power. Agreeing to Koo's visit was a way of helping the KMT in the coming elections by giving it credit for being able to improve cross-strait relations. A Chinese strategist, Yu Keli,[63] revealed this motivation when commenting on Ma Yin-jeou's victory over Chen Shui-bian as Taipei mayor. He said that Ma's victory was related to China's tacit support in agreeing to Koo's China visit.[64]

China also hoped that the KMT victory this time would diminish the prospect of the DPP's victory in the 2000 presidential election. Since it had no trust in Lee whatsoever, it placed high hopes on the presidential election, and was prepared to engage in serious talks with the new president, so long as he was not a hard-line advocate of Taiwan's independence. Therefore, by entertaining Koo's visit, China tried to maintain some "reasonable" ties with the KMT, before Lee left office in 2000. Through these ties, it hoped to influence the *zhong sheng dai* (the younger generation) of the KMT leaders after Lee Teng-hui, such as Soong Chu-yu, Lien Chan, and Ma Yin-jeou. These younger leaders had some policy differences with Lee despite their public support for him. Soong had an open conflict with Lee on the issue of freezing the Taiwan provincial government and on Taiwan's mainland policy. Unlike Lee, Soong, Lien and Ma had not made any remarks about reunification that would be considered as provocative to China and helpful to advocates of Taiwan's independence. China was interested in Lien Chan's proposal in late 1995 (but not implemented because of Lee) for setting up a special zone for direct trade and shipping links with China, apart from the government's plan for an offshore transhipment centre. He had called for efforts to boost exchanges with China to secure a win-win situation. He had laid down the principles of "three No's", that is, "no Taiwan independence, no immediate unification, and no confrontation", and "three wants", namely, "want peace, want exchanges, and want a win-win situation". He had also once urged for the re-opening of dialogue between Beijing and Taipei, saying that talks *could include any issue.*[65]

For their own political interests, these younger leaders generally did not encourage the *benshengren* (natives of Taiwan) to marginalize the *waishengren* (the mainlanders in Taiwan). China, of course, liked to see more *waishengren* and those who had strong feelings towards China to remain in power. It once had a preference for a coalition between Lien, Soong, Ma, and those KMT leaders who had been marginalized by Lee on the reunification issue.[66]

To meet the DPP challenge, this KMT younger generation would like to "play the China card" to seek tactical political co-operation from China in order to demonstrate to the voters in Taiwan their capability to maintain cross-strait stability. This was where Beijing could exert its influence.

This expectation had been plunged into doubt because of the wide support within the KMT for Lee's "two states" theory. In the past, Lee had occasionally made controversial remarks, which the KMT government had been quick to dilute by describing them either as "being misquoted" by the press or "a slip of the tongue", or personal opinion. This time, it was different. This "two states" theory had not only been prepared for a long time within the KMT but was also formally endorsed by it, with the support of many of its leaders, including the younger ones. This prompted Beijing to have serious doubts about one primary element of the basis of its "peaceful reunification strategy" — whether the KMT could in future be trusted with reunification. This doubt and frustration was revealed when, for example, Chinese Vice-Premier Qian Qichen for the first time used the expression, "Taiwan separatist forces with Lee Teng-hui at the core".[67] In the past, China had only targeted Lee himself without mentioning or hinting at other KMT leaders. This time, it also criticized, though without mentioning names, Koo Chen-fu, Su Chi and other Taiwan officials, warning them that no good would come about if they followed Lee any further.

An Eroding Social Basis for Reunification

Another "trust" that formed the basis of China's "peaceful reunification" strategy, was the trust of the people in Taiwan, which had also been plunged into doubt by the high percentage of people in Taiwan who supported Lee's "two states" remarks. For example, in an opinion poll conducted by TVBS on 11 July 1999, more than 56 per cent of respondents sided with Lee, while only 22 per cent disapproved of his remarks. Thirty-eight per cent said that they realized that Lee's words would lead to tension, while 45 per cent foresaw no strains with China. Some 43 per cent believed Taiwan's ties with China had moved in the right direction during Lee's tenure, while 25 per cent disapproved of his policy.[68] In another poll, taken by the *United Daily* on 11 July 1999, 71 per cent said that Taiwan was a sovereign country, 13 per cent disagreed, and the rest had no opinion. Forty-nine per cent agreed with Lee that relations with China were "state-to-state" matters.[69] A poll commissioned by the KMT showed over 60 per cent backing the categorization of Taiwan–China relations as "special state-to-state" ties rather than as "political entities".[70] Though many Taiwanese thought that it was neither feasible nor absolutely necessary and preferred to maintain the status quo for the moment, they were pleased that their President had finally spoken out for what they saw as the political reality, that Taiwan was nothing other than a sovereign state.

Beijing felt that it could not be more tolerant towards Taiwan. Feeling wronged, many Chinese asked this writer the following questions during interviews: would the United States be as tolerant and be willing to practise a "one country, two systems" formula on its own soil, and allow the co-existence of a communist government? How many central governments in the past two thousand years of Chinese history have made so many concessions as China had done so far? If it were the CCP who had lost the Civil War and retreated to Taiwan, would the KMT government in Beijing (or Nanjing) be willing to treat the CCP regime as another independent sovereign state or another central government of China? They felt that the concessions and trade benefits extended to the people in Taiwan did not really work. They complained that when China made concessions, Taiwan did not return the favour. Instead, it mistook this as a signal that China was weak, that it could not do anything about Taiwan and was in need of Taiwan. Thus, it would demand more, and often the impossible. They complained: "We don't know when and where it will end its endless demands". They highlighted what Lee Teng-hui once said in a private talk with other Taiwanese officials: "You [Beijing] want reunification? Then, you must first of all recognise the fact of [Taiwan] being independent. ... Once the CCP is thus trapped, then it will have no more control of what happens next".[71] Many Chinese interviewed for this study were concerned that Taiwan would not return the favour with any further concessions. However, whenever China's response was strong, even though it was directed against Lee Teng-hui alone, the Taiwanese would support Lee all the more, as was the case when China denounced Lee's "two states" theory. In response, more people in Taiwan identified themselves as "Taiwanese" instead of "Chinese". A public opinion poll, conducted after Lee's announcement of his "two states" theory, found a record high of 44.8 per cent of the respondents considering themselves Taiwanese rather than Chinese, representing an increase of 7.9 per cent over the last such poll conducted in April. In this poll, 39.9 per cent of the respondents said that they considered themselves both Taiwanese and Chinese, a decline of 5.5 per cent from the April survey. Only 13.1 per cent said that they considered themselves solely Chinese.[72]

"Wait and See" Posture

China believed that Taiwan would not retract the "two states" position so long as Lee was in power. It therefore placed its hopes on the new President. Hence, it took a "wait and see" posture. It exerted measured pressure, only in stern rhetoric but not resorting to force. In this way, it sent a stern warning to Taiwan, while leaving Lee with no excuse to postpone the presidential election, and no justification for a U.S. military intervention.

By mid-September, China appeared satisfied with the international response to Lee's "two states" position. The United States, Japan, the European Union (EU), Russia, Canada, Australia, together with more than one hundred other countries quickly reaffirmed their "one China" policy. U.S. President Bill Clinton took the initiative to call Chinese President Jiang Zemin, assuring him of his support for the "one China" policy. U.S. officials tried to coax or pressure Lee into modifying his statement. At a Clinton–Jiang summit on the sidelines of the APEC summit meeting in Auckland in mid-September 1999, President Clinton concurred that Lee had created trouble for U.S.–China relations. He told the APEC forum that the United States recognized only one China.[73]

Furthermore, in September, Taiwan's diplomatic allies failed, for the seventh year, to get the U.N. General Assembly to consider its membership. The General Assembly's steering committee decided not to include the issue on the Assembly's agenda.[74] What was noteworthy was that the United States, Britain, France and Spain affirmed, for the first time, a "one China" position in the steering committee.[75] This was the first time that the five permanent members of the U.N. Security Council affirmed their "one China" position on the same occasion in the steering committee.[76]

With this international response, China did not feel cornered to rush into immediate military actions, but chose to wait for the outcome of the presidential election in Taiwan on 18 March 2000, before deciding on its next move.

Notes

1. "Taiwan Redefines China Relations", Associated Press Newsline, 10 July 1999; *Lianhe Zaobao* (Singapore), 11 July 1999, p. 2; and *Chung Kuo Shih Pao*, 11 July 1999.
2. David Briscoe, "U.S. Calls for China–Taiwan Dialogue", Associated Press Newsline, 12 July 1999; and *Lianhe Zaobao*, 11 July 1999, pp. 2 and 11.
3. Ibid.

4. *Chung Kuo Shih Pao*, 13 July 1999. The Chinese words *"guo jia"* can be translated into either "countries" or "states".

5. Michael Laris, "Taipei Softens Wording But Reiterates It's Coequal", *International Herald Tribune*, 22 July 1999.

6. "Taiwan Moves to Sell 'Two States' Policy World-Wide", *Straits Times* (Singapore), 15 July 1999. *Lianhe Zaobao*, 14 July 1999, p. 16.

7. "Ziwo Biaobang, Yugai Mizhang" [A Wild Bragger and A Poor Liar], *Renmin Ribao*, 6 August 1999, p. 4.

8. Ching Cheong, "Teng-Hui Pushing Changes to Constitution", *Straits Times* (Singapore), 14 July 1999. Under the present constitution, Taiwan is referred to as the "freedom area of China", while the mainland is described as "ROC territories other than Taiwan".

9. "Taiwan Moves to Sell 'Two States' Policy World-Wide", *Straits Times* (Singapore), 15 July 1999.

10. In September, China's President Jiang Zemin listed two preconditions for Wang's visit to Taiwan. One was retraction of the "two states" statement. The other was that Lee could only meet Wang in his capacity as chairman of the KMT.

11. Ivan Tang, "Beijing Anger at Congressman", *South China Morning Post*, 14 August 1999.

12. "Taipei Denies Mainland Jets Crossed Line", *South China Morning Post*, 14 August 1999.

13. Ching Cheong, "Press Coined '2 states' Idea, Says Teng-Hui", *Straits Times* (Singapore), 28 July 1999.

14. Annie Huang, "Taiwan President Warns China", Associated Press Newsline, 28 July 1999. See also, "China Rejects Taiwan President", Associated Press Newsline, 29 July 1999.

15. See Koo's statement in *Chung Kuo Shih Pao*, 30 July 1999. It generally reiterated what Lee Teng-hui had said. Regarding the "special state-to-state relationship", he said: "First, the shared cultural and ethnic origins have cultivated a very unique affection between the two states. Second, the intensifying cross-strait exchanges in civil, commercial as well as other sectors are unparalleled when compared with other divided countries, past and present. Third, and most importantly, both sides should have the common will to pursue a unified China in the future by engaging in negotiations on the basis of parity." See also, "Unification with China Still the Goal", *Straits Times* (Singapore), 31 July 1999.

16. See the MAC's statement of 1 August 1999, in *Chung Kuo Shih Pao*, 1 August 1999.

17. Annie Huang, "Taiwan President Warns China", Associated Press Newsline, 28 July 1999.

18. Annie Huang, "Taiwan President Stands by Statehood", Associated Press Newsline, 20 July 1999.

19. Jason Blatt, "Taipei Dialogue Offer Aims to Cool Tensions", *South China Morning Post*, 14 July 1999.

20. See also Koo's statement in *Chung Kuo Shih Pao*, 30 July 1999. Koo said: "We believe one China is in the future, but at the moment the sides are coexisting as equals". Annie Huang, "Taiwan Reaffirms Statehood Claim", Associated Press Newsline, 30 July 1999.

21. "Yige Zhongguo Shi Wuke Zhengbian De Shishi" [One China Is an Indisputable Fact], *Renmin Ribao*, 12 August 1999.
22. Ibid. Emphasis added.
23. Ibid.
24. Ibid. Emphasis added.
25. Ibid. Emphasis added.
26. Two major official statements from Taiwan to explain Lee's "two states" theory are Koo Chen-fu's written explanation of 30 July 1999, in *Chung Kuo Shih Pao*, and the MAC's statement of 1 August 1999, also in *Chung Kuo Shih Pao*.
27. Tom Raum, "Albright: US–China Tensions Easing", Associated Press Newsline, 25 July 1999.
28. Ching Cheong, "Taipei Plans to Suspend Charter", *Straits Times* (Singapore), 7 September 1999.
29. "Ziwo Biaobang, Yugai Mizhang [A Wild Bragger and A Poor Liar], *Renmin Ribao*, 6 August 1999, p. 4.
30. "Bo Li Denghui de 'Lianguolun'" [Refute Lee Teng-hui's 'Two States' Theory", *Renmin Ribao*, 10 August 1999.
31. Taiwan uses the word "unification" while mainland China uses the word "reunification", though in Chinese they are the same words "*tong yi*".
32. "Taipei Denies Policy Shift to 'Two Chinas'", Reuters Newsline, 23 November 1993.
33. "White Paper on Cross-Strait Relations", Reuters Newsline, 14 July 1994. Emphasis added.
34. *Straits Times* (Singapore), 9 November 1997, p. 23.
35. "President Defiant on Ties to Mainland", *South China Morning Post*, 18 February 1999.
36. Jason Blatt, "Taipei 'to Face Beijing Force'", *South China Morning Post,* 11 August 1999.
37. *China Times Express* (Taipei), quoted in "Two Likely Reasons for Controversial Declaration", *Straits Times* (Singapore), 13 July 1999.
38. Blatt, op. cit.
39. This section is an expansion of the article by the author, "China Eyes Taiwan: Why Is A Breakthrough So Difficult", *Journal of Strategic Studies* 21, no. 1 (March 1998): 65–78.
40. *Lien Ho Pao* [United Daily News] (Taipei) (overseas edition), 23 December 1995, p. 1; 22 December 1995, p. 2. See also "Taiwan: China Fires 3 Missiles Over Taiwan, Says Report", Reuters Newsline, 25 December 1995.
41. Zhang Shan and Xiao Weizhong, *Erzhi Taiduo* [Containing Taiwan's Independence] (Beijing: China Social Publishing House, 1996), pp. 168–69. See also Zheng Jian, *Gudao Chanmeng* [Lingering Dreams over the Isolated Island] (Beijing: Qunzhong Publishing House, 1997), p. 373.
42. Zhang and Xiao, op. cit., pp. 167–68.
43. Ibid. Chinese President Jiang Zemin also mentioned "*yi gang si mu*" and other proposed arrangements for Taiwan's reunification in his talk with the visiting former president of Taiwan's Tsinghua University, Shen Junshan, in the early 1990s. See *Jiushi Niendai* [The 1990s] (Hong Kong), no. 8 (1996): 108–9.

44. *Lien Ho Pao* (overseas edition), 23 December 1995, p. 1; and 22 December 1995, p. 2. See also "Taiwan: China Fires 3 Missiles Over Taiwan, Says Report", Reuters Newsline, 25 December 1995.

45. From my interviews with Chinese strategists in Beijing and Shanghai in 1996–98.

46. For example, see Shen Cheng, *Lian'an Mishi Miwenlu* [Stories of Secret Missions] (Taipei: Shangzhou Publishing House, 1995).

47. *Renmin Ribao*, 15 January 1988, p. 1.

48. *Renmin Ribao*, 9 July 1988, p. 1.

49. Wang Mingyi, *Lian'an Hetan* [Peace Talks Across the Taiwan Strait] (Taipei: Caixun Publication House, 1997), pp. 39–40.

50. Ibid., pp. 36–37.

51. Xu Jiatun is a former member of the Central Committee of the CCP, and former director of China Xinhua News Agency in Hong Kong in the 1980s — the informal Chinese "Ambassador" to Hong Kong and now self-exiled in the United States because of the Tiananmen incident of 1989. See Xu, *Xu Jiatun Xianggan Huiyilu* [Years in Hong Kong] (Taipei: Lien Ho Pao Publishing House, 1994).

52. Ibid., pp. 328 and 342.

53. Wang Mingyi, op. cit., p. 17.

54. Ibid., pp. 18–20.

55. Ibid., pp. 61–72.

56. *Renmin Ribao*, 19 August 1993.

57. For these secret communications and Lee's remarks, see *Chung Kuo Shih Pao*, 19 July 2000, 20 July 2000, and 21 July 2000; *Lianhe Zaobao*, 20 July 2000, p. 33; "Chinese and Taiwan Officials Had Secret Talks", *Straits Times* (Singapore), 20 July 2000; Catherine Sung, "Secret Envoy Story Called a China Ploy", *Taipei Times*, 21 July 2000; and "Historic 1993 China, Taiwan Talks Took Five Years of Groundwork", Agence France Presse, 19 July 2000.

58. The Lake Incident happened on 1 April 1994, when a tourist ship *Hairui* was robbed by a group of gangsters on Qiandao Lake [Lake of a Thousand Islands] in Zhejiang Province, China. The robbers set the ship on fire and twenty-four Taiwanese tourists died. Before China caught the criminals and executed them in mid-May 1994, Taiwan launched a big anti-China wave. It claimed that the incident was politically motivated, and accused the PLA of master-minding the murder and trying a cover-up. Taiwan's MAC threatened to terminate all cultural and educational exchanges with China. The DPP made good use of the incident by calling for the abandonment of the "one China" policy, freezing all cross-strait talks, and declaring Taiwan's independence. In an official press release from the presidential office, Lee Teng-hui called the CCP a group of "bandits" and "hooligans". See Zheng, *Gudao Chanmeng* [Lingering Dreams over the Isolated Island], pp. 471–72. This incident was simply an action by individual criminals. Taiwan could not find evidence to support its accusation that the Chinese Government and the PLA had organized the murder. It later only complained about the inefficiency of the Chinese in handling the incident.

59. Zheng, op. cit., p. 480.

60. "Su Duikou Renshi Ying Huanyou Zeng Qinghong" [Mr. Su Chi-cheng's Counterpart Should Include Mr. Zeng Qinghong], *Chung Kuo Shih Pao*, 19 July 2000.

61. Li Jiaquan, ed., *Li Denghui Zhuzheng Taiwan Zhihou* [After Lee Teng-hui Stepped into Power] (Beijing: Yanshi Publishing House, 1997).

62. *Huanzhu Gege* [My Fair Princess] is a Chinese TV series that caused a big sensation throughout Taiwan in early 1999.

63. Yu was deputy director of China's Institute of Taiwan Studies in Beijing, an élite think-tank for Beijing's Taiwan policy-making.

64. China Central TV (Beijing) (overseas), News Program, 7 December 1998.

65. "Two Takes on Cross-Strait Ties", *Straits Times* (Singapore), 20 February 1998.

66. For example, see Yan Xuetong, "Lian'an Zhengzhi Tanpan de Zhenjie yu Qianjing [Crux and Prospect for Cross-Strait Political Negotiations], *Lianhe Zaobao*, 30 March 1998, p. 13.

67. "Committed to Peace", *Straits Times* (Singapore), 20 August 1999.

68. "President Backed in Poll", *South China Morning Post*, 14 July 1999.

69. "Taiwanese Back Their President", *South China Morning Post*, 14 July 1999.

70. *Straits Times* (Singapore), 15 July 1999.

71. Zheng, op. cit., p. 616.

72. This poll was commissioned by the MAC and conducted by the China Credit Information Service. See "Highest Percentage Ever Consider Themselves Taiwanese", Central News Agency, 3 September 1999.

73. Ching Cheong, "Sino–US Summit Smoothes over Cross-Strait Tensions", *Straits Times* (Singapore), 16 September 1999.

74. "UN Doesn't Include Taiwan on Agenda", Associated Press Newsline, 15 September 1999. The request to place U.N. membership for Taiwan on the Assembly agenda was sponsored by Burkina Faso, El Salvador, Gambia, Grenada, Honduras, Liberia, the Marshall Islands, Nicaragua, Saint Vincent and the Grenadines, Senegal, Solomon Islands, and Swaziland. See "U.S. Speaks Against Putting Taiwan on U.N. Agenda", Reuters Newsline, 15 September 1999.

75. China Central TV (overseas), News Program, 16 September 1999. *Lianhe Zaobao*, 17 September 1999, p. 2.

76. Russia has always supported the "one China" policy in the steering committee.

4

Taiwan Under
President Chen Shui-bian

Taiwan's 2000 Presidential Election

Taiwan's presidential election, held on 18 March 2000, saw the defeat of the
Kuomintang (KMT) government, for the first time after fifty-five years in power,
by the pro-independence Democratic Progressive Party (DPP). The election
race drew a field of five: the KMT's Lien Chan, the then Vice-President, and
Siew Wan-chang, the then Premier; the DPP's Chen Shui-bian and Lu Hsiu-lien;
independent candidates Soong Chu-yu and Chang Chao-hsiung; the New Party's
Li Ao and Feng Hu-hsiang; and independent candidates Hsu Hsin-liang and Chu
Hui-liang.

Though not as dominant as it was in the 1996 presidential election, the issue
of cross-strait policy still remained a very significant one in the election. Its
debate attracted particular attention after President Lee Teng-hui announced his
"two states" theory in July 1999.

On Unification/Independence

The three front-runners in the election (Lien, Soong, and Chen) had de-
emphasized the unification/independence issue, as many voters were afraid
of military conflict with China. Though once a vocal advocate of Taiwan's
independence, Chen Shui-bian was far less fervent in public about independence.
He vowed that he would not declare Taiwan's independence (unless Beijing
moved to retake Taiwan by force) and abandon the title of the Republic of China
(ROC).

Nevertheless, his "Long Live Taiwan Independence!" cheer during the
campaign made people suspect that his new stance was merely for political

expedience. His remarks often appeared ambiguous, evasive, and self-contradictory. While vowing not to promote a referendum on Taiwan's independence, he also supported the concept of having the Taiwan people determine their own destiny. While on one occasion he promised not to write Lee's "two states" theory into the Constitution, on other occasions he advocated amending the Constitution to give legal effect to the theory. He also did not make clear any commitment to change the pro-independence clause in his Party Charter.

Soong stated that Taiwan, with security and dignity, should seek to find a mutually beneficial model for integrating with mainland China. He suggested that the two sides sign a thirty-year non-aggression agreement in the presence of international witnesses. After this, they could come together, following the European Union model, for another twenty years. Finally, a referendum should be held to decide which direction cross-strait relations should take.

On the "Two States" Theory and Taiwan's Identity

None of the three leading candidates mentioned the "one China" principle. They did not accept China's "one country, two systems" formula for reunification. They agreed that the ROC was an independent sovereign state and upheld, in one way or another, Lee's "two states" theory. Lien said that the theory was an accurate description of the status quo. As for Soong, although criticizing the theory for having unnecessarily led to a deterioration of cross-strait relations and damaging the trust between Taiwan and the United States, he nevertheless defined cross-strait ties as "quasi-international relations of corresponding sovereignty", or, in another English version, as "mutual non-jurisdiction and independent sovereignty". Chen claimed to be the only real defender of Lee's "two states" theory, and challenged both Soong and Lien to mention the theory to Chinese President Jiang Zemin. He even re-worded the theory as "special relations between two separate states".[1]

On the "Three Links" with China

In order to win more votes, all the candidates criticized Lee's "go slow and be patient" policy and promoted the earlier "three links"[2] concept to assure Taiwan's security. Soong said that the ban on the "three links" with China had weakened Taiwan's potential advantage as an Asia-Pacific regional operations centre, and he vowed to lift it. He advocated a conditional establishment of the "three links" with the immediate implementation of a "mini three links", that is, between mainland China and Kinmen and Matsu islands.

Though previously a supporter of Lee's "go slow and be patient policy", Chen now criticized it. He suggested that, based on the principles of reciprocity, market regulations, and equality, Taiwan should reduce the restrictions on the "three links" and on investment in China.

Lien showed his distance from Lee by saying that the "go slow and be patient" policy was not an unchangeable principle, and he would consider setting up a direct trade zone between China's Fujian Province and Taiwan's outlying islands of Kinmen and Matsu.

On Political Negotiations

All the three front-runners were in favour of a resumption of cross-strait talks, willing to enter political negotiations with Beijing under certain conditions. Chen suggested that Taiwan and China could conduct comprehensive talks or dialogue, but the issue of Taiwan's sovereignty was non-negotiable. Moreover, he suggested that any result reached at the talks was invalid before the Taiwanese people sanctioned it. Soong was willing to enter political dialogue with Beijing but he took a similar position to Chen's, suggesting that the Taiwan people had the final say on any potential agreement reached with Beijing. Lien expressed willingness to enter the medium-phase in the Guidelines for National Unification,[3] that is, to conduct political talks with China on unification. All three insisted on parity in negotiations with China.

On National Defence

Regarding national defence, all the three main candidates avoided taking extreme positions. Chen and Lien issued their policies on national defence while Soong remained evasive.

There were many similarities between Chen and Lien in this respect. They both suggested a consideration of confidence-building measures (CBMs) with Beijing. Lien proposed the establishment of a mechanism of notifying and verifying military exercises conducted by each side, together with communications hotlines. Chen proposed disengagement zones in the Taiwan Strait and a code of conduct at sea and in airspace, particularly in the Taiwan Strait and the South China Sea. Soong mentioned CBMs and hotlines, but did not elaborate.

Both Chen and Lien claimed to accept the United States' offer of the Theatre Missile Defence (TMD) system. Chen proposed abandoning a pure defence policy and proposed the development of intermediate-range surface-to-surface missiles. Lien suggested the acquisition of long-range, surface-to-surface missiles. Their defence concepts implied going beyond warfare on the coastline and the western plains of Taiwan. For them, the best operational strategy was to conduct warfare beyond the main island of Taiwan, and to acquire the military capability to deter China and retaliate against targets such as Shanghai and Beijing. They were keen on a comparative edge which they believed Taiwan enjoyed in information warfare, and supported the idea of carrying out offensive information operations against China. With digital or computerized armed forces, Lien and Chen argued that Taiwan should be able to maintain a streamlined defence structure. Lien proposed to reduce the number of armed forces personnel to below 320,000, while Chen argued for a further reduction to 250,000.

Soong was more cautious and even sceptical about the TMD and longer-range missiles. Though he had once said that he would support any measures conducive to the increase of Taiwan's defence capabilities, including joining the TMD, he had reservations about Taiwan's role in it.

On Foreign Policy and Relations with China

All the three leading candidates claimed to pursue wider international recognition for Taiwan and stressed the notion of "Taiwan first" in dealing with China. Chen said he would seek a settlement to the cross-strait dispute under the framework of the Charter of the United Nations and considered signing a peace treaty with the mainland. He favoured signing a non-aggression pact, but under three conditions, namely, that China and Taiwan had the same status; that there would be peaceful means to resolve differences; and that there would be no preconceived notion about a future China. He also suggested the exchange of permanent representative missions in Beijing and Taipei.

Both Chen and Lien expressed willingness to undertake a "journey of peace" to China to "meet with any Chinese Communist leaders". Chen also said that he would invite Chinese President Jiang Zemin, Premier Zhu Rongji, and top Chinese negotiator Wang Daohan to visit Taiwan.

Lien vowed to continue the current pragmatic diplomacy, while maintaining stable relations with China. He put forward four basic principles in solving "disagreements and conflict" between the two sides, namely, mutual respect, incrementalism, peace, and regular and open communications. He also proposed a ten-point policy towards mainland China.[4]

China's Concerns

The initial Chinese strategy during the election campaign was to show no preference for any candidate lest it backfired. However, privately, they took the view that "none of them (the three leading candidates) would be easy for China to deal with [*du bu shi sheng you de deng*]", but anyone of them would be better than Lee Teng-hui. Lien and Soong were both against Taiwan independence, but they would also take a strong position against Beijing. Lien would still be under Lee's control for some time. Soong, under attack from both the KMT and the DPP, could not afford to appear soft in dealings with Beijing. However, they were better than Chen Shui-bian, under whose rule, pro-independence forces in Taiwan would grow rapidly.

Beijing set up an ad hoc 24-hour office headed by the Director of the Central United Front Affairs Department, Wang Zhaoguo, and the Director of the State Council Taiwan Affairs Office, Chen Yunlin, to closely monitor the election campaign. On 28 January 2000, Vice Premier Qian Qichen laid out China's basic positions:

- The two sides of the Taiwan Strait must engage in political talks under the "one China" principle;
- "Taiwan independence" can only mean war;
- The framework is "peaceful reunification" and "one country, two systems" as well as the "one China" principle;
- Under the "one China" principle, in negotiations on reunification, the two sides could discuss any issues, such as entry into the World Trade Organization (WTO), the "three links", ending the state of hostilities, Taiwan's international participation, its political status, and other topics;
- China would adopt a more liberal approach towards its "one country, two systems" policy with Taiwan, than with Hong Kong and Macao;
- China is now willing to discuss the issue of "international space for economic, cultural and social activities for Taiwan that suits it"; and
- Other countries should not do anything that would cause tensions or impede the reunification process. The United States should not sell Taiwan advanced weaponry (including the TMD), and the U.S. Congress should not pass the "Taiwan Security Enhancement Act".[5]

Beijing called once again (after nearly ten years): "We place our hopes on the Taiwan authorities and even more on the Taiwan people".[6] This was a clear sign of Beijing's willingness to work with the new Taiwanese leader. (At that time, China did not expect that Chen Shui-bian would win the election.)

China's White Paper on Taiwan

On 21 February 2000, the Taiwan Affairs Office and the Information Office of the PRC State Council issued an 11,000-word White Paper entitled "The One

China Principle and the Taiwan Issue".[7] After Lee Teng-hui's announcement of the "two states" theory, Beijing felt that it should put forward a theoretical and comprehensive response. This effort resulted in the White Paper.

Much of the document explained the "one China" principle and "one country, two systems" formula for reunification. It said that the ROC's historic position was terminated in 1949 and the PRC became the sole legal government exercising sovereignty over all of China, including Taiwan. It emphasized that the Taiwan government was a local government.[8] It warned against "foreign interference in China's internal affairs" and against foreign countries forging military alliances with Taiwan or selling weapons to the island. It was strongly critical of the United States' TMD plan for East Asia.

The Paper blamed Lee Teng-hui for the deterioration of cross-strait ties. It said: "Lee Teng-hui has become the general representative of Taiwan's separatist forces, a saboteur of the stability of the Taiwan Strait, a stumbling-block preventing the development of relations between China and the United States and a troublemaker for the peace and stability of the Asia-Pacific region".

The White Paper was basically a sum-up of China's positions since its previous and first White Paper on the Taiwan issue in 1994. What is interesting is that the new Paper proposed to resume cross-strait dialogue on an equal footing, and with a flexible agenda. It did not insist, as it had done before, on Taiwan rescinding the "two states" theory. However, the international media largely overlooked these points, but focused on the "three situations" (or three "ifs") under which China said it would use force on Taiwan: namely, a grave turn of events leading to the separation of Taiwan from China in any name; foreign invasion and occupation of Taiwan; and an indefinite delay of the peaceful settlement of reunification through negotiations.

Earlier Chinese documents had only listed two situations: that is, "Taiwan's independence" and "foreign intervention". Occasionally, Chinese officials had talked about two more situations: firstly, large-scale social turmoil against mainlanders by local Taiwanese; and secondly, possession by Taiwan of nuclear weapons. In October 1999, in a meeting with a visiting delegation from Taiwan's Institute of International Relations, Chinese strategists (from the Institute of Taiwan Studies of the China Academy of Social Sciences [CASS]) added four situations: (1) writing the "two states" theory into the Constitution; (2) drafting something like a basic law to declare independence; (3) changing Taiwan's title of the ROC and its flag; and (4) holding a referendum on independence.[9]

This White Paper was the first formal and open document in which Beijing disclosed the situation under which force would be used — that is, an indefinite delay of negotiations for reunification.[10] It did not say how long Beijing would wait before resorting to force. The reason for adding the third "situation" was obvious; it was intended to step up the pressure on the Taiwan government, rather than to really use force. Otherwise, it would not have had to issue such a White

Paper. Taiwan had already given Beijing many excuses to use force, such as the "two states" theory, and China really did not need to list another "situation" as an excuse.

The White Paper was also, as the Chinese admitted, deliberately timed ahead of Taiwan's presidential election to put pressure against independence.[11] Accompanying the White Paper was a *Renmin Ribao* [People's Daily] editorial on the same day, and a *Jiefangjun Bao* [The PLA Daily] editorial the day after. Though not identifying Chen Shui-bian by name, they attacked "the leader of the group that has always advocated Taiwan's independence" and alleged that a position paper that Chen had written the previous December on Taiwan's Constitution was a declaration of independence.[12] They accused him of deception. "One minute he is brazenly howling 'Long live Taiwan independence' while the next he is using beautiful and pleasant words to lie that he wants 'good will, reconciliation, vigorous co-operation and everlasting peace' with the mainland". They warned: "Under no circumstances should we be fooled by his sweet talk".[13] As the election day drew near and promised no obvious win for either Lien or Soong, Beijing issued sterner and clearer warnings in an attempt to influence voters away from Chen. Chinese strategists warned that war between the mainland and Taiwan would be hard to avoid if Chen was elected. Even if Chen did not declare the island independent, cross-strait relations would remain tense and confrontational, which could eventually lead to war.[14] On 15 March, three days before the election, Chinese Premier Zhu Rongji issued a widely televised warning that "Taiwan independence means war".[15]

Washington's Concern

Leading Chinese experts on Taiwan in both Beijing and Shanghai, such as Xu Shiquan, president of the Institute of Taiwan Studies of CASS, and Zhang Nianci, director of the East Asia Institute in Shanghai, had accused the United States of "covert support" for Chen Shui-bian. They said that when the three-way struggle for the presidency (between Lien, Soong, and Chen) promised no obvious winner, the Americans made overtures that steered "hesitant" voters to cast votes for Chen "at the last moment".[16]

Washington denied any role. It claimed that no matter who won the presidential election, it would accept the result. However, it expected the "new government" to act in a responsible and practical manner, encourage cross-strait dialogue, and reduce tensions between Taipei and Beijing.[17] It said that the United States would adhere to the "one China" policy and warned the presidential candidates that to provoke Beijing any further would risk a loss of U.S. support.

By doing this, Washington showed that it did not want a crisis during the upcoming U.S. presidential campaign.[18] As 2000 was also an election year in the United States, China had already become a hot topic. If a Taiwan crisis erupted, China could be the determinant issue in the American presidential campaign at the political expense of the Democratic presidential candidate who would find it difficult to face opposition challenges on the current Administration's policies towards China, Taiwan, and East Asia.

With the successful lobby by the DPP over the years, Washington was much less worried than before about a provocative Chen Shui-bian. In fact, it was concerned that Lee Teng-hui would make another major initiative before the election that would push cross-strait tensions out of control, and get the United States involved in a military conflict. Thus, it exerted pressure on him.

Because Lee sometimes refused to meet those Washington officials whom he called "Beijing's running dogs", this time Washington sent a House of Representatives delegation to visit Taiwan in January 2000. It was headed by Matt Salmon, Lee's close friend and a member of the International Relations Committee and its Asia and the Pacific sub-committee of the Congress.

While in Taipei, Salmon told their host that the United States did not want provocative comments from Taiwan's leadership to interfere with its fragile relations with China. During his meeting with Lee, Salmon asked Lee to remain cautious and prudent in speeches regarding cross-strait ties. He also told Lee that the United States would not provide any "answer" to cross-strait issues. "Such issues can be resolved only by the people on both sides of the Taiwan Strait themselves." He did not want to see his country "sucked into a needless conflict". Directly referring to Lee's "two states" theory, Salmon said: "I believe the comments he made in July were extremely hurtful to relations".[19]

Washington exerted pressure on China too. It feared that Beijing might step up the pressure against Taiwan either by bowing to internal political pressure among the Chinese leadership or by releasing domestic economic and social tensions. It warned Beijing that any use of force against the island would be regarded "with grave concern".[20] Any action similar to what it had done before Taiwan's 1996 presidential election would result in its hope of receiving the Permanent Normal Trade Relations (PNTR) encountering strong opposition in the U.S. Congress. The Congress postponed its voting on China's PNTR to one week after the new Taiwan president's inauguration, so as to await Beijing's reaction.

China did not, however, hold military exercises in the Taiwan Strait as it had done in 1996. Washington noted that the Chinese had been "relatively restrained" and there seemed to be no indication of any increased state of military readiness. As noted by Admiral Dennis Blair, commander-in-chief of the U.S. Pacific Command, "The rhetoric is more heated than the military".[21] New U.S. high-resolution satellite photographs showed little evidence of a Chinese military build-up at airfields within striking or non-refuelling range of Taiwan.[22] Top U.S. intelligence and military officials believed that China did not have the means to launch an invasion of Taiwan, and would not have that capability for some time. President Clinton said that Beijing was just "playing hardball" to try to influence the election.[23]

Chen Shui-bian's Election

On 18 March 2000, 82.69 per cent of eligible voters in Taiwan participated in the presidential election. Chen won 39.30 per cent of the vote, followed by Soong with 36.84 per cent, and Lien with 23.10 per cent.

International Response

According to some U.S. strategists, "Washington was not ready for Mr. Chen's victory".[24] Some even suspected that the Clinton Administration had privately hoped that either Lien or Soong — or for that matter almost anyone except Chen — would be elected the President.[25]

Nevertheless, U.S. President Bill Clinton issued an official statement congratulating Chen Shui-bian. He said the election "clearly demonstrates the strength and vitality of Taiwan's democracy". He noted that the two sides should renew peaceful dialogue. "The United States strongly supports such dialogue and is committed to promoting peace, stability and prosperity in the region". The United States would continue to have close unofficial ties with Taiwan's people through the American Institute in Taiwan "in accordance with the Taiwan Relations Act and our one-China policy".[26]

Clinton reaffirmed the "one China" policy. This was nothing new. What was new and of significance was that this was the first time that a U.S. President had issued an official statement to comment on and congratulate the presidential winner in Taiwan, whose government the United States does not officially recognize. This is a huge step from 1996 when only a U.S. spokesman commented briefly on Lee Teng-hui's presidential election victory.

Many other countries also reaffirmed their "one China" policy and expressed the hope for peace and stability across the strait. Among them, the Japanese and Australian responses, for example, were made at a higher government level than they were in 1996.[27]

Beijing was, perhaps, most satisfied with Russia's response, which was made by an unnamed Foreign Ministry official through Interfax News Agency. He emphasized Russia's refusal to recognize Taiwan's independence. He said: "Moscow builds its relations with Taiwan on two basic principles, the main one of which is the principle of 'Four No's'." "The 'Four No's' are 'no' to Taiwan's independence, 'no' to the concept of 'two Chinas' or 'one China, one Taiwan', 'no' to Taiwan's participation in international organisations in which only sovereign states can be members and 'no' to arms sales for Taiwan".[28]

China's Response

Before the election, China worked to achieve what it termed the "three not's": Lee Teng-hui should *not* stay for another term; the "two states" theory should *not* be incorporated into the Taiwan Constitution; and Chen Shui-bian should *not* be elected. Its prediction had long been for a Lien Chan win. From the end of February 2000, it began to worry about Chen's win.

As soon as Chen was announced as the winner on the evening of 18 March, the CCP Political Bureau held an urgent meeting that same evening. It instructed both the central and state Taiwan Affairs Offices to issue a short statement (announced on Chinese TV and Radio at 10 o'clock that same evening) that Beijing would "listen to what Chen says and watch out for what he does", and that the election result "will not change the status of Taiwan as a part of China".[29]

The next day, an enlarged meeting of the Political Bureau was held. At the meeting, Jiang Zemin put forward a sixteen-character basic policy line, namely, *renzhen guancha* [observe closely], *naixin dengdai* [wait with patience], *buji buzao* [guard against impetuosity], and *baochi gaoya* [maintain high pressure].[30] On 20 March, Jiang Zemin made a public statement: "We said before, and we still take the view now, that whoever is in power in Taiwan is welcome to the mainland for talks. Meanwhile we may also go to Taiwan. But there must be a basis, i.e., the one China principle must be recognised. Under this prerequisite, we can talk about anything".[31]

In late March, Chinese leaders called the directors of Taiwan affairs of various provinces for a meeting in Beijing. China issued a new policy, called the policy of thirty-two characters, which read "*tongyi sixiang* [unify thinking], *jianchi yuanze* [uphold principle], *lengjing guancha* [observe calmly], *fandu cutong* [oppose independence and promote reunification], *yizhan cuhe* [adopt force to promote peace], *buji buzao* [guard against impetuosity], *baochi yali* [maintain pressure], and *liangbian tanpan* [bilateral talks].[32]

China claimed that recognition of the "one China principle" was the real test of whether the Taiwanese leaders were advocating independence or reunification. It was prepared to hold talks with Taiwan's new leader on any issue, as long as that leader recognized the principle of "one China". It would wait for Chen's inauguration speech on 20 May to see if he agreed to the "one China" principle to decide its next step. It could not accept Chen's stance that "one China" was "a topic for discussion", rather than a guiding principle.[33] Meanwhile, China maintained high pressure on Taiwan. However, despite some heated rhetoric, there was no obvious military build-up by Beijing. This followed the internally circulated central guideline of *"dou er bu po, ya er bu bian"* [contending but not destroying; coercing but not crashing].[34]

How Did China Read the DPP?

China has long had a deep distrust of the DPP for openly advocating Taiwan's independence, as written in its Party Charter. Beijing refuses to have any ties with it, at least official ones, so long as it advocates Taiwan's independence.

Think-tanks in China began research on the DPP soon after it was founded in September 1986 and proposed, no later than 1992, to contact it. Beijing acceded to the proposal in 1993. In March that year, the DPP leader, Chang Chun-hong, met Chen Andong, deputy director of the Third Division of the CCP United Front Work Department in Shenzhen, China. Wang Daohan had also on several occasions met Chang Chun-hong, Chen Zhongxin (in Chinese *pinyin*) and other DPP leaders, but not in their official capacities.[35] In 1994, the CCP United Front Work Department announced its policy:

> As long as these people are not acting on behalf of the DPP, they are welcome to start investment projects in the mainland or to conduct fact-finding tours. But they will not be entertained if they come here to discuss the issue of Taiwan independence. The mainland China is maintaining some contact with the DPP, but it cannot be considered a contact between two parties. China is maintaining personal contact with individual members of the DPP but not with the party as a whole.[36]

Since 1995, there has been some adjustment to Beijing's policy towards the DPP. For example, President Jiang Zemin, in his eight-point proposal in January 1995, invited representatives from *"all the parties* and groups" in Taiwan to participate in the reunification talks, no longer mentioning negotiation with the KMT as the other participant, as it had done before.[37] In May 1996, Jiang noted that as long as the DPP gave up its stand on Taiwan's independence, the mainland could have dialogue with it.[38] He repeated this statement with some modification at the Fifteenth CCP National Congress in September 1997. He said that China "welcomes *all the parties* in Taiwan and people of all the circles, *except those who stubbornly stick to Taiwan's independence*, to visit the mainland to exchange views on cross-strait relations and reunification matters".[39]

As early as 1996, some Chinese strategists had argued in internal deliberations that the prospect of the DPP as the ruling party might not be a bad thing for Beijing. First, the KMT might feel forced to liberalize its mainland policy as this would help maintain its mandate. Secondly, this would intensify conflict between the KMT and DPP. Thirdly, to be the ruling party, the DPP would have to compromise its pro-independence stance to achieve stable relations with China, in order to win confidence from nervous voters and maintain international investors. This would intensify internal divisions within the DPP. Fourthly, this would also aggravate its conflict with both the New Party (NP) and the Taiwan Independence Party. Fifthly, this would deepen the apprehension of the United States and other countries of a premature and uncontrolled conflict between China and Taiwan that might destabilize East Asia. These countries would also exert pressure on any future DPP government. Thus, the DPP would not go too far, nor become too radical, even if it was voted into power. What was more, it did not have enough financial and personnel resources, compared to the KMT, to rule effectively, and Beijing would then be in a better position to influence Taiwan's politics.[40]

Despite these different voices, Beijing still preferred to keep what it called a "grey area" from the DPP, with its old rival, KMT, still in power. The DPP once sent their "representatives" to visit China as tourists, but discussed political matters under the auspices of economic issues. Their "excessive demands" might have made the Chinese side feel that it was not yet time to "make a deal" with the DPP.

Understanding Chen Shui-bian

Since his election, Chen has shifted from being a radical advocate of Taiwan's independence that he and the DPP had stood for during the past years. This shift has relieved popular worries over a military clash across the Taiwan Strait. Chen's new position has helped to reduce the high tension that had erupted following Lee Teng-hui's announcement of the "two states" theory in July 1999.

However, the question is whether this is just a tactical adjustment to allow a temporary breathing space for Chen to consolidate his power before he becomes strong enough to challenge Beijing on the reunification issue, or whether the shift will lead to abandonment of his pursuit of Taiwan's independence. The difference between the two opposite choices would determine peace or war in future. In the following sections, Chen's major policies will be examined to illustrate the trend of the shift and its significance.

Chen's Inauguration Speech: On the "One China" Principle

The crux of the cross-strait tension is whether the Chen government will resume its "one China" position, which the previous KMT government had held for more than five decades. Chen and the DPP have so far refused to accept the "one China" position.

In his inauguration speech on 20 May 2000, Chen mentioned "one China" only once. He said: "Leaders on both sides possess enough wisdom and creativity to jointly deal with the question of a future 'one China' [*gongtong chuli weilai 'yige Zhongguo' wenti*]".[41] By so saying, he actually declared that there was not "one China" at that time, which coincided with his earlier position that both sides should take "one China" as an issue for discussion, not as a principle as espoused by China.[42] As for the "future one China", Taipei and Beijing would jointly deal with it. He did not say whether or how this "future one China" would include Taiwan. His promise to "deal with the question of a future 'one China'" does not mean that he will promote Taiwan's reunification with the mainland, either now or in the future.

Chen has refused to accept the "one China policy" on the grounds that the people in Taiwan would not agree to Taiwan being part of the PRC. This argument does not sound strong. First, China's "one China principle" had previously been stated in three sentences: there is only one China in the world; Taiwan is a part of China; and the government of the PRC is the sole legal government representing the whole of China. However, in January 1998, Beijing changed this definition in its proposal to Taiwan:

> Before the realisation of reunification and in handling affairs concerning cross-straits relations, especially during the talks between the two sides, the One-China Principle should be upheld, namely, that there is only one China in the world, Taiwan is a part of China and China's sovereignty and territorial integrity is not to be separated.[43]

Here, Beijing replaced the third sentence of the earlier definition of the "one China principle" ("The government of the PRC is the sole legal government representing the whole of China"), with a new one: "China's sovereignty and territorial integrity is not to be separated". In August 2000, Beijing went further to replace, at Taiwan's request, the second sentence of the definition ("Taiwan is a part of China"), with a new one: "Taiwan and the mainland are both part of China".[44] Obviously, Beijing wanted to make it easier for Taiwan to accept the "one China principle" by changing its definition.

On 25 April 2000, Tang Shubei, secretary-general of China's ARATS, noted: "We hope that the Taiwan side accepts the one China principle, i.e., the practice since 1949".[45] The "practice since 1949" is that while the PRC claims to be the sole legal government representing China, the ROC claims to be the one. By this gesture, Tang actually sent a clear message to Chen that China hoped the new government would follow its predecessor in agreeing to the "one China principle" though it may claim this "one China" to be the ROC (Chen has not actually done this yet).

Shortly before Chen's inauguration, *Liang'an Guanxi* [Cross Strait Relations] (a journal of the PRC State Council) pointed out: "'One China' should be upheld as a principle, though its content, namely what and who is this one China, could be discussed".[46]

In his inauguration, Chen also failed to accede to the Chinese request to state that he is Chinese [*zhongguoren*]. He used the word *huaren* instead (in saying "all the *huaren* both overseas and at home"). The English word "Chinese", when referring to the people, is translated from two separate words, *huaren* and *zhongguoren*, which actually carry different political connotations. For example, Singaporeans of Chinese descent call themselves *huaren* (Chinese) but not *zhongguoren* (also Chinese) because Singapore is not part of China, but the people are of Chinese origin. By refusing to call himself a *zhongguoren* [Chinese], Chen came under strong suspicion that he was denying Taiwan as being part of China. His deputy, Vice President Lu Hsiu-lien, and MAC Chairperson, Tsai Ying-wen, also publicly denied that they were *zhongguoren* (Chinese).[47] They even refused to follow Lee Teng-hui's example by saying that they were Taiwanese as well as Chinese.

At his inauguration, Chen announced the "five not's", namely, *not* to declare independence, *not* to change the national title, *not* to push forth the inclusion of the "two states" description in the Constitution, *not* to promote a referendum to change the *status quo* with regard to the question of independence or unification, and *not* to abolish the National Unification Council and the Guidelines for National Unification.[48] But he placed the "five not's" under two conditions. First, he stipulated that this applied "during my term". In other words, he did not indicate what would occur after the first "four years". He certainly needs stability for the first few years to establish a strong power base at home before he can challenge Beijing. Secondly, he also stated that the "five not's" stood "as long as the CCP regime has no intention to use military force". The "intention to use military force", instead of the "actual use of military force", allows for wide interpretation. What is more: "not to declare independence" does not mean "not to promote independence"; "not to include the 'two states' theory into the Constitution" does not mean that he rejects the theory. (In fact, Taiwan's MAC stated that dropping the wording of the "two states" theory did not mean that the government was abandoning the theory, and would not change the fact of China and Taiwan being "two states"); and "not to abolish the National Unification Council and the Guidelines for National Unification" does not mean that he is going to use the guideline as the basis of his mainland policy. (In fact, Chen's later statement that unification should not be the only choice for Taiwan is not compatible with the guidelines that list unification as the only target.)

Chen's "conciliatory" gestures have also appeared to China as "one step backward two steps forward". For example, he put forward three principles in opening cross-strait dialogue, that is, to negotiate on the basis of equality; to resolve disputes by peaceful means; and to establish no pre-set conditions on the future of cross-strait relations.[49] A close study into the original Chinese text of these principles reveals something significant. For example, most international media reported his second principle as to "resolve disputes by peaceful means".[50]

However, its original Chinese text reads "to solve disputes by applying United Nations peaceful means and according to the United Nations Charter".[51] The UN Charter [Article 2(7)] prohibits intervention in the domestic affairs of a member state. By insisting on adopting the UN Charter to solve the dispute, which in the strict legal sense is the outcome or extension of a civil war within one member state of the United Nations, Chen only made Beijing more suspicious of his intention to treat Taiwan as another UN member state.

As for the principle "to negotiate on the basis of equality", Chen did not elaborate on whether his "equality" was more compatible with China's notion that "the two sides shall negotiate on equal footing", or with Lee Teng-hui's notion of two sides being "two equal political identities", which finally evolved into the "two states" theory.

As for the third principle of "no pre-set conditions", it is actually an incorrect English translation. The original Chinese words "*bu yu she fan xiang*" should be translated as "no pre-set direction". His complete sentence reads: "no pre-set direction for the possible development [in cross-strait relations] in future". In other words, reunification should not be the only choice, and Taiwan's independence should also be one option. Again, this is what China does not agree to. In the past, Taiwan had only talked about how and when unification should be achieved but never compromised unification as the sole target, as is listed in its Guidelines for National Unification.

Despite Chinese pressure, Chen reaffirmed this position three months later and went even further. He declared on several occasions in late August and early September that the 1991 National Unification Guidelines had been adopted "not through a democratic process", and were therefore "not an unchangeable totem". Stressing that unification was only "a choice" and not "the only choice" for Taiwan, he said he would consult the people on how to revise those guidelines.[52] He noted: "It is against people's will to list unification as the only choice, as the KMT government has done, for Taiwan's future and in cross-strait relations development".[53] He showed his reservation in holding the chairmanship of the National Unification Council.[54]

The ruling DPP also claimed that under "present subjective and objective circumstances, modifying the National Unification Guidelines is inevitable".[55]

1992 Consensus of "One China"

Chen at first refused to acknowledge the 1992 consensus (reached between Beijing's ARATS and Taipei's SEF) on "one China". Later, he said that there was no "1992 consensus on one China", but only a "1992 spirit", which, he explained, "means dialogues, exchanges and shelving disputes".[56] He called on Beijing to resume cross-strait talks based on such a "spirit", instead of the "1992 consensus on one China" as Beijing demands.

As a matter of fact, on 16 November 1992, Taipei and Beijing did reach a verbal consensus on the "one China" principle in a discussion between the ARATS and the SEF. China's ARATS said: "Both sides of the Taiwan Strait adhere to the one China principle, seeking national reunification. But the political content of the one China will not be involved in their talks on practical matters".[57] Taiwan's SEF said: "In the process of both sides of the strait making common efforts to seek national unification, although both sides adhere to the one China principle, they have a different understanding of what is this one China".[58]

Obviously, both sides did reach a consensus on one China, though each side had a different interpretation of this "one China". KMT chairman Lien Chan, former MAC chairman Su Chi, Taipei Mayor Ma Ying-jeou and other officials in the previous KMT government involved in the ARATS-SEF meetings have also publicly acknowledged that the "one China" consensus is a fact.[59]

Adhering to the "one China" principle and the 1992 consensus on one China, the two conditions that Beijing is now demanding of Chen's government, is currently at the centre of the tussle across the Taiwan Strait. To the ruling DPP, acknowledging "one China" means, as Vice-President Lu Hsiu-lien describes, "capitulation". Hence, the new government has tried hard to keep away from this "one China" issue while trying to avoid unnecessary tension in the strait. Therefore, it has resorted to ambiguity and play of words, as reflected in its announcement of the "three acknowledgements and four suggestions", and Chen's New Year speeches, which will be examined below.

Three Acknowledgements and Four Suggestions

To avoid the "one China" issue, Taipei came out in November 2000 with a recommendation for "three consensus and four suggestions", which was drafted by the Supra-Party Panel on Mainland Affairs. The "three acknowledgements" were:

- The current state of cross-strait affairs is the result of the developments of history;
- The PRC and Taiwan neither mutually represent one another nor belong to each other; and
- Any change to the current cross-strait situation should be approved by the people of Taiwan through democratic measures. People are the pillar of a nation and the purpose of a nation is to guarantee their security and benefits. Seeing that languages on both sides of the Strait are similar and the physical distance between the two is small, the people on both sides of the Strait should work to uphold and enhance this.

The "four suggestions" were:

- To improve cross-strait relations, to deal with cross-strait disputes, and to deal with China's "one China" principle according to the ROC Constitution.
- To create a new mechanism or adjust current measures to continually co-ordinate the different opinions on national development or cross-strait relations, which would include all political parties as well as the public.
- To appeal to the PRC to respect both the dignity and the "space" of Taiwan and to end military threats and work together with Taiwan to sign a peace agreement. In this way, confidence can be built and a win-win situation will be established.
- To declare to the world that the government and people of Taiwan insist on peace, democracy, and prosperity as cornerstones to co-operation with the international community. With this in mind, Taiwan will construct new cross-strait relations with sincerity and patience.[60]

The panel is headed by Academic Sinica President Lee Yuan-tseh, who advises the President on Taiwan's mainland policy. It is not representative since all the three major opposition parties have refused to be part of it. As its roles are similar to the National Unification Council, it is subjected to criticism from the opposition parties that the functions of the two are overlapping. Chen intends to defunctionalize the National Unification Council.

The recommendation of the "three acknowledgements and four suggestions" urged the President to use the ROC's 1947 state constitution to find a way to accommodate Beijing's insistence on "one China" without actually having to utter those words. Beijing immediately criticized this recommendation.[61] The three major opposition parties in Taiwan derided the recommendation as a "conclusion without conclusions".[62] The KMT dismissed the recommendation as "irrelevant", a "play of words" and "a manifesto of non-agreement" among the panel members.[63] The People's First Party (PFP) said that the panel had "come full circle" without making any breakthrough in getting Chen out of the political mire of his own making.[64] The New Party said that the recommendation managed only to "agree to disagree", far from solving the problems plaguing Chen, "no less puzzling than the questions themselves".[65]

Actually, the recommendation was aimed "inward" more than "outward". In other words, rather than to please Beijing, Taipei actually used the ambiguous wording in the recommendation to prevent an internal national split on the divisive "one China" issue, which Beijing could use to divide and rule. There have long been disagreements in Taiwan regarding how to proceed with cross-strait relations, and the DPP holds that this lack of consensus has made it difficult for the people of Taiwan to develop a strong consciousness of, and confidence in, their nation. This has had a severe impact upon the DPP's efforts at nation-building.

One reason for Beijing's opposition to this recommendation was its failure to give a clear endorsement of the "one China" principle and the 1992 consensus of "one China". The essential point of this recommendation was to call on Chen Shui-bian to "respond to Beijing's 'one China' claim ... according to the Republic of China Constitution". Here, there are two key points. First, by asking the President to "respond to *Beijing's* 'one China' claim", it has actually described this "one China" claim as something belonging to Beijing only and Taipei is just responding and does not, at least at present, hold this "one China" position.

Secondly, instead of a clear endorsement of the "one China" policy, it asks the President to respond "according to the Republic of China Constitution". Does the Constitution contain a framework for "one China"? For this question, MAC vice-chairman Chen Ming-tung gave a vague answer: "This is a constitutional issue, which should be interpreted by constitutional bodies. The MAC won't comment on that".[66] The ruling DPP claimed that any decision made by the panel on the "one China" position would be against public opinion.[67] Obviously, Beijing could not be satisfied by the vague position on the "one China" principle.

Chen Shui-bian's New Year Speeches

One point of the recommendation of "three acknowledgements and four suggestions" was to ask Beijing to resume cross-strait talks without Taipei clearly agreeing to the "one China" principle but only based on a broad ROC Constitution, which allows wide interpretation. This was once again manifested in Chen's New Year speeches.

For the New Year of 2001, Chen Shui-bian made two speeches, one on the eve of the New Year and the other on the first day. In them, Chen proposed revising the "no haste, be patient" policy with a new approach of an "active opening and effective management". As for the key issue of the "one China" principle, he said: "According to the ROC Constitution, 'one China' was *originally* not a problem". He proposed: "The two sides should start from economic, trade and cultural integration, and build mutual trust on a gradual basis so as to seek lasting peace and build a new mechanism for political integration".[68] He continued: "It has always been my personal view that peoples on the both sides of the Taiwan Strait *originally* belonged to one family. ... Since wanting (*sic*) to live under the same one roof, [we] should understand and help each other, ... ".[69]

This was the first time that Chen had proposed a long-term framework, however abstract and ambiguous it was, for cross-strait relations. A careful analysis is needed, as done below, to illustrate its implications.

Trends in Cross-Strait Relations

Compared with his earlier radical support of Taiwan's independence, Chen has made a great effort in adjusting his policy since assuming office as President. This has helped to reduce the tension across the strait which many people had expected to escalate when the pro-independence DPP won the election. His flexibility has surprised many Taiwan observers.

However, as the discussion above has shown, despite the flexibility, he has so far been ambiguous on key issues, such as the "one China" principle, the 1992 consensus, and reunification. For example, he used the ROC's Constitution to respond to Beijing's insistence on "one China", saying in his New Year speeches: "According to the ROC Constitution, 'one China' was *originally* not a problem". The word "originally" is important here. It implies that "one China" is a problem at present, although originally it was not. It was not an accident that he used the word "originally" for the second time in his New Year speeches when he said "It has always been my personal view that peoples on both sides of the Taiwan Strait *originally* belonged to one family." He left open the question whether they now still belong to the same family. He continued, "Since wanting (*sic*) to live under the same one roof, [we] should understand and help each other … " Here, Chen deliberately avoided making clear *who* wanted to live under the same roof. In other words, it could mean that it is not Taiwan but Beijing that wants the people on both sides of the strait to live under the same roof. "Living under the same roof" does not necessarily mean reunification, as he used the ambiguous word "integration" in the same speech — "The two sides should start from economic, trade and cultural integration, and build mutual trust on a gradual basis so as to seek lasting peace and build a new mechanism for *political integration*."

Here, the word "integration" is subject to wide interpretations. It could mean a federation, confederation, or even commonwealth. Chen later added that the European Union was the best model for Taiwan and China.[70] Obviously, Chen was asking for Beijing's recognition of Taiwan as nothing less than a separate sovereign state, and not Taiwan's reunification. DPP Chairman Hsieh Chang-ting explained that the word "integration" was to indicate that the political entity of Taiwan would not disappear. It was different from unification, but "*duo zhong you tong, tong zhong you duo*" [independence among unification and unification among independence].[71] "'Integration' does not necessarily mean 'unification' while 'unification' must mean 'integration'".[72] The MAC Chairperson Tsai Ing-wen refused to spell out exactly what the government meant by the phrase "political integration". She asked the people not to pin down its meaning too precisely but to allow a certain degree of flexibility in its interpretation.[73]

Both the MAC Chairperson and the ruling DPP Chairman emphasized that integration was "only a process", "not the final status", which was uncertain.[74] However, in exchange for this uncertain and fluid status, Taiwan wants something that is specific and immediate, that is, recognition of Taiwan's full and equal sovereign status, and abandonment of the right of the use of force. Chen Shui-bian said that any form of political integration should be subject to the ROC Constitution, and Taiwan's national sovereignty, safety and dignity should not be compromised. He also specifically reiterated his insistence that Beijing renounce the use of force against Taiwan.[75] As one Taiwanese strategist suggested: "Once the integration process kicks off, China will in fact have admitted that Taiwan has a certain form of sovereignty or autonomy. Taiwan will therefore naturally have the right to drop out of the integration process at any time ..."[76] On a public occasion, Chen explained that for the word "integration", "we can make our own interpretation that is favourable to us. To use the phrase doesn't necessarily mean that we are going to be unified by the other side".[77]

In the same speeches, Chen also rejected, as Lee Teng-hui had done, Beijing's demand to start political talks and dialogues, saying, "The two sides should start from economic, trade and cultural integration" first, in order to "build mutual trust on a gradual basis" before "seeking lasting peace and building a new mechanism for political integration".

Nevertheless, Chen should be given credit for his flexibility that has so far helped to relax the cross-strait tension. However, the question is: "what next?" The future of cross-strait relations depends on at least two factors. First, how will Chen elaborate on and concretize his currently broad and abstract cross-strait framework of "integration"? Secondly, will the ruling DPP toe Chen's policy line? Not to stay on these two courses would invalidate Chen's good intentions and cause Beijing to interpret his overtures as a tactic to buy time and a cover-up for his pursuit of independence.

How Does China Read Chen Shui-bian?

With Chen's surprise election, China, as Chinese scholars have put it, has to step out of the "grey area" to face the DPP "eyeball-to-eyeball" ("*duan bin xiang jie*"), earlier than it had expected. To Beijing, Chen has long been an advocate of Taiwan independence, but he is also, to use the expression of one Chinese leader, "*zhi suo jin tui*" (flexible and pragmatic). A CCP Politburo member drew the following distinction between Lee Teng-hui and Chen: "Lee Teng-hui is driven by a set of misguided beliefs and is hard to change. While being a Lee disciple, Chen Shui-bian often waffles. He may flip-flop according to circumstances".[78]

Since his election, Chen Shui-bian has made some "conciliatory" gestures to Beijing. However, Beijing has doubted his sincerity. His flexibility does not mean the abandonment of his pursuit of independence, but, as Chinese

Vice-Premier Qian Qichen has said, it is only a "change from a pursuit of overt independence to a covert one". Qian said that this was because of his current weak power bases at home.[79] Chinese strategists have acknowledged that Lee Teng-hui was also "very conciliatory" when he was weak as the executive. After consolidating his control over any challenges in late 1993, he became more hardline. Beijing suspects that Chen may follow Lee's lead. Obviously, Beijing's bitter memories of Lee Teng-hui have greatly influenced its reading of Chen's gestures.

In fact, there are differing voices among Chinese strategists. Some have argued that Chen is personally not as ideological regarding Taiwan's independence as Lee Teng-hui is. Given Taiwan's political reality, he has done what he could to shift from independence. However, Beijing is still taking a hard position. This, as expressed by the Chinese strategists, is less targeted at Chen himself, but more at "the independence force as a whole led by the DPP". In other words, even if Chen personally gives up the pursuit of Taiwan's independence, it would be of little use to Beijing because the ruling DPP and the independence forces as a whole have not yet collapsed.

"Flexible and pragmatic" as he is, Chen Shui-bian is unlikely to change too much and too quickly. The DPP will not allow him to do that.

The DPP is a loose political alliance made up of various factions. No leaders or factions can wield dominance. Leaders of different factions are voted into the party chairmanship in turn, and for short terms (one year for each term, originally, and two years for each term at present). The chairman does not have more power than the Central Standing Committee because it is a collective leadership based on consensus. The DPP's decision-making process has been based on difficult inter-faction bargaining and consensus making, which is being made more and more difficult with the ever growing power of local party branches (as more and more local leaders in cities and counties are from the DPP which has won more local elections, and produced more DPP legislators).[80] Under this power structure, Chen needs a consensus if he wants the DPP's political support. If he changes his China policy too much, he would find it difficult to obtain consensus from the DPP, whose members are mostly in favour of Taiwan's independence. At present, without the DPP's support, Chen's political position would be in danger.

Political reality does not encourage Chen to shift too much in the short term from the "left", that is, independence fundamentalists, to the middle, or even the "right", that is, pro-unification. Those in the middle, that is, those who want to keep Taiwan's status quo, comprise a large part of the votes. If Chen moves too far to the "middle", he will lose the support from his basic DPP supporters at the left. They have long supported almost everything he says and does while the new votes he may get from those in the "middle" are not certain because they only support Chen when he adopts what they think are correct policies. In other words, they are only issue-supporters, but do not always support whatever he does like those at the "left". With this political reality, Chen will hesitate to move too far or too quickly to the "middle".

The social scenario in Taiwan also encourages Chen to stay with the "leftists", at least not to go beyond the "middle". During the 1996 presidential election, 21.2 per cent of the votes went to the DPP candidate, and it rose to 39.3 in 2000. Young voters, aged 20–39, comprise 50.5 per cent of the total (24.8 per cent aged 20–29, and 25 per cent aged 30–39),[81] some 6 per cent more than in 1996. These young voters have little emotional ties with the mainland, and the majority of them voted for Chen. The population of mainlanders has decreased to only 13 per cent.[82] *If* it can avoid a premature conflict with Beijing, tide over the first few critical years by remaining united, and do a better job than the KMT in internal governance and the economy, in a matter of one or two terms, the DPP will find no serious challenge from other parties at home. Of course, it is a big *if*.

Taiwan's Weaknesses

Under this situation, Beijing will likely continue its pressure on the Chen government. Instead of a political disaster for Beijing, Chen's election has exposed some inherent weaknesses of Taipei that Beijing can make use of, and its current Taiwan policy has thus been adjusted. This section will examine these weaknesses before discussing the reorientation in China's Taiwan policy.

A Fragile Democracy

Taiwan's democracy is weak in three essential areas: civil society, core values of the society, and state building.

Civil Society

In a mature civil society — the base for a stable democracy — the intelligentsia as well as businessmen are comparatively highly independent, politically. This is not the case for a young democracy like Taiwan, as vividly demonstrated in its rampant "black gold" politics. Hence, a change of government in Taiwan will affect the interests of these businessmen and intelligentsia much more than in a stable democracy like the United States. Their political fight-back, as we can see in post-election politics in Taiwan, will be much fiercer than what is generally expected of a stable democracy.

In a mature civil society, there should also be strong "civil power", that is, broad and horizontal social connections within the social system rather than the vertically connected social structure along family and/or ethnicity lines, as is the case now in Taiwan. As a result, despite the impressive progress of democracy on the surface, its foundation remains weak. Hence, the dramatic change of government in 2000 has inevitably brought about huge political and social upheavals that will not easily quieten down.

Societal Core Values

A stable democracy cannot be built on severe conflict of societal core values; if this occurs, it may lead to social and political chaos. Indeed, the United States remains stable despite continual deep divisions and debate over issues such as men–women relationships, the origin and sanctity of human life (abortion, capital punishment), race relations, and the balance of central and state powers. However, none of these issues are as divisive and volatile as the debates in Taiwan on independence or unification, and being Chinese or Taiwanese. These debates started openly from the early 1990s, and have now become even more divisive with the pro-independence DPP becoming the ruling party. What is more, the United States has strong state building to accommodate those debates, while Taiwan has a weak one and faces a big neighbour that, out of its determination to unify, consistently plays the "united front" tactics on Taiwan.

For example, the number of overseas ROC citizens who came back for the celebration of the ROC's 2000 National Day was a record low. In the armed forces, dozens of generals offered to retire after Chen's election. Even though the loyalty of Taiwan's military to the Constitution and to their commander-in-chief has never been doubted, Chen is faced with the problem of how to work with a military that fundamentally opposes the DPP position on Taiwan independence, with the fact that an overwhelming majority of the officer corps did not vote for him.[83] Chen Shui-bian pointed out: "Taiwan's danger does not lie on the side of China or the United States but on Taiwan itself. In other words, the danger is, there is no consensus regarding who is the enemy, who is the friend."[84]

State-Building

The political mess after Chen's election has demonstrated Taiwan's weak state building, which cannot easily accommodate "rule by rotation" and "coalition government" — both of which are common features in many stable democracies. Taiwan's state system is peculiar. Its presidential system is neither based on that of the United States nor that of France; neither is its Cabinet system based on that of the United Kingdom. The new president, with only 39.30 per cent of the votes and without the second voting to give him a convincing mandate of more than half of the votes, has very limited power. These constitutional flaws have somehow stalled and will likely — at least for the near future before a relevant constitutional revision and a new political landscape take place — stall the efficient functioning of the new government. This becomes a vicious cycle: the weak state building intensifies the division over societal core values, and vice versa.

A Weak Governance

Apart from the above-mentioned three essential areas, Taiwan's weakness also comes from the ruling DPP's lack of sufficient competent technocrats and experience for effective governance. Furthermore, the DPP's party culture, the product of long years as the grassroots opposition, makes it difficult for the party to adapt quickly to its new role as the ruling party. It still often resorts to the methods it used when it was the opposition, such as mobilizing the pro-independence native Taiwanese to come all the way from southern Taiwan to demonstrate in Taipei to show the "people's voice" in order to put pressure against the KMT-dominated legislature. As the ruling party, it should refrain from such tactics, as this will only intensify the social division and tension. A party needs these masses at the grassroots level for votes. However, once voted into power, it should rely on social élites for effective governance and help unite the masses at the grassroots level with those élites. Hence, the DPP should help to unite mainlander Taiwanese with native Taiwanese instead of setting them against each other, as it often does for winning an election. A widening division between the social élites and the masses, and between the mainlander Taiwanese and the native Taiwanese can only plunge Taiwan into deeper instability.

A Weak Cohesion

Taiwan's weakness also lies in its weak political cohesion. When Lee Teng-hui was in power, he had a strong cohesion behind him and, therefore, had the confidence to say "no" to Beijing: As the KMT chairman, he controlled the KMT. As the first native Taiwanese president, he often enjoyed support from native Taiwanese and the DPP. For Chen Shui-bian, however, with severe political fighting between the DPP and the opposition parties and even within the DPP, he stands on weak ground *vis-à-vis* Beijing.

Confusion and Division of the DPP

Chen's election has actually hindered the development of Taiwan's independence movement. If the DPP had remained out of power and continued to mobilize at the grassroots level, the independence movement would probably have been stronger. After being voted into power, Chen has had to shift from the "left" (Taiwan independence) to a position he calls "middle road". The DPP chairman Hsieh Chang-ting said: "As a ruling party, it is inevitable for us to adopt a "middle road", in order to follow current social trends and win recognition from mainstream voters." [85] The Taiwan independence movement has thus been confused, divided, and stalled. Hsieh's announcement that the DPP did not rule out unification further divided the DPP, as did Chen's call for political integration with China. Hsieh added: "The public may no longer distinguish the DPP from other parties in terms of our advocacy of Taiwan independence or our stance on cross-strait relations." [86] This has jeopardized the independence movement. The DPP is now losing some of its traditional supporters, those who favour independence. [87]

The DPP is slipping fast into corruption, confusion, and division. It has long consisted of different factions. The major reason why it did not break up in the past was that those factions shared two things: the first was their aim to obtain state power, which required unity among the opposition. The other was their ideological appeals, that is, for Taiwan's independence and democracy. The DPP used the appeal for Taiwan independence to get votes from local Taiwanese who resented mainland China and viewed the KMT as an "alien regime". It used the appeal of democracy to get votes from both local and mainland Taiwanese, who disapproved of the non-democratic one-party rule by the KMT.

Taiwan's independence and democracy were life-long pursuits for only some DPP leaders. To the rest, they were only political means to obtain state power. In other words, while they were the ends for some leaders, they were the means for others. The pursuit of state power was the only aim that all the factions shared, which accounted largely for their previous unity. Once in power, factional differences and tension developed rapidly. The appeal of democracy, though effective in the past, cannot be used now as the KMT is no longer the ruling party. The Chen Shui-bian government also cannot openly appeal for Taiwan's independence in view of the Chinese and international pressure, and therefore has to claim to move from the "left" to the "middle road". The result is confusion among those who advocate Taiwan's independence and loss of their support. A survey by Taiwan's cable television TVBS, conducted on 15 March 2001, found that about 30 per cent of Chen's supporters said that they had regretted their decision to vote for Chen. [88]

After losing its two ideological appeals, the DPP is now resorting more and more to vested interests as a means for internal cohesion, as the KMT had done before. This leads to corruption, which is anathema to those DPP ideologists who value independence more than power. The DPP's unity is thus becoming more and more fragile.

A Deteriorating Economy

Enormous political and social dislocations have occurred since Chen's election. They have bitten deeply into Taiwan's economy, which is now facing its worst crisis in almost thirty years. International and local confidence in Taiwan's economy has been deteriorating. Taiwan's stock market has plunged from 8,900 points when President Chen Shui-bian stepped into office on 20 May 2000 to around 3,446.26 by the end of August 2001. It economy, according to Taipei's Directorate-General of Budget, Accounting & Statistics, contracted 4.21 per cent in the third quarter of 2001, and a further contraction of 2.68 per cent is forecast for the fourth quarter. For the entire year, the economy is expected to shrink 2.12 per cent, the first negative growth in Taiwan since 1951, and down from the average of more than 6 per cent that Taiwan enjoyed over the past thirty years.[89] Export and domestic investments have fallen sharply. The unemployment rate has reached a record high.[90] Funds have been moving massively from Taiwan into the mainland. In May 2001, Taiwan's leading economic indicator, considered a predictor of short- and medium-term economic conditions, fell to the lowest since September 1985. Since the end of 2000, Taiwan has been having a contracting economy.[91]

Notes

1. Lee Teng-hui's description was "special state-to-state" relations; see the section on the "two states" theory.
2. The term "three links", commonly used since the early 1990s, was once expressed in the 1980s as "three direct links". It refers to direct trade, transportation, and postal services between China and Taiwan.
3. The Guidelines for National Unification, promulgated in 1991, set a three-phase process to achieve final unification. The "medium phase" is characterized by two sides establishing official communication channels on equal footing. Direct postal, transport, and commercial links should be allowed, and both sides should develop jointly the southeastern coastal area of the Chinese mainland, and then gradually extend the development to other areas to narrow the gap in living standards between the two sides. Both sides should assist each other in international organizations and activities. Mutual visits by high-ranking officials on both sides should be promoted.
4. For the ten-point policy, see *Chung Kuo Shih Pao* and *Taipei Times*, 18 February 2000.
5. *Renmin Ribao*, 29 January 2000.
6. See President Jiang Zemin's speech at the new year party, and Vice-Premier Qian Qichen's speech on 28 January 2000. *Renmin Ribao*, 31 December 1999, and 29 January 2000.
7. For the text, see *Renmin Ribao*, 22 February 2000.
8. The White Paper was drafted by Yu Keli, Deputy President of the Institute of Taiwan Studies of the China Academy of Social Sciences (CASS). In his draft, he did not

use the expression that "the Taiwan government was a local government". The central leaders later added it. For further reading of how the White Paper came about, see Xin Rong's article in *Jing Bao* [Mirror Monthly] 273, no. 3 (2000).

9. China's Institute of Taiwan Studies of CASS issued the warning when the Taiwanese delegation visited the Institute. Vivien Pik-Kwan Chan, "Delegation Warned on 'Two States' Policy", *South China Morning Post*, 30 November 1999.

10. Chinese Vice-Premier Qian Qichen insisted that the threat to attack Taiwan if the island indefinitely delayed talks on reunification was not new. Deng Xiaoping first delivered the warning in an October 1984 speech. See "Threat of Attack Is Not New, Says Qian", *South China Morning Post*, 1 March 2000. However, the speech by Deng was not made public.

11. See the interview of Zhang Mingqing, Information Bureau Director of the Taiwan Affairs Office, in "Timing of Threat Deliberate: Chinese Official", *Straits Times*, 28 February 2000.

12. In December 1999, the DPP passed a resolution to "draft a law to reflect Taiwan's new constitutional reality".

13. Mark Landler, "China's Sniping Heeded by Some Taiwan Voters", *New York Times*, 9 March 2000.

14. "Threats May Backfire, Says DPP Candidate", *South China Morning Post*, 3 March 2000. See also Mary Kwang, "Chen's Win Will Rule Out Peace, Say Scholars", *Straits Times* (Singapore), 15 March 2000.

15. For Zhu's remarks, see *Renmin Ribao*, 16 March 2000. According the assessment by Xu Shiquan, President of the Institute of Taiwan Studies of CASS, Zhu Rongji's warning had knocked off about 2 per cent of the votes from Chen Shui-bian. This warning had little positive effect on voters in the south of Taiwan, most of whom are traditional supporters of Taiwan's independence. However, it had some effect on the people in the north of Taiwan, who want to maintain peace and the status quo. They consequently switched their votes from Chen. From a seminar by Xu Shiquan at the East Asia Institute, National University of Singapore, 19 December 2000.

16. For Xu's suspicion, see "Talk Must Be Backed Up by Firepower", *Straits Times* (Singapore), 1 April 2000. For Zhang's suspicion, see *Lianhe Zaobao*, 30 April 2000, p. 20.

17. "US Commitment to People, Not Politician", *Lien Ho Pao*, 11 January 2000.

18. For example, Richard Bush, managing director of the American Institute in Taiwan, delivered this message to Taipei on 15 December 1999. See "Washington Sends a Message to Taipei", STRATFOR.COM., Global Intelligence Update, 16 December 1999. Goh Sui Noi, "Warnings for Presidential Hopefuls", *Straits Times* (Singapore), 17 December 1999.

19. "Congressman Predicts Cross-Strait Dialogue to Resume after Election", Central News Agency, 17 January 2000. "Congressmen to Teng-hui: Mind Your Words", *Straits Times* (Singapore), 15 January 2000.

20. John Leicester, "China, U.S. Swap Taiwan Warnings", Associated Press Newsline, 29 February 2000.

21. See speech by Adm. Dennis Blair, commander-in-chief of the U.S. Pacific Command, at the Senate Armed Services Committee in early March 2000. Tom Raum, "Blair: China Not Fighting Taiwan", Associated Press Newsline, 7 March 2000.

22. Tom Raum, "New Images Question Chinese Threat", Associated Press Newsline, 12 May 2000.

23. Robert Kagan, "How China Will Take Taiwan", *Washington Post*, 12 March 2000.

24. From Douglas Paal, a former official in the U.S. Department of Defence. See Douglas H. Paal, "Turbulence Ahead in the Beijing-Taipei-Washington Triangle," *International Herald Tribune*, 12 April 2000, p. 8

25. Dennis V. Hickey, "The Election of Chen Shui-bian and Its Impact on U.S. Policy toward Taiwan" (Paper delivered at the 42nd annual meeting of the American Association for Chinese Studies, University of San Francisco, 27–29 October 2000). http://www.taiwansecurity.org/IS/Hickey-1000.htm.

26. "Clinton Wants Taiwan, China to Meet", Associated Press Newsline, 18 March 2000.

27. For Japan, it was made by Japanese Prime Minister Keizo Obuchi to reporters. For Australia, its Foreign Minister Alexander Downer announced it on a TV programme. For these international responses, see a survey by the *Straits Times* in "Around the World", *Straits Times* (Singapore), 20 March 2000.

28. Ibid.

29. Pan Xitang, "Xuanhe Lian'an Guangxi De Weiji Yu Zhuanji" [Crises and Opportunities in Cross-Strait Relations after the Presidential Election], *Lianhe Zaobao*, 17 April 2000, p. 21. William Foreman, "Opposition Wins Taiwan Election", Associate Press Newsline, 18 March 2000.

30. Pan, op. cit.

31. *Zhongguo Guofang Bao* [China Defence Daily] (Beijing), 24 March 2000, p. 2.

32. *Sing Tao Jih Pao* [Sing Tao Daily] (Hong Kong), 20 April 2000; and *Chung Kuo Shih Pao*, 20 April 2000.

33. Jason Blatt, "Principle Stumbling Block", *South China Morning Post*, 7 April 2000.

34. MAC News Briefing, no. 0173, 21 April 2000, p. 1.

35. *Lianhe Zaobao*, 30 September 1997, p. 17.

36. "China: Chinese Party Official Speaks on Unofficial Links with Taiwan's Democratic Progressive Party", Reuters Newsline, 9 August 1994.

37. See Jiang's eight-point proposal in *Renmin Ribao*, 31 January 1995, p. 1. Emphasis added.

38. "Former Parliamentary Leader Urges Beijing to Move towards Peace Talks", *Sing Tao Jih Pao*, 6 May 1996, p. A2, cited in Reuters Newsline, 7 May 1996. Emphasis added.

39. *Lianhe Zaobao*, 13 September 1997, p. 26. Emphasis added.

40. From the author's interviews with Chinese strategists in China in 1998 and 1999.

41. News from Taiwan's CTN TV and CNN, 20 May 2000.

42. "Chen Reaffirms 'Three Noes' to Show Goodwill in Cross-Strait", Central News Agency, 16 April 2000; and Catherine Sung and William Ide, "Chen Says No Consensus on 'One China'", *Taipei Times*, 14 April 2000.

43. See China's White Paper on Taiwan, *Renmin Ribao*, 21 February 2000.

44. Todd Crowell, "Now, a Beijing Peace Offensive", *Asiaweek*, 28 July 2000. "Beijing Redefines Dogma in Overture to Taiwan", Reuters Newsline, 27 August 2000.

45. *Chung Kuo Shih Pao*, 26 April 2000.

46. *Liang'an Guanxi* [Cross Strait Relations] (Beijing journal), April 2000. Cited in *Lianhe Zaobao*, 12 April 2000, p. 24.

47. Lu said: "If 'one China' means the PRC, then we are of course not Chinese". *Lianhe Zaobao*, 23 April 2000, p. 21; and *Chung Kuo Shih Pao*, 23 April 2000. Tsai gave a

formal statement when asked whether she was Chinese. She said: "From a political aspect, I am citizen of the ROC and you may as well call me *huaren*. But I am Taiwanese in terms of culture and blood relationship, among which, I am not denying, the Chinese [*zhongguoren*] are one of the segments." See *Chung Kuo Shih Pao*, 30 May 2000.

48. Taiwan's CTN TV and CNN news, 20 May 2000.

49. Jason Blatt, "Chen Outlines Principles for Dialogue with Beijing", *South China Morning Post*, 6 May 2000.

50. For example, see "Taiwan Makes a Goodwill Gesture to China", *Straits Times* (Singapore), 6 May 2000. For further reading, see *South China Morning Post*, and major newspapers in the United States of the same date.

51. See *Chung Kuo Shih Pao*, 6 May 2000; and *Sing Tao Jih Pao*, 6 May 2000.

52. Mark Landler, "Risking China's Ire, Taiwan Leader Questions Unification", *New York Times*, 2 September 2000. "Taiwan President: Reunification is Not Taiwan's Only Choice", Associated Press Newsline, 18 August 2000.

53. *Lianhe Zaobao*, 4 September 2000, p. 4.

54. On 17 August, during a visit to the Dominican Republic, Chen said that there was room for discussion over whether he should chair the National Unification Council. The Council is charged with deliberating policy principles and guidelines for unification with the mainland. It was set up in October 1990 and meant to be chaired by the President of Taiwan. "Chen attacked for not chairing reunification body", *South China Morning Post*, 28 August 2000.

55. Goh Sui Noi, "Taipei removes signs calling for reunification", *Straits Times* (Singapore), 22 August 2000.

56. Lawrence Chung, "Chen still hopes for cross-strait dialogue", *South China Morning Post*, 1 August 2000.

57. *Renmin Ribao*, 21 February 2000.

58. Ibid.

59. Goh Sui Noi, "Lien Tells Chen About 'One China' Consensus", *Straits Times* (Singapore), 28 October 2000. Lien said that as one of the participants of the 1992 proceedings that led to cross-strait talks in Singapore in 1993, he knew for a fact that there was consensus on "one China", which was that the two sides would express verbally what each meant by "one China". For Su Chi's acknowledgement, see "Ex-MAC Chief Claims 'Spirit of 1992' Is Invented by Foreigner", Central News Agency, 14 October 2000.

60. See Lin Chieh-yu, "President's Advisors Make Suggestions", *Taipei Times*, 27 November 2000.

61. Zhang Mingqing, spokesman for the Taiwan Affairs Office of the PRC State Council flatly rejected this recommendation as "word games". "What they are doing is playing games with words". He said: "Those suggestions are neither here nor there, neither fish nor fowl". "We are resolutely opposed to any person or any so-called committee refusing to recognise 'one China'". See "China Flatly Rejects Taiwan's Ice-Breaking Bid", Reuters Newsline, 30 November 2000.

62. "Presidential Task Force Recommendations Criticized by Opposition", Central News Agency", 27 November 2000.

63. Ibid.

64. Ibid.

65. Ibid.

66. MAC News Briefing, no. 0206 (27 November 2000), p. 2.

67. Ibid.

68. "Chen Extends Olive Branch to Beijing: 'One-China' principle 'no problem for Taiwan's constitution'", *South China Morning Post*, 1 January 2001. "China Deserves the Back Burner", *Taipei Times*, 2 January 2001. Emphasis added.

69. *Chung Kuo Shih Pao*, 1 January 2001. Emphasis added.

70. Lin Mei-chun, "President backs Siew's 'common market' concept", *Taipei Times*, 27 March 2001.

71. "'Political Integration' in Line with DPP Policy: Hsieh", *China Post* (Taipei), 8 January 2001.

72. *Chung Kuo Shih Pao*, 7 February 2001.

73. "MAC Head Discusses Future of Unification Guidelines", *Lien Ho Pao*, 22 February 2001. *Chung Kuo Shih Pao*, 28 February 2001.

74. See a speech by MAC Vice-chairman Chen Ming-tung, reported in "'Integration' a Step to 'Future One China', MAC Official", Central News Agency, 18 February 2001. Hsieh Chang-ting's speech was reported in *Chung Kuo Shih Pao*, 7 February 2001.

75 "Chen: 'Integration' to Follow Constitution", Central News Agency, 22 February 2001. Brian Hsu, "Chen appeals to Beijing to stop threats of force", *Taipei Times*, 14 February 2001.

76. David Huang, "'Integration' the key to strait woes", *Taipei Times*, 13 February 2001.

77. *Lianhe Zaobao*, 20 March 2001, p. 31.

78. Willy Wo-Lap Lam, "Top Cadre Hopes Chen Will Be More Flexible", *South China Morning Post*, 7 April 2000.

79. See Qian's talk at Beijing University on 26 May 2000, reported by CTN TV, 26 May 2000, and *Chung Kuo Shih Pao*, 27 May 2000.

80. For the DPP organization and its decision-making process, see Julian J. Kuo, *Minjindang Zhuanxing Zhi Tong* [The DPP's Ordeal of Transformation].

81. *Lianhe Zaobao*, 17 March 2000, p. 1.

82. Ibid. The term "Mainlanders" refers to those Chinese that came from the Chinese mainland to Taiwan after the KMT lost the civil war in 1949.

83. Alexander Chieh-cheng Huang, "Militarization of the Cross-Strait Relations: Security Challenges to the Chen Shui-bian Administration", in http://www.dsis.org.tw/peaceforum/papers/2000-05/CSM0005003e.htm.

84. "Guoren Diwo Bufeng Shi Lian'an Wenti Guanjian" [The Crux of the Cross-Strait Issue is that We Cannot Distinguish Enemies and Friends], *Chung Kuo Shih Pao*, 26 July 2000.

85. Goh Sui Noi, "Taiwan's DPP marks anniversary quietly", *Straits Times* (Singapore), 28 September 2000.

86. Ibid.

87. Ibid.

88. "Voters Turn against Year-Old Taiwan Government: Poll", Agence France Presse, 18 March 2001.

89. "Taiwan's Economy Faces Four Uncertainties", Editorial, *Commercial Times* (Taipei), 19 November 2001.

90. Mure Dickie, "Taiwan's Growth Sinks to 1%", *Financial Times*, 26 May 2001.

91. Taipei's Council for Economic Planning and Development made the announcement in June. "Economic indicator index falls to 15-year low", *Taipei Times*, 28 June 2001.

5

China Responds

As a long-term strategy, Beijing will continue to insist on the "one China" principle, and push for political negotiation on reunification, earlier "three links", as well as cross-strait cultural and educational exchanges. It will continue to encourage Taiwanese business people to invest in the mainland. Internationally, China will continue to improve its relations with its Asian neighbours and avoid a head-on collision with the United States so that any radical push by the DPP towards independence could only have very limited impact. So long as it can maintain internal stability and sustain its economic growth and military modernization, China believes that time is on its side. Before the time comes, Beijing will try hard to keep its head cool against any impetuous and premature actions.

Political Pressure

Chen's surprising election did not shock Beijing into taking military actions. Even before the election, it had already made the assessment that Chen, if elected, would avoid an immediate showdown on the issue of independence. As early as the National Conference on the Taiwan issue in late March 2000, Beijing had already told the participants (directors of the Taiwan Affairs Offices in various provinces of China) of its assessment that Chen would continue Lee's separatist policy and foster the growth of indigenous Taiwanese nationalism. He would try to perpetuate the current state in which there was neither reunification nor declared independence. This would allow time for the independence movement to gradually erase the cultural and sentimental ties between mainland China and Taiwan, and to reduce resistance against separatism at home.[1] Beijing was prepared for a "long-term struggle with Taiwan's independence forces".

At the Beidaihe meetings of the Central Committee of the CCP in July–August, a consensus was reached that as long as Chen did not declare independence, and it was unlikely in the near future, there would be no need to take military action on Taiwan.[2] The meetings set the general guidelines of China's Taiwan policy. Though the details still remain unknown, it is clear that there is no dramatic change in its Taiwan policy. President Jiang Zemin received U.S. Congressman Archer during the meetings and told him that there would be no change in the basic policy of peaceful reunification under the "one country, two systems" formula.[3]

At the meetings, President Jiang Zemin reportedly said that the more Beijing was confronted by major threats, the more it should adhere to Deng Xiaoping's teaching to focus on economic development first,[4] as time would then be on China's side in dealing with the Taiwan issue.

In the late 1970s, Chinese leader Deng Xiaoping had designed this long journey towards modernization in three stages. Stage 1 (1980–2000) was to quadruple the 1980 gross domestic product (GDP) by 2000, which had been successfully accomplished. Stage 2 (2001–2020) was to again quadruple the 2000 GDP by 2020. This meant that by 2020, the GDP should be in the order of US$4 trillion (using the average exchange rate in the 1990s), the world's largest in aggregate terms. At the end of Stage 3 (2021–2050), China's per capita income should be close to that of the United States in 2000.

These long-term targets have been translated into specific five-year plans. The tenth five-year plan (2001–2005) that China's NPC adopted in March 2001 is a crucial step towards achieving these targets. During this period, China's annual GDP growth should be above 7 per cent, to ensure its interim target of doubling the 2000 GDP by 2010. With this plan, Beijing does not want to see its agenda being hijacked by a premature solution of the Taiwan issue, especially by military means.

A close examination of China's diplomatic behaviour in the 1990s shows that it may have lost its temper but not its head. It wants nothing to distract it from its modernization focus. When it occasionally made angry responses, such as to Lee Teng-hui's trip to the United States, and to the U.S.-led NATO bombing of its embassy in Belgrade, it was mainly a bluff, a tactic of "offensive for defensive".

Beijing is well aware that, as President Jiang Zemin had said at the Beidaihe central meetings in July–August 2000, "an important lesson to be learnt from the failure in our work towards Taiwan, which saw a deterioration from one China to two Chinas, is that only until we are fully prepared to reclaim it by force would there be a chance for peaceful unification".[5] Before that day comes when it is fully prepared, China has to bite the bullet and practise "united front" tactics, using other political forces in Taiwan to constrain the DPP's push for independence. Being on weak ground, Chen and the DPP badly need breathing space at present to develop internal cohesion and for power consolidation. Beijing will not give them that.

It resorts to "united front" tactics to intensify the political conflicts so as to weaken, divide, and even paralyse the DPP. The DPP itself, as Beijing hopes to see, may also evolve, with Taiwan independence fundamentalism being marginalized. In other words, the DPP may become a party for democracy, but not for independence. Chinese Vice-Premier Qian Qichen reportedly laid down, in mid-2000, five guidelines:

- to seek concessions from Chen by applying pressure on many fronts;
- to foster alliances among anti-independence forces in Taiwan;
- to expand contacts and dialogue with all political parties in Taiwan outside the DPP orbit;
- to exert great efforts to win over the Taiwan people; and
- to stick firmly to the "one-China" principle.[6]

For the short-term, Beijing will resort to both well-calculated pressure (on the DPP) and concessions (to the opposition):

- to limit Chen's political space and choices;
- to confuse the DPP (and the United States as well) of, and keep them further away from challenging, Beijing's real bottom-lines and vulnerable points;
- to divide the pro-independence forces and to help foster a coalition between pro-reunification forces;
- to diminish the prospect of the DPP winning the 2001 legislative and local elections so that Chen will be faced, for the rest of his term, with a stern structural constraint — that is, the legislative dominated by the opposition; and
- to emasculate Chen's will and capability to push for independence by besetting him with *neiwai jiaokun* (internal trouble and external pressure).

Practising the "United Front"

Beijing says that once Taiwan accepts the "one China" principle, anything can be discussed, including the national title, the national anthem, Taiwan's legal and political status, and its retention of military forces. It will immediately invite Chen to visit China and Jiang Zemin will also visit Taiwan. Beijing has once again modified the definition of the "one China" principle. It had previously been composed of three sentences:

- There is only one China in the world.
- Taiwan is a part of China.

- The government of the PRC is the sole legal government representing the whole of China.

In January 1998, Beijing changed its definition to:

- There is only one China in the world.
- Taiwan is a part of China.
- China's sovereignty and territorial integrity is not to be separated.[7]

The latest definition is

- There is only one China in the world.
- Taiwan and the mainland are both part of China.
- China's sovereignty and territorial integrity is not to be separated".[8]

This definition is similar to what is listed in Taiwan's "Guidelines for National Unification", adopted by the KMT government in 1991. Under this "one China" principle, Beijing made three demands:

- Both sides should return to the 1992 consensus between Beijing and Taipei regarding "one China".
- Leaders in Taipei must recognize themselves as being "Chinese".
- The DPP must scrap the independence clause from its Party Charter.

The redefinition of the "one China" principle and the various demands are all easy for the opposition (that is, the KMT, PFP and New Party), but difficult for the ruling DPP to accept. This has intensified the internal political confusion in Taiwan.

Beijing desires a coalition or political co-operation between Soong's PFP and Lien's KMT. Otherwise the opposition will stand no chance in defeating the DPP either in the 2001 legislative and local elections or in the next presidential election. What is more, the KMT will collapse, with many of its talents joining the DPP. Owing to this concern, Beijing has extended its invitation to both Lien and Soong to visit China together and promised to deal with them with "the utmost sincerity".[9]

Beijing also encourages exchanges between cities, local officials, and political parties across the strait, leaving Chen Shui-bian and his ruling DPP in the cold for not taking a clear stance on the "one China" principle. In June 2000, Beijing terminated exchanges between the ARATS and the SEF, communicating directly instead with a Taiwanese set-up headed by a New Party legislator. This was followed by Beijing's reception of opposition PFP co-founder Liu Sung-pan. In July 2000, a formal New Party delegation, led by Feng Hu-hsiang, became the first political party from Taiwan to visit Beijing. Beijing's visitors included KMT vice-chairman Wu Po-hsiung, in November 2000. The meeting was unofficial, but nevertheless marked the highest level contact between the two parties since the communists won the civil war in 1949.

Beijing is courting opposition legislators in Taiwan to handle civic exchanges, thereby letting them gain political and economic benefits. In Matsu, local officials have even signed an agreement, without authorization from Taipei, with a local government in mainland China. Deputy mayor of Taipei City, Bai Hsiu-hsiung, visited China in September 2000, and in early 2001 to attend the Taipei-Shanghai City Forum. He had talks with officials of both Shanghai and Nanjing on concrete city-to-city exchange programmes in the cultural, educational, sports, and social welfare fields. Hsinchu mayor, Tsai Jen-chien, visited Nanjing in October 2000 to attend an international technology forum; he was the first elected local government official from Taiwan to visit China. In November, Hsinchu County Commissioner, Lin Kuang-hua, attended an international Hakka association forum held in Xiamen. During the six months from 18 March 2000, when Chen was elected, to September, Beijing invited about one-third of Taiwan's 221-member legislature to visit China.[10] All these activities have prompted SEF chairman, Koo Chen-fu, to express concern over the "localisation of cross-strait affairs".[11]

Beijing has even begun courting Chen's rivals within his own party, offering them invitations as well. In July 2000, Xiamen mayor Zhu Yayan invited his Kaohsiung counterpart Hsieh Chang-ting, who is also the DPP chairman, to visit Xiamen.[12] Hsieh applied for Taipei's permission but it was rejected. In March 2001, Hsieh expressed his desire again to visit the mainland to conduct city-to-city exchanges in his capacity as major of Kaohsiung.[13] Beijing said that it was willing to co-operate with those who had "advocated, engaged in and pursued Taiwan independence as long as they gave up their 'splittist' stance".[14] "[It] welcomes whoever embraces the 'one China' principle, including those who said and did wrong things in the past".[15]

More of the same is expected to follow shortly. Shanghai CCP chief Huang Ju invited Taipei mayor Ma Ying-jeou to visit China. He later visited Hong Kong, his birthplace, in February 2001, to attend the second annual "Taipei-Hong Kong City-to-City Forum". KMT Vice-Chairman, and formerly Defence Minister — between 1994 and 1999 — Chiang Chung-ling, visited his native province of Zhejiang in China in April 2001. In May 2001, former Taiwan Premier and KMT Vice-Chairman Vincent Siew Wan-chang visited China. Beijing reportedly planned to invite the chairmen of the KMT, PFP and the New Party to visit China in 2001 to discuss cross-strait affairs.[16]

Such strategy has sown discord and created confusion in Taiwan, raising alarm on an island wary of divide-and-rule tactics. It may not bring about an immediate collapse of the Taiwan independence movement, but it intensifies the break-up of Taiwan's societal core values, causes social division and political confusion. All these will bite deep into the essentials that the DPP relies on in its confrontation with China. Beijing believes that this political pressure is necessary, otherwise Chen will move from the middle road, where he is currently standing, back to the "left" — that is, radical Taiwan independence. This political pressure goes with growing economic engagement, military deterrence, and international blockade.

Economic Engagement

Since the late 1970s and especially since the early 1990s, Beijing has been heavily courting Taiwan's business with trade opportunities and incentives. After the promulgation of the Law of the People's Republic of China for the Protection of Investment Made by Taiwan Compatriots in the early 1990s, it set forth, in December 2000, detailed rules concerning cross-strait trade.[17] These laws and rules, and follow-up policy initiatives by both the central and local governments, provide legal protection for Taiwan business in the mainland, and special trade privileges.

With such governmental encouragement, the strong complimentary nature of the two economies, and the attraction of a huge Chinese market, cross-strait trade and investment have been growing rapidly and steadily. At the end of 1999, Taiwan's investors had funded more than 43,500 projects on the mainland, worth more than US$43.8 billion, since the late 1980s.[18] According to Taipei's data, Taiwan investment in China in the first ten months of 2000 nearly doubled, swelling by 98 per cent, compared with that of 1999, to reach US$2 billion.[19] Even in the absence of the three links, more than three million people from Taiwan visited China in 2000, and cross-strait trade reached more than US$32 billion.[20] By November 2000, it had totalled US$188.22 billion compared with only US$46 million in 1978. Taiwan's US$26.16 billion exports to China in 2000 represented a 25 per cent increase from 1999.[21] Taiwan is now the fifth largest trading partner and the second largest source of imports for the mainland, while the mainland (including Hong Kong) is the second largest export destination of Taiwanese goods. Taiwan enjoys the highest trade surplus among the mainland's trading partners.[22] According to Taiwan's Board of Foreign Trade, its trade surplus with the mainland rose 20 per cent year-on-year to US$18.28 billion in the first eleven months of 2000, as exports to the mainland totalled US$24.03 billion, an increase of 24.3 per cent, while imports from the mainland rose 40.5 per cent to US$5.75 billion.[23] Its trade with the mainland surged 27.2 per cent to US$29.77 billion, compared with the same period one year earlier.[24] Its exports to the mainland accounted for 17.6 per cent of the island's total exports.[25]

In the past, most of the Taiwanese firms that invested in the mainland were in traditional industries, such as textiles and garment manufacturing. Since the late 1990s, however, more and more high-tech companies have invested in China,

Table 1
Taiwan's Economic Dependence on Mainland China
(In US$ billions)

Year	Value of Taiwan's Exports to Mainland China ($)	Shares of Exports to the Mainland as Percentage of Taiwan's Total Exports
1987	1,226.50	2.28
1988	2,242.20	3.70
1989	3,331.90	5.03
1990	4,394.60	6.54
1991	7,493.50	9.84
1992	10,547.60	12.95
1993	13,993.10	16.47
1994	16,022.50	17.22
1995	19,433.80	17.40
1996	20,727.30	17.87
1997	22,460.30	18.39
1998	19,900.00	18.00
1999	22,500.00	17.90

Sources: Mainland Affairs Council, Taipei, "Cross Strait Trade", at http://www.gov.tw/english/ora01.htm

Table 2
**Taiwan's Trade Surplus with Mainland China as a
Percentage of Its Total Trade Surplus**
(In US$ billions)

Year	Taiwan's Trade Surplus with Mainland China ($)	Taiwan's International Trade Surplus ($)	Mainland Surplus as Percentage of Total Surplus
1990	3,629.20	12,495.20	29.04
1991	6,367.60	13,299.10	47.88
1992	9,428.60	9,479.30	99.47
1993	12,889.50	7,869.80	163.78
1994	14,163.80	7,697.20	184.01
1995	16,342.40	8,116.30	201.35
1996	17,667.50	14,704.40	120.35
1997	18,540.00	7,672.30	241.65
1998	16,200.00	10,531.00	153.83
1999	16,700.00	10,900.00	153.21

Sources: As in Table 1.

and the trend is moving so rapidly that Taipei has warned that as high-tech industries are the core of Taiwan's international competitiveness, they should stay put. However, these words of caution did not slow down the flow. In July 2000, Taiwan's Advanced Semiconductor Engineering took the lead to invest NT$7 billion in IC (integrated circuit) packaging and testing in China. It was followed by Quanta, Taiwan's largest computer notebook maker, which said in September that it planned to invest between US$19 million and US$32 million in a plant in Shanghai to build motherboards and computer peripherals.[26]

The slow-down in global computer sales was forcing Taiwan's electronics and information industries to move more rapidly to take advantage of economic production conditions in China to remain competitive. For the first time, investment in China in 2000 accounted for half of Taiwan's total foreign investment. More than half of the investments was made by high tech companies. According to Taiwan's Institute for Information Industry, over 70 per cent of IT (information technology) hardware produced in China was from plants with Taiwan investment. In late December 2000, Taiwan's Institute for Information Industry announced that China would surpass Taiwan in 2000 to become the third largest IT hardware producer after the United States and Japan.[27]

Although Taiwanese firms are prohibited from producing laptops on the mainland, by 2000, all but one of Taiwan's major laptop manufacturers had parts plants in the mainland. Grace Semi-Conductor Manufacturing, a Taiwan-PRC joint venture that broke ground for an eight-inch fabrication plant in Shanghai in November 2000, involves investments that go well beyond the capital and technology ceilings authorized by Taiwan.

In December 2000, Jiang Mianheng and Winston Wang signed a landmark agreement to build a US$1.63 billion chip foundry in Shanghai. The pact was important not only because of the power of their respective fathers, Chinese President Jiang Zemin and Wang Yung-ching, chairman of Taiwan's largest conglomerate, Formosa Plastics. It was significant also because it did so with Taiwan's strategic production of microchips, the dynamo of Taiwan's economy. It was also because Formosa Plastics had signed letters of intent to invest during a visit to China by Wang Yung-ching in September 2000. It had pledged to forfeit the threshold of Taiwan investment in China and to invest in petrochemical ventures on the mainland, which could trigger an exodus of petrochemical firms to China.[28] It plans to invest about US$300 million to build four petrochemical plants producing polyvinyl chloride and other plastic materials in China. It had already signed a contract with China to acquire land needed for the plants on Meishan island off China's eastern Ningpo port. Meanwhile, it also plans to open a branch office in Shanghai to manage the investment projects of its three flagship enterprises — Formosa Plastics Corp, Nan Ya Plastics Corp, and Formosa Chemicals & Fiber Corp. Nan Ya Plastics operates nine petrochemical plants in China.[29]

Taiwan already makes the bulk of computer components like disk drives and power adapters in the mainland. Eight out of ten Taiwanese scanners, and nearly half the monitors, are assembled there. According to the Market Intelligence Centre, a research group in Taipei, in 2000, Taiwan produced 25 per cent of desktop personal computers (PCs) on the mainland.[30] However, these numbers understate the reality, since many PC components are basically built in China but shipped to Taiwan or the United States for final assembly.

Compal Electronics, the second largest maker of laptop computers, said that it would move 15 per cent of its manufacturing to China in 2001, another 50 per cent in 2002, and the rest within three years.[31] Compal, Arima, and First International have opened factories to assemble laptop computers near Shanghai. To avoid breaking the rules set by Taipei, they are making components, rather than assembling entire machines. However, at least two companies are reportedly already producing complete laptops in China.[32] Many Taiwanese companies have also set up offshore companies to make their investments in China.

According to a poll by the Taipei Computer Association in February 2001, up to 90 per cent of Taiwan-based high-tech firms had invested or planned to invest in mainland China.[33] It is almost certain that investments by Taiwan's high-tech industries in the mainland will continue and expand. It may lead to a chain reaction that will cause an exodus of down-, medium- and upper-stream firms to the mainland.

In view of the vast growth potential in the mainland after the country's entry to the World Trade Organization (WTO), the flow Taiwan's investments into the mainland would accelerate. Together with the flow, many of Taiwan's brightest, especially young engineers and entrepreneurs, are finding a new job market in mainland China. According to Taipei, in the two years of 1999 and 2000, more than 40,000 Taiwanese left to work in mainland China and about 230,000 Taiwanese were in China by early 2001.[34] According to various opinion polls, more Taiwanese are now willing to migrate to the mainland.

Factors for the Economic Flow

The main factors that account for the sustained economic flow from Taiwan to the mainland include:

- strong complimentary nature of the two economies;
- sustained booming Chinese economy with its abundant cheap land and raw materials, cheap but also well-educated labour, and big market; political stability, common language and culture, improved infrastructure, and favourable government policies;

- worsening economy in Taiwan and a slumping international market; and
- tension in cross-strait relations. (It may appear ironic that to many Taiwanese businessmen, the higher the tension across the strait, the better their investment will be protected and encouraged, with more privileges, in the mainland.)

Taiwan is now facing its worst economy in almost thirty years. International and local confidence in Taiwan's economy has been deteriorating. According to one survey conducted in late 2000 by the *Commonwealth*, a renowned economic monthly in Taiwan that does the survey every other year, Taiwan's attractiveness to foreign investment has plunged from third place in 1998 to the last but one spot among eleven Asian countries.[35] The survey showed that up to 76.55 per cent of polled foreign enterprises recognized the deterioration of the investment climate in Taiwan, a sharp increase of 23 per cent compared to two years earlier. Only 15.1 per cent of the foreign firms surveyed expressed willingness to expand their investments in Taiwan, the lowest figure of its kind in six years, and a decline from 36.7 per cent registered in 1994.[36] Some 60 per cent of the polled foreign firms expressed dissatisfaction with the administration performance of President Chen Shui-bian, while 50 per cent showed little confidence in Premier Chang Chun-hsiung's handling of the current political and economic crises.[37]

In early 2001, Taiwan's statistics bureau revealed the stunning data showing that Taiwan's economy grew only 1.06 per cent year-on-year in the first quarter of 2001, its most feeble performance in twenty-six years.[38]

Officials in Taipei also unveiled sharp falls in industrial output and export orders, record low broad money supply growth, and an unemployment rate touching record levels. Domestic investment had plunged as computer-chip makers scaled back billion-dollar plants and small companies hunkered down.[39]

The factors responsible for this poor economic performance include (1) a bubble economy; (2) unsatisfactory economic upgrading; and (3) a slump in the international market. The abrupt and unexpected change of government from the KMT to the DPP, at a time when the DPP was not yet fully prepared for national governance, and in a society where state-building and democracy are still not mature enough has not helped. Hence,

- the government lacks governing experience, and competent administrators with the vision and, consequently, policy to guide the economy to meet future challenges, and even to meet the needs of normal industrial development;
- the government lacks good co-ordination among various government units, and policy consistency; and
- fierce power struggle between the government and opposition parties has seriously weakened the performance of the government.

Economic Pressure

Enormous pressure has therefore come from the affected industries for Taipei to liberalize its restrictions on investment in the mainland. At present (mid-2001), Taipei still bans the three links with the mainland, and places restrictions on Taiwan investment there under the so-called "go slow, be patient" policy (first instituted in September 1996), under which Taiwanese are barred from investing in infrastructure building and some high-tech industries in the mainland. They cannot invest in any project there exceeding US$50 million, and cannot pump more than 20 per cent of their total assets into their mainland projects.

Taiwanese businessmen are unhappy with these limitations as they increase the costs of business, cut down business competitiveness, and reduce economic opportunities. A poll conducted in February 2001 showed that a mere 3.5 per cent of the polled companies supported the government's "go slow, be patient" approach to investment in the mainland.[40]

Consequently, pressure is mounting on Taipei to reopen direct shipping and commercial links with the mainland. Taiwan's legislature passed a bill in March 2000 and made a petition with a large number of signatures in November, calling on the government to restore the "three links".[41] With accession of both Taiwan and China to the WTO, the government will have to address the ban on direct links and the "go slow, be patient" policy.

The "Mini Three Links"

With the steadily growing economic and political pressure at home, Chen Shui-bian finally agreed to open the outlying Kinmen, Matsu, and Penghu islands to direct communication and transportation with Xiamen and Fuzhou on the mainland, for what was described by the MAC as "small scale trade", or "mini three links" as they are popularly called.[42] Kinmen and Matsu islands are less than 10 kilometres off China's southeast coast. Illegal trade in vegetables, seafood and other goods has long flourished between the two sides.

In March 1992, China's Fujian province made two proposals. The first was limited direct links between Xiamen and Kinmen, as well as Manigang and Matsu. The other was the construction of harbour facilities at Manigang, Xiamen, and Meizhouwan for cross-strait shipping. Beijing also proposed running an undersea cable from Xiamen to Kinmen and lifting visa requirements for Taiwan residents flying to Fuzhou or Xiamen. In January 1994, Beijing unilaterally passed the Regulations on Small-scale Trade with Taiwan, and set the status of the trade as "non-official direct trade and economic exchanges that supplement indirect cross-strait trade." This small-scale trade was considered, according to Taiwan's laws, as smuggling and therefore illegal.

In June 1994, Taiwan's Kinmen-Matsu Local Alliance made a proposal to Taipei to open "mini three links" between Kinmen, Matsu, and mainland China. It asked Taipei to research the feasibility of such links, or at least direct links for tourists, goods, and mail. It proposed unilaterally but gradually to open direct links, restricted to a small number of areas — first sea links, then air links; and exchange of goods first, and then people.

Transshipment was implemented between Taiwan's Kaohsiung and China's Fuzhou and Xiamen on 19 April 1997. This does not constitute direct links, as goods are not allowed to pass through customs into Taiwan, and the number of ports open to cross-strait trade has not increased.

Taiwan's legislature passed the Offshore Island Development Act in March 2000, calling for the "mini three links". On 12 June, the legislative again passed a resolution for the opening of the "mini three links", asking the government to evaluate the "mini three links" within three months and to make blueprints within the following three months.[43] By September, the MAC had completed the evaluation. In mid-December, Taipei announced the regulations. Under the rules, only residents of Kinmen and Matsu (not the residents on Taiwan island and other surrounding islands) will be allowed to travel directly to Xiamen and Fuzhou in China to visit relatives and friends there. Residents of China (mainly those who were born in Kinmen and Matsu or have relatives there) will be allowed to travel to Kinmen and Matsu for as long as a week. Kinmen will limit Chinese visitors to 700 a day, with Matsu restricting the number to 100 a day.[44] Taipei agreed to allow trade between Kinmen/Matsu and the mainland, rather than allow the two islands to serve as a mid-point for trade between China and Taiwan itself. The rules permit only Taiwanese vessels to ply between the two sides, while Chinese ships would be barred from docking at Taiwanese piers.[45] It was just one-way transportation from the Taiwanese side.[46]

On 2 January 2001, two ferries from Kinmen (*Taiwu* and *Wuchiang*) and one ferry from Matsu (*Taima*) made round trips to Xiamen and Fuzhou — the first legal transits since 1949. The ROC national flag was removed from the boats when entering the waters of Xiamen and Fuzhou, following the "Hong Kong model".[47]

Taipei's intention was clear. It wanted Beijing to move away from its "wait and see" posture to resume dialogues between the two sides without accepting the "one China" principle. Should the "mini three links" turn out to be a disaster, it would be convincing evidence against those who opt for unlimited direct transport, trade, and postal links, which is popularly called "big three links". The loss of the two outlying small islands, either politically, economically or strategically, does not matter to some DPP leaders who have long been advocating cutting Taiwan off from these two islands that, geographically and historically, belong to China's Fujian province.

For months before the first direct sailing took place, Beijing avoided official comment on the "mini three links". If it had openly endorsed the initiative by

Taipei, Chen would have garnered more credit while he still refused to acknowledge the "one China" principle as demanded by Beijing as the essential prerequisite for resuming contacts with Taipei. However, if Beijing had blocked this initiative, it would have had to stop the existing unauthorized trade and travel, which Beijing had favoured for two decades. When Taipei announced its regulations for the "mini three links" in mid-December 2000, Beijing made no comment. Then, in late December, a week before the first sailing, Beijing took two steps: first, it banned reporters from visiting the mainland ports in order to minimize publicity. Secondly, it authorized a Fujian provincial official to indicate that Beijing would support the initiative.

Taiwan's Minister of Transportation and Communications Yeh Chu-lan called the "mini three links" "special state-to-state" links.[48] This raised Beijing's suspicion of Taipei in using the sailing to demonstrate to the world that cross-strait ties were part of the "special state-to-state relations" that Lee Teng-hui had pronounced one year before. Therefore, China's Vice-Premier Qian Qichen openly defined the "mini three links" as "special domestic links", "an internal affair within one country".[49] China's Minister of Communications, Hong Shanxiang, said that cross-strait shipping routes would be reserved for Taiwanese and Chinese ships only after both sides had been admitted into the WTO.[50] China's Civil Aviation Administration also expressed a similar position for direct cross-strait flights.[51] Later, Deputy Secretary-General of Taiwan's presidential office, Chen Che-nan, conveyed a message to Beijing through a secret channel that Yeh Chu-lan was only expressing her personal view, which President Chen Shui-bian did not agree. Beijing, therefore, made a concession by labelling the "mini three links" as "bi-coastal links" [*liang'an hangxian*] instead of "domestic links" [*guonei hangxian*] as it had termed before. Nevertheless, Chen Shui-bian rejected this labelling.[52]

Beijing noted that shipping companies from each side, instead of the governments in Beijing and Taipei, should conduct the negotiations. Both sides should keep clear of political issues in order for the three links to be put in via agreements between enterprises, associations, and non-state organizations.[53]

This raised Taipei's suspicion that Beijing was trying to split the new government and lower it to a *de facto* local government of China. Consequently, Taiwan's MAC Vice-chairman Chen Ming-tong insisted that the SEF was currently the only authorized body that should negotiate with China on behalf of Taiwan. He called on Beijing to restore official dialogue with Taiwan soon to facilitate negotiations on opening up direct cross-strait trade, transport, and postal links.[54]

China is unhappy that the new links are limited to just selected ports in Fujian and the outlying Taiwanese islands of Matsu and Kinmen, which does not constitute real and complete "three links".[55] In its view, the "mini three links" is merely a move to decriminalize the current smuggling and illegal sea trade between the people of both sides (which has been existing for decades), without greatly expanding cross-strait trade.[56] Beijing would like earlier "big three links", under the "one China" principle. It claims to be fully ready to open up all harbours for direct cross-strait shipping, waiting for Taiwan to further lift its ban.[57]

In the 1980s and the early 1990s, Taipei used the "three links" as bargaining chips for Beijing's political concession. Now, the table has been turned around. Economically, Taiwan now needs the "three links" more than mainland China. Beijing now does not seem to be in a hurry, and it stresses agreement on the "one China" principle for opening the "big three links". In other words, Taipei should not expect to get economic benefits from the "big three direct links" without a paying a political price.

Chen's Economic Strategy and China's Economic Response

The massive flow of Taiwan investment into the mainland has alarmed Taipei of a gradual but deadly "hollowing out" of its economy. Chen Po-chih, Chairman of Taipei's Cabinet-level Council for Economic Planning and Development, did not appear worried in public however. He noted that at present, Taiwan's overall investments in mainland China account for only 1 per cent of Taiwan's gross domestic product (GDP). "As Taiwan still has a 2 per cent excess savings rate, its mainland investment would not have a serious impact on the nation's domestic capital supply. When the outbound investment ratio exceeds 2 per cent of its GDP, Taiwan's domestic investment and economic development would be affected".[58]

However, the real outflow of funds and high technology may be more than the official record. For example, at the end of 2000, only about US$200 million worth of loans from Taiwan's major banks were recorded as flowing to the mainland, far lower than the actual amount, which was estimated as at least US$71.54 billion.[59] It is an open secret that many Taiwanese, in order to circumvent government restrictions, have invested in the Chinese mainland in the name of companies (either their own or others') that are set up in other countries. According to a report lodged by Finance Minister Yan Qingzhang (in Chinese *pinyin*) in the Taiwan legislature, by late 2000, only 0.63 per cent of the funds invested in the mainland had flowed back to Taiwan.[60]

Taiwan's economic dependence on China has been increasing over the past decade (see Tables 1 and 2). According to the MAC, Taiwan's economic dependence rating on China has already reached 24 per cent, bordering on the "warning" level. If it exceeds 30 per cent, China, as Chinese strategists believe, will have the power to influence Taiwan's politics.[61]

To hold back the trend, Taipei has taken a series of measures, including stricter control on the outflow of its currency to the mainland.[62] It has called for "three priorities" in the government's agenda — priority of Taiwan, priority of investment, and priority of economy — to enhance and strengthen Taiwan's economic foundation and competitiveness.[63] It has also launched "8,100 public construction and investment projects" to stimulate the slumping domestic demand in order to reverse the trend of investment outflow. This stimulus package is the government's NT$810 billion budget for public infrastructure and investment for the fiscal year 2001. However, this package has been widely criticized by industries and academics as nothing more than a fine-sounding slogan that provides little actual help.[64] Stimulating domestic demand cannot be taken as the primary solution to Taiwan's overall economic slump. The experience since the late 1990s has demonstrated that increased government expenditure has made little contribution to domestic economic growth. Taipei must come up with clear industrial policies, improve the investment environment, encourage local industries to upgrade, and restore public confidence.

Taipei is now evidently aware that its ability for sustained confrontation with China depends upon its economic development. It, however, seems to be short of effective means to cope with the Chinese challenge brought about by the sustained and vigorous growth of the Chinese economy.

In the early 1970s, after the first world oil crisis, Taiwan adopted a correct economic development strategy — that is, it developed its electronics industry, while China was deep in the domestic turmoil of the Cultural Revolution. This correct development strategy benefited Taiwan with huge economic resources and social stability, which it skilfully used in its political bargaining with China for nearly thirty years.

China's Cultural Revolution is now over, and it is trying hard to catch up. A rising China coupled with a depletion of Taiwan's economic resources will tell loudly in the long run on its political confrontation with China.

With this awareness, Taiwan once had a plan to become a regional economic centre. However, without China's co-operation, it is impossible for Taiwan to become such a centre. Instead, it wants to become a regional centre of science and technology. Taipei wants to develop a "digital economy" and transform the island into an information society, to ensure that the island plays an important role in the global Internet society.

The government plans to turn the island into a technologically advanced information society by 2010, as well as to develop it into a knowledge-based regional operations centre by 2020. Through the National Information Infrastructure Initiative, started in 1994, the government aims to provide the economy with an environment for Internet industries to flourish. Chen Shui-bian said that the goal was to turn Taiwan into a "green silicon island".[65] Taiwan's Council of Economic Planning and Development has put out a knowledge-based economic plan, which includes 57 projects over the five years from 2000 to 2005.[66]

Taiwan, however, is faced with a very bumpy road to realize these ambitions. Not only is China now intensifying its efforts to become a major power in high technology, but Hong Kong has recently also mapped out its plan to be a regional technology centre. Taiwan's basic science research cannot match that of the United States and even China. Its application science and technology also cannot match that of Japan and the United States. With these two ceilings, 95 per cent of its industries being medium and small-sized, the fast decline of its economic resources through an economic "hollowing out", poor economic management, arms race with the mainland, and expensive "check diplomacy" against an increasingly competitive China and the world market, Taiwan will find its technological upgrading very difficult. Taiwan's businessmen will likely continue to make money, as most of them are small in size and therefore flexible. However, its industries as whole will not easily climb the ladder of high technology, either globally or regionally. What is more, with a slumping external market, China, with its great economic potential — a huge domestic market with many different levels and forms of economies — can continue its economic growth if it can successfully stimulate its domestic demand. Taiwan cannot however. With insufficient depth, once Taiwan's prime industry loses the competition, it will collapse much faster than larger countries.

At present, Taiwan's economy is faced with four serious challenges, namely, (1) government incompetence and fierce political infighting; (2) economic upgrading; (3) a slumping international market; and (4) a bubble economy. It will take a long time for Taiwan to sort them out before its economy can leap forward again. China will not give Taiwan an easy time. It will make sure that Taiwan does not become a regional economic centre, a financial centre, a transportation centre, and even science and high technology centre. It will keep a close watch on Taiwan's economic development in order to overtake it. In the coming years, its strong economic growth will rapidly narrow the economic gap between the two sides. By then, even if China cannot overtake Taiwan economically and in terms of GDP per capita, the latter will have much less economic resources to support its social stability and its military modernization, hence its political confrontation. In view of the trend of economic globalization, it is difficult for small economies, such as that of Taiwan, to develop fast enough without attaching themselves to one of the big economies, such as the North America Free Trade Agreement (NAFTA), the European Union, or China. This is one important reason why many big Taiwanese enterprises are opposing the "go slow, be patient" policy and moving into the mainland despite sharing different ideologies with the mainland. There is no reason to hope that this economic trend will reverse.

The WTO Competition

Taiwan has also asserted an interest in entering the World Trade Organization (WTO). In fact, the Republic of China was a founding member of the General

Agreement on Tariffs and Trade (GATT), the forerunner to the WTO, in 1947 but resigned its position in 1950. Between 1965 and 1971, Taiwan took part in the GATT as an observer. When the ROC was deprived of its U.N. membership in 1971, it also lost its GATT observer status.

Both Taipei and Beijing are now in the process of applying for WTO membership. In 1992, when the GATT restored Taipei's observer status, it also agreed to respect Beijing's wishes to postpone the admission of Taiwan until after China joined.

As a result, Taiwan has emerged as one of the strongest proponents for granting China membership in the WTO. However, Taipei's concern is broader than that. Taiwan has moved so much of its manufacturing to the mainland in recent years that any tampering with normal trade relations between the United States and China also has the potential to circumscribe Taiwan's economy severely. The goods produced by Taiwanese enterprises in the mainland are generally not sold in China or in Taiwan, but are exported to the United States. The failure of China to secure PNTR trading status with the United States would mean serious economic losses to Taiwan, and China's entry into the WTO almost means Taiwan's own entry.

On 15 November 1999, the United States and China signed an agreement on China's accession to the WTO. Meanwhile, Taiwan completed talks with twenty-six WTO contracting parties and signed accession pacts with all of them, except Hong Kong. Taiwan and China are expected to enter the WTO by late 2001.

One point of contention between Beijing and Taipei is that Taipei wants to see its relations with Beijing, after accession to the WTO, as equal to those between other full members of the WTO — that is, as separate independent states. Beijing, on the other hand, wants to ensure that other states treat Taiwan's status as a matter of China's internal politics and not as an international issue. It wants Taiwan to join the WTO as a customs territory of China instead of as "the Separate Customs Territory of Taiwan". Taiwan's stand has U.S. support. In September 2000, U.S. President Clinton told Chinese President Jiang Zemin: "Taiwan will join the WTO under the language agreed to in 1992, namely as the Separate Customs Territory of Taiwan (commonly referred to as Chinese Taipei). The United States will not accept any other outcome".[67]

The second point is that if it enters the WTO, Taiwan must make a decision: open direct trade links with China or sink any chance of salvaging the relationship with its giant neighbour by continuing to bar two-way trade.

The WTO was established in the spirit of free trade and as Taiwan hopes to reap the benefits of membership, it can hardly expect to be allowed in while it maintains its decades-old ban on direct trade with China. The ban is clearly inconsistent with Article 1 of the 1994 GATT, which states that most-favoured nation-status must be extended to all other WTO members.

It should be pointed out, however, that restrictions on direct communication and transport links with China can be maintained after WTO entry if they are listed in Taiwan's accession application. The only way for Taiwan to maintain the restriction on trade, however, would be to have the "right of exclusion" (the non-application formula, under Article 13 of the WTO Agreement) by arguing that national security would be jeopardized by lifting the ban. This would permit Taiwan to declare Beijing excluded from privileges accorded to other WTO members under provisions contained in the WTO's charter once the two are admitted as full members.[68] The question is whether Taiwan will be able to have the "right of exclusion".

If the right of exclusion is waived, Beijing could force Taiwan to further relax its ban on the three direct links, which Taiwan has heretofore refused on grounds of security. Otherwise, Taiwan has to give equal treatment to China as it accords other WTO full members without discrimination against the three direct links. Taipei would feel greatly disadvantaged if Beijing becomes a full member while it itself is kept outside the WTO. However, it would also feel so if it does not have the "right of exclusion" after becoming a full WTO member. Taiwan, then, must grant China the most-favoured-nation (MFN) treatment, and other rights given to other WTO member nations. This means that Taiwan will no longer be able to establish discriminatory clauses against goods, services, and funds and personnel related to the trade in goods and services. Taiwan's "Statute Governing Relations between the People on the Two Sides of the Taiwan Strait" includes various limits that do not conform to the regulations or spirit of the WTO. For instance, Chapter 2 of the Statute limits exchanges of personnel, funds and organizations, and Article 70 further sets limits on laws on both sides of the strait. These must be revised to conform to the WTO. This would have far-reaching effects on the types of cross-strait exchanges, and if funds, organizations and personnel from China are able to come to Taiwan freely, it will force the government to rethink its present China policy.[69]

Other obligations that Taiwan will automatically assume after its WTO entry include:

- allowing direct investments by individuals and companies from China;
- opening direct trading links with China, including financial and commercial exchanges;
- permitting employees of Chinese companies and multinational corporations to stay and reside in Taiwan;
- opening direct links with China, and relaxing restrictions on investments by Taiwan firms to China;
- lifting the restriction on visits by mainland Chinese nationals to Taiwan including work permits. Academic institutions in the mainland may also be allowed to set up branches in Taiwan and accept students to study in China.[70]

If Taiwan wants to have the "right of exclusion", it would be difficult for it to enter the WTO as two-thirds of the members must approve such application for the right. If Taiwan chooses to use the "right of exclusion" against China, then the latter can invoke a similar clause against Taiwan. Cross-strait trade would then not be governed by the rules of the WTO, which could hurt Taiwan's economy as it is significantly smaller than China's. China can lock Taiwanese firms out of its market without any retaliation by the WTO.[71]

Some scholars have pointed out that even if Taiwan is unable to invoke the "right of exclusion", it can still invoke other WTO clauses, such as the Safeguard Clause, against China after joining the WTO. However, there are strict limits to the use of the Safeguard Clause, and countries must provide proof of concrete damage. Furthermore, the Safeguard Clause is only for temporary economic relief and the country that invokes the clause must pay for damages resulting from such usage. Taiwan runs a huge trade surplus with China, making it unlikely that Taiwan will be able to convince other nations of a threat that demands the use of the Safeguard Clause.[72]

Taiwan's options are, therefore, limited. What is feasible for Taiwan is to choose the venue for discussions about the three links with China. In other words, after entry, Taiwan can solve trade disputes with China within the WTO, thus avoiding trade retaliatory measures by China.

It could also invoke Article 21 of the WTO agreement, which would allow it to restrict specific trade rights for China that jeopardize national security. A less confrontational approach could follow the Japanese model, imposing informal trade and investment barriers such as phytosanitary (plant health) regulations. Although China could lodge complaints against such commercial obstacles just as Washington has done against Japan in various venues, it would take years to break down each of these constraints. In addition, because so much of the commercial interaction in Asia is multinational, Taipei might be able to call upon foreign investors to assist.[73]

Military Deterrence

In Beijing's mind, the cross-strait tussle has always been a China–U.S. issue in essence, although called "the Taiwan issue" in public. If China had been capable of "persuading" or "deterring" the United States from intervention, by now there would not have been a "Taiwan issue". Beijing does not have any intention to initiate a war with the United States; it merely wants to deter the United States from intervention in what it sees as an internal issue. It believes that without the U.S. support of Taiwan, it could solve the Taiwan problem without the actual use of force, although there might be some need for deterrence.

China Enhances Strategic Capabilities

For the purpose of deterrence, China is further developing its intercontinental ballistic missiles — *Dongfeng*-31,[74] and futuristic *Dongfeng*-41 — that will be equipped with low-power propulsion technology, a new technological breakthrough that can alter the path of offensive missiles.[75] In other words, the two missiles can change their flight directions from designed points at different angles, thus making them difficult to be intercepted. The *Dongfeng*-31 missile is already commissioned, with a range of 8,000 kilometres. The *Dongfeng*-41, to be commissioned in 2005,[76] has a range of around 12,000 kilometres. Both are to be mounted on MIRV or MRV.[77] They (at least the *Dongfeng*-31) are solid-fuelled, vehicle-mounted, vehicle-erected and vehicle-launched, thus giving China a stronger strategic deterrence than it previously had.

The People's Liberation Army (PLA) currently has seventy-seven submarines in service. Among them are seventeen nuclear attack submarines (designated 091 and 093), and five 092 or *Xia*-class ballistic missile nuclear submarines (SSBN). It started the 094 SSBN project at the end of the 1980s and three 094 SSBNs have been commissioned recently. Another three SSBNs are believed to follow. Compared with the 092, the 094 is much safer, quieter, and more mobile. It is equipped with a C41SR system and the *Julang* (*Great Wave*)-2 missiles (that is, *Dongfeng*-31), with a range of 8,000 kilometres. The 094 launch missiles from under water; while the older 092 model cannot do submerged-launching. The 094 reportedly carries sixteen missiles each that can be MIRVed or MRVed, with from three to six warheads mounted on each. In other words, one 094 can launch ninety-six missiles. If the PLA builds at least six 094s, as reported, they can attack 576 targets all over the world at the same time.[78] As a strong deterrence against U.S. aircraft carriers, the PLA is reportedly using Russian Victor III design to upgrade two nuclear attack 093 submarines. They will be commissioned in 2005 and 2007 respectively. The PLA is also developing a new submarine-launched cruise missile based on its C-801 cruise missiles.[79]

China has spy satellites that continuously monitor the U.S. and Taiwan military. They could be used to guide "saturated" missile attacks against, for example, aircraft carriers well in advance before they approach China's coast. China has recently built two fixed missile launch sites, named the "Long Wall Project", in its southeastern Jiangxi and Fujian provinces. It plans to build more of such launch sites to form a formidable "wall of missile bases" capable of launching long-range missiles, such as the *Dong Feng*-31.[80] The PLA can fire *Dong Feng*-31 at a U.S. navy aircraft carrier group shortly after the group leaves its base in Hawaii. The "Long Wall Project" is basically a deterrent against U.S. military intervention.

China has not only the capability to detect and track most satellites but also anti-satellite (ASAT) capability. It has a highly developed electro-optic industry and the ability to field laser weapons. Chinese experts in their local newspapers revealed that China had acquired the capability to destroy a satellite's optical sensors with lasers.[81] It is close to fielding a parasitic ASAT(anti-satellite) mini-satellite that could attach itself to a satellite to distort information, alter data, and shut down vital operations of the opponent's satellite.[82] It may also be developing jammers against Global Positioning System (GPS) receivers. China's ASAT capability will pose a serious challenge to the space-based laser weapons that the United States is now developing as part of its National Missile Defense (NMD) system to knock down China's missiles at their boosting stage.

In January 2000 the PLA initiated Project 1-26 to develop exotic high-tech weapons. This project involves dual-use space and information technology, and exotic weapons such as miniaturized namo weapons.[83] To complicate the U.S. aircraft carrier intervention, the PLA is fielding a new Passive Coherent Location (PCL) system, a revolutionary new anti-aircraft early-warning defence system that can detect U.S. stealth aircraft, including the F-117 bomber and even the futuristic F-22 fighter.[84] Apart from purchasing the Russian *Sovremenny* class destroyer, whose sea-skimming supersonic medium-range SS-N-22 *Sunburn* missile is designed specifically to get through a U.S. Navy destroyer screen to attack a carrier, the PLA is also improving its own surface-to-surface missiles (SSM) and cruise missiles. Its cruise missile is now both accurate and difficult to intercept: with a range of 2,000 kilometres, it is capable of hitting a target accurately to within 5 metres (the Chinese Academy of Science confirmed this Western report),[85] while being able to change directions three times at angles greater than 35 degrees on flight.[86] In the exercise in May 2001, the PLA successfully launched its air-launched cruise missiles.

The PLA also claims to have an arsenal of secret weapons, "the most advanced in the world, including laser weapons to disable the laser guidance systems of America's F-17s".[87] It has been working on a new generation of nuclear weaponry for the past ten years based on a new theory of nuclear physics.[88] According to Danny Stillman, a well-known American nuclear physicist from the Los Alamos National Laboratory,[89] "they [the Chinese] are right up with us on [nuclear] weapons design. My expertise is diagnostics of nuclear weapons testing, and they're ahead of us in that. They have instrumentation that we have never developed".[90]

The PLA has developed neutron bombs and miniaturized nuclear warheads. It had developed the concept of a miniaturized nuclear warhead as early as in the mid-1970s, but did not have the computer capability to design it until the late 1980s. It successfully tested the device in 1992.[91] Now, its tactical nuclear warhead can be as small as 500 tonnes of TNT, making it a very effective tactical deterrence against U.S. aircraft carrier intervention.[92]

Weapons for a Taiwan Strait Crisis

To boost its military pressure over Taiwan, the PLA has placed high priority on the development of land-attack cruise missiles (LACM) for medium to long-range missions. It had only one theatre missile brigade in 1995; the number has since grown to three and is expected to be seven between 2005 and 2010.[93] China's official aerospace publications recently indicated that the PLA had developed two such land-attack missiles: *Chang Feng* and *Chang Feng*-1. Similar to the U.S. *Tomahawk* LACM, the Chinese versions employ technologies such as GPS/Inertial mid-course guidance and, most critically, terrain contour matching to increase its accuracy. The range of *Chang Feng* missiles is believed to be 600 kilometres and accurate to within 15 metres. *Chang Feng*-1 has a range of 1,300 kilometres and accuracy to within 5 metres. When the PLA fields these cruise missiles and more advanced *Hong Niao* LACM (*Hong Niao*-3 can cover 2,500 kilometres), Taiwan's military advantage will be harder to preserve.[94]

China has recently deployed Russian-made S-300PMU1 and S-300 PMU2 surface-to-air missile batteries, which have a minimum range of 90 kilometres. They could severely challenge Taiwan's air operations in the Taiwan Strait as they are deployed in Longtian opposite Taiwan. China has also successfully developed a series of its own anti-aircraft missiles, including the *Hongqi* (*Red Flag*)-9 and the *Hongqi* (*Red Flag*)-7. Other such missiles deployed include SA-2, SA-10 and SA-15.[95]

China has also acquired the co-production licence of the Russian *Zvezda* Kh-31P missile. The missile is specifically designed against U.S.-made *Patriot* and *Aegis* systems. It is reportedly developing FT-2000/2500 missiles (dubbed as a killer of the Airborne Warning and Control System [AWACS]) based on Russia's S-300PMU missiles, which are capable of homing in on radiation emitted by Taiwan's E-2s. Such a development would pose a serious threat to Taiwan's air space and ground radar stations. China has also acquired Russian-designed anti-AWACS missiles, dubbed KS-172/AAM-L; these are capable of being launched from a jet fighter. Taiwan's E-2Ts, future P-3s, and land-based and sea-based missiles would then be subject to China's anti-radiation missile threats.[96]

The PLA has increased its inventory of M-9 and M-11 ballistic missiles and started deploying another 200 to 300 state-of-the-art missiles targeted at Taiwan.[97] According to a recent Pentagon report, China could amass more than 650 of such missiles targeting Taiwan by the year 2005, thereby neutralizing Taiwan's air superiority within forty-five minutes.[98] Taiwan is more feared for its M-11 than its M-9. The M-11 can fire a wide variety of warheads, ranging from nuclear and chemical warheads to electronic magnetic pulse (EMP) warheads. The missile can decelerate while homing towards the target so as to explode at the most suitable altitude to effect the greatest destruction against ground targets. The missile, with improved global positioning system(GPS) technology, can hit with a margin of error of around 5 metres.[99]

The PLA air force has its own AWACS,[100] and may soon acquire a few Russian *Beriev* A-50E. This system is capable of co-ordinating up to thirty of China's aircraft at one time and tracking 200 targets over an 800-kilometre radius, much farther than the 300 kilometres of Taiwan's E-2T.[101] The A-50, coupled with the Su-27SK, Su-30MKK, and Su-27UBK advanced jet fighters deployed in the air bases in Wuhu, will greatly improve the PLA's air control. The Chinese AWACS' capability could also be integrated into its land-based and sea-based missile launching systems, increasing the accuracy of its missiles against Taiwan.[102]

Similarly, the PLA's deployment of advanced diesel-electric submarines, such as the Russian-designed 636 series, and destroyers, such as the *Sovremenny* equipped with "*Sunburn*" and possibly longer-range *Yakhont* missiles, will further improve its naval capability. The PLA Navy (PLAN) is reportedly considering buying two more *Sovremenny*-class destroyers. To boost its sea lift capability, the PLAN has renovated part of its huge commercial fleet for both civilian and military use. Apart from conducting many military activities — such as personnel and armoured vehicle transportation, surveillance, electronic interference, mining, building floating bridges, and medical service — the PLAN ships can fire rockets as far as 180 kilometres (more than the width of the Taiwan Strait), with container-based vertical-launched missiles, anti-air missiles (including *Hongqi* 61 and *Feimeng* 80), and the shoulder-launched anti-air missile, *Hongying* 5A.[103]

The PLA is further developing information and electronic warfare capabilities, such as computer hacking (by introducing misleading information, altering data, shutting down vital operations in an opponent's computerized control and command systems, or planting computer viruses), electronic weapons (procuring state-of-the-art intercept, direction finding, and jamming equipment), directed-energy weapons (laser guns to paralyse satellites, microwave beams, particle beams, high energy radio frequency [HERF], acoustic cannons, plasma guns, high energy ultrasonic weapons, subsonic wave weapons), and non-directed energy weapons (electronic magnetic pulse [EMP] and its miniature technology). These weapons can greatly enhance the PLA's edge over Taiwan and complicate U.S. intervention. The PLA has acquired the technology to make EMP miniature warheads, which could shut down all electronic systems on Taiwan, from communications systems to cars or petrol stations, before an invasion, without casualties and without affecting neighbouring regions.[104] The PLA's capability for information warfare is also enhanced by its recent launch (in both October and December 2000) of navigation satellites.[105]

According to a U.S. congressional report, the PLA has rapidly advanced its joint-force operations. Its recent exercises have demonstrated "significant new joint-service war-fighting skills 'under high-tech conditions' that are steadily altering the balance of power in the Taiwan Strait". The most impressive is the PLA's progress in the communication as well as command-and-control areas. It has made rapid advances in utilizing a national "plug-and-play" fibre-optic civilian telecom network to thoroughly secure its military communications.[106] The PLA has also built a nation-wide fibre-optic network, made of "eight verticals" (North-South fibre-optic lines) and "eight horizontals" (East-West fibre-optic lines).[107]

Diplomatic Pressure

A Grand U.S. Strategy of Asia and China

China's diplomatic pressure on Taiwan will continue. Its success depends, to a large degree, on U.S.–China relations, which will be examined below.

As I see it, the U.S. post-Cold War global strategy is a two-ocean strategy, simultaneously reaching across the Pacific and Atlantic oceans to assert world leadership. This strategy resembles a human figure, with the United States as the head, the rest of North and South America as the body, and two arms extending across the two oceans to hold leadership in Eurasia. Controlling the Eurasian continent (or the "grand chessboard", as Zbigniew Brzezinski, former U.S. national security adviser, has called it) is of fundamental strategic interest if the United States is to retain its sole superpower status in the new century.[108]

In the U.S. Asia–Pacific strategy, the hand reaching towards China has five "fingers": U.S.–Japan relations, U.S.–Australia relations, U.S.–Korea relations, U.S.–ASEAN relations, and U.S.–Taiwan relations. These five fingers are positioned so as to prevent the formation of a strong East Asian power bloc, either by a dominant local power, such as China or Japan, or by a cohesive and exclusive East Asian community. They are also designed to prevent China from threatening the major sea-lanes that are vital to U.S. global strategic interests.

This strategy has a "southern anchor", as termed by William Perry, then U.S. Defence Secretary, referring to U.S.–Australia relations. It also has a "northern anchor", that is, U.S.–Japan security relations.[109] U.S.–Korea relations are also of tremendous long-term importance in this strategy. In 1997, then U.S. Defence Secretary William Cohen acknowledged as much when he stressed that U.S. troops in both Japan and South Korea should stay there, even if North and South Korea reunify.[110] Indeed, it would be much more difficult for the United States to withdraw its military presence from Northeast Asia, that is, those in Korea or Japan, than from its Southeast Asian bases, such as those that were in the Philippines. Conflict is potentially more volatile and destructive in Northeast Asia than in Southeast Asia and, more importantly, a cohesive power centre in

Northeast Asia would be a far greater threat to U.S. global leadership. (A power centre in Southeast Asia would be difficult to achieve and toothless.) Moreover, without a cohesive Northeast Asia, an East Asian power bloc is impossible.

The strategic finger of U.S.–Taiwan relations has also worked well so far. Relations between China and Taiwan took a sudden downturn following Lee Teng-hui's U.S. visit in 1995. On the U.S. side, it is unlikely that Washington will overlook the strategic value of the Taiwan card to support an early and smooth reunification of Taiwan into China.

The hand-shaped strategy has done its job, so far, in helping to prevent the creation of an exclusive regional power bloc in East Asia. Thanks to the financial crisis in East Asia in the late 1990s and the consequent overwhelming influence of the International Monetary Fund and the United States in countries such as Thailand, Indonesia, and Korea, the "five fingers" have been further strengthened.

The U.S. "hand-shaped" Asia–Pacific strategy has thus been strengthened beyond challenge, and no prospect of a strong East Asian power bloc is anywhere in sight. The United States has, by and large, realized its near-term strategic target in East Asia, that is, *political pluralism*, which, in a way, could be interpreted in strategic terms as there is no East Asia power block —either strategic, political, economic, or cultural. A big local power must be divided into smaller ones, or geopolitically constrained.

This "political pluralism" is only a step leading to the mid-term target, that is, to build the countries into U.S.-led regional security co-operation mechanisms. In other words, the five strategic "fingers" will now pull together (only after the U.S. confidence in the sure influence of each of these fingers) in good co-ordination as a "fist" under firm U.S. leadership. This "fist" will work in good co-ordination with U.S.-led NATO advances on the other side of the Eurasian continent.

Clinton's China Policy

The Clinton Administration's China policy was part of a larger Asian strategy that kept America fully engaged, maintained the region's strength and dynamism in an era of globalization, and encouraged China's own constructive engagement in the region. This provided the prospects for encouraging China's internal reform and external co-operation and for creating the conditions to cope with the consequences should China ultimately seek to confront the United States across the region.[111]

For nearly thirty years, Republican and Democratic administrations — despite disagreements on many particulars — have based their overall policy on six strategic premises to seek a reform-minded China that acts co-operatively with the United States, both in the region and globally. The six core premises are:[112]

1. The United States and Asia benefit from the type of stability that comes from China's meeting the needs and demands of its people. Major governmental breakdown in China would produce tragedy at home and severe problems for the region and the United States.
2. Market-based economic development — and the associated formation of a middle class and increased integration with the outside world — will, in the long run, produce liberalizing effects in China.
3. America has a fundamental interest in China's acceptance of international norms and rules. The United States makes the greatest progress when Beijing officially adopts these norms and rules and when it works with China to achieve rigorous implementation.
4. The United States has a strong national interest in having China believe that it is not inescapably hostile.
5. Diplomatically, the United States must pursue a "one China" policy.
6. Maintaining peace and prosperity in Asia is in America's core economic and security interests, and active U.S. engagement in the region is vital to pursuing that goal.

Bush Starts to Detour

The new Bush Administration has complicated the scenario. It is questionable whether President Bush and hawks in his administration will accept these six premises. The first premise is to avoid a broken, though not necessarily weak, China. However, this is not an endorsement of the political status quo in China. In fact, it encourages China to rapidly reform its political system and prods its leaders to adopt the liberalizing reforms.

The second premise posits a belief held by previous administrations that market-based economic reform in China will, in the long run, certainly produce liberalizing effects in China, as Washington desires.

The third premise acknowledges that the United States has achieved considerable progress in areas such as non-proliferation. Less than full compliance on implementation, such as in human rights, should not negate this basic premise as long as the process moves substantially forward towards the direction Washington wants to see.

The fourth premise encourages China to be more liberalized, more rule-abiding, and more co-operative so as to cut down considerably the cost of the U.S. Asia policy. On both sides, words and actions affect each country's perceptions of the other's attitudes and intentions. Adopting such harsh rhetoric as the Bush Administration is currently doing, which cites China as a strategic competitor instead of a strategic partner, can help to make it one.

To sum up the first four premises, the previous Democratic and Republican administrations had a strong belief in, and therefore encouraged, a "peaceful evolution" inside China. In other words, their frontline was drawn inside China.

For the "hawks" in the Bush Administration, however, their "battleline" seems to be drawn around China, mainly because of their doubt whether the "peaceful evolution" will work eventually. Even if it works, a democratic, but strong, China will also likely pose a serious strategic challenge to the U.S.' global leadership. Their initial strategic reorientation is demonstrated in their actions to turn China from a "strategic partner", as the previous Administration had defined it, to a "strategic competitor", as well as the expanded arms sales to Taiwan. It is also demonstrated in their claim for a broader commitment to defend Taiwan, and their proposal to shift the defence focus from Europe to East Asia, with China as the thinly-disguised main target, in the same manner as their proposed NMD and TMD intend to do.

The re-drawing of the "battleline" by these "hawks" in the Bush Administration is demonstrated by their heavier alliance with Japan, their initiatives to strengthen the de facto alliance with Taiwan, and their action to forcefully stall the bold initiatives by South Korean leader Kim Dae Jung for a more vigorous process towards peaceful reunification on the Korean peninsula.

For the fifth premise, the U.S. "one China" policy taken by the previous Administrations was not meant as a favour to China. Such restraints on American diplomacy help America's ability to successfully pursue policies that are built on the first four premises. Now, the Bush Administration has started to withdraw these restraints. This point will be discussed in detail in the following section.

For the sixth premise, the previous Administrations believed that the United States could benefit from China's active and constructive engagement and integration throughout Asia. Asia's peace and prosperity would be in America's interest. Now, the new security strategy, as upheld by the "hawks" in the Bush Administration, will divide Asia into two hostile camps if it is officially adopted. If this happens, this premise will also have been fundamentally denied.

If these six premises are compromised, circumvented or denied, the Bush Administration will certainly bring about a new Asia and China policy, sooner or later.

Bush's Taiwan Policy: Arms Sales and Security Commitment

President Clinton took the initiative to propose to Beijing to build a "strategic partnership" between the two countries. The new U.S. President, George W. Bush, calls China a "strategic competitor", not a "strategic partner". The Secretary of State in the Bush Administration, Colin Powell, claims to "treat China as it merits. A strategic partner China is not. But neither is China our inevitable and implacable foe. It is a competitor and a potential regional rival, but also a trading partner".[113] The Bush Administration, as Colin Powell puts it, stresses "the importance of strong relationships with its Asia–Pacific allies and friends, particularly Japan". As for its relations with China, Colin Powell continues to say, "All else in the Pacific and East Asia flows from those relationships.[114]

The Bush Administration has so far clearly tilted towards Taipei with stronger political and military support. In June 2001, the Administration for the first time proposed three suggestions for initiating a dialogue across the Taiwan Strait. They are: (1) the two sides should resume direct dialogue; (2) they should begin with economic issues; and (3) they should increase understanding in order to enhance mutual trust.[115]

This is a clear rejection of Beijing's request that the two sides of the strait should, apart from economic negotiations, also have political negotiation or dialogue under the "one China" principle. Taipei should accept the consensus, reached between Beijing and the KMT government in 1992, regarding the "one China" principle. In his visit to Washington in March 2001, Chinese Vice Premier Qian Qichen told the White House once again that President Jiang Zemin had invited Chen Shui-bian to visit China, but under the "one China" principle.[116] Now, the Bush Administration has asked Beijing to resume its dialogue with Taipei "without preconditions".[117] This is the first time that Washington has openly expressed support for Taipei's position that no preconditions be set for cross-strait dialogue.

The Bush Administration has also called upon Beijing to acknowledge the Chen Shui-bian government that was created through democratic elections, and to promote cross-strait dialogue with a higher degree of sincerity. It repeated the U.S. long-standing stance that any disagreement in the Taiwan Strait must be resolved through peaceful means. It warned that if the Chinese leaders ignore their international responsibilities in such areas as human rights, weapons proliferation, and trade, the United States would use all available methods to compel mainland China to move in a more constructive direction.[118]

U.S. Arms Sales to Taiwan

The Bush Administration reaffirmed the "one China" policy, but failed to repeat the "three no's" policy as President Clinton had done.[119] It supported continued U.S. arms sales to Taiwan and a clearer U.S. defence commitment to Taiwan.

On 23 April 2001, President Bush decided to offer Taiwan the largest arms package since the 1992 sales of 150 F-16 fighters. Bush denied Taiwan the most expensive and controversial items on Taiwan's shopping list: four *Arleigh Burke*-class destroyers equipped with advanced *Aegis* radar systems and the *Patriot*-3 anti-missile systems. (But he stated that he would reconsider the outstanding *Aegis* request if China continued to deploy missiles aimed at Taiwan.) Bush approved two other weapons systems that China strongly protests against: eight submarines and twelve P-3C *Orion* anti-submarine patrol aircraft (a different version of the same model involved in the recent spy plane incident with China).[120]

China's navy and air force have only very limited anti-submarine capability compared with most other navies, including Taiwan's. While China outnumbers Taiwan in modern submarines, the former has no modern anti-submarine patrol aircraft while the latter has a few. The twelve new P-3Cs, which are among the best anti-submarine weapons in the world, would be a substantial addition to Taiwan's anti-submarine warfare (ASW) capability. Taiwan also outnumbers China in warships with advanced anti-submarine weaponry.[121]

Also offered for sale were four *Kidd*-class missile destroyers. The *Kidd*-class destroyers lack the capabilities of the *Aegis* radar and do not have the ability to launch standard air defence missiles from vertical launch tubes. Nonetheless, they provide Taiwan's answer to the four *Sovremenny*-class destroyers China is acquiring from Russia. They are also twice as big as any existing Taiwanese warship and much more capable than most Chinese destroyers.

Submarine- and surface-launched *Harpoon* anti-ship missiles and new torpedoes were also offered to help Taiwan against China's anti-access and naval blockade strategies.

The amphibious assault vehicles and *Paladin* artillery systems offered raise the spectre of a future military confrontation that includes Taiwanese operations on the mainland. The technical briefing on PAC-3, while only the first step in upgrading Taiwan's current *Patriot* anti-missile force, takes direct aim at China's missile build-up across the strait, effectively doing what China sought to avoid in fighting the *Aegis* radar sale.

The sales list is noteworthy in two respects: first, it is the largest arms sale the United States has ever made to Taiwan (at an estimated cost of more than US$7 billion) since 1992. It is a clear violation of the Sino–U.S. communiqué of 1982 that requested the United States to gradually reduce its arms sales to Taiwan from the 1979 level in both quantitative and qualitative terms.

Secondly, it is the first time that offensive weapons are included. Previous administrations deemed submarines offensive rather than defensive weapons, and thus the sale would constitute a violation of the understanding with Beijing. The main obstacle, however, is that the United States no longer makes diesel-powered submarines and would have to use German or Dutch or other countries' plans.[122]

The inclusion of eight submarines has crossed a line subtly observed by the United States of not selling offensive weapons. This is the first time that the United States has circumvented its Taiwan Relations Act, under which U.S. arms sales to Taiwan should be restricted to purely defensive ones.

Taiwan's "Offshore Engagement Strategy"

As the new government in Taiwan has adopted a new military strategy — that is, "offshore engagement strategy" — the U.S arms sales were particularly noteworthy as they may provide a footnote to the U.S. attitude towards Taiwan's new military strategy.

The Concept of an "Offshore Engagement Strategy"

When Lee Teng-hui was in power, Taiwan's military strategy focused on "strong defence at home". Lee, in his last years in office, tinkered with the strategy that also emphasized Taiwan's offensive capability. At first, he called for a "strong defence posture and effective deterrence". Later, he urged "effective deterrence and a strong defence posture". The re-ordering indicated that he was prepared to adopt a more pro-active and more offensive military line. Chen's "offshore engagement strategy" is an extension of Lee's military line.

Before 2001, the idea of an "offshore engagement" was still a very contentious issue. Since the inception of the DPP government, Taiwan's military has quietly put its "offshore engagement" strategy into practice.

The policy committee at the DPP's headquarters first formulated the strategy, and Chen spelled it out during his presidential election campaign in 2000. The new strategy abandons the old idea of "fighting the enemy on the beaches". It aims at "winning a decisive battle outside Taiwan" and emphasizes having the necessary offensive capability to strike deep into the Chinese mainland as deterrence. The answer to how far it will strike into the Chinese mainland has been deliberately left ambiguous.

From the very beginning, the "offshore engagement" strategy has met strong opposition from conservatives both inside and outside the Taiwan military. A hot debate on the topic arose after Chen elucidated the strategy during a speech made at the 76th anniversary of the army academy in June 2000. In the face of opposition to the term "offshore engagement", the military chose not to openly announce its adoption as a strategy but nevertheless put the concept into practice. The military prefers to use the term "offensive capability", the substance of which is identical to Chen's conception of "offshore engagement".[123]

The Rationale and Implications

The change in the strategic posture is due to Taiwan's realization that China's growing economic and military power would render its previous "effective deterrence" strategy less and less effective. Taiwan, therefore, wants to prepare, through this new strategy, for an asymmetrical war.

To achieve this purpose, Taiwan would enhance its capability to launch a pre-emptive attack far into the Chinese mainland on China's command and control, communication and intelligence, and logistics points, as well as major economic centres. Taiwan, therefore, has made efforts to obtain weapons of longer range and with massive destruction and information warfare capability.

Taiwan's Development of Longer Range Weapons and for Mass Destruction

Building Air-Offensive and In-Flight Capability

To give effect to the new strategy, Taiwan has approved a NT$7 billion programme to upgrade its indigenous defence fighter (IDF) to a joint counter-offensive platform (JCP).[124] With minor modifications to the fighter, the derivative JCP would be capable of carrying offensive weapons. Taiwan has budgeted billions of dollars for the Lushan project to develop the IDF into a stealth plane.[125] It has also started a programme to refit the IDF with in-flight refuelling capability. Extended flying ranges could give Taiwan the ability to strike targets deep in the Chinese mainland. Taiwan is very keen on developing in-flight refuelling capabilities. It has asked Washington for permission to buy a number of KC-135 aircraft. The KC-135 is the only aircraft capable of providing in-flight refuelling for Taiwan's F-16s. Taiwan also introduced the Hsiang Sheng Project, which aims at restoring the in-flight refuelling function of the *Mirage* 2000-5 now serving its air force.[126]

Enhancing Missile Capability

Taiwan has bought *Harpoon* AGM-84A air-launched anti-ship missiles from the United States and has successfully fired them from its own F-16 fighters. With these missiles, the F-16s can attack China's highly valuable military facilities along its southeastern coast from a significant distance, or a target far into the Chinese mainland. Taiwan also has surface-launched versions of the *Harpoon* missile, which is currently deployed on its *Knox*-class frigates. The seekers on these missiles have been significantly upgraded with software provided by the United States.[127]

Taiwan has placed the development of ballistic missiles as one of its top priorities. It has upgraded the domestically built *Tien Kung*-IIA air defence missile to a simplified ballistic missile, which is named *"Tien Chi"*.[128] Some experts believe that Taiwan has successfully developed a medium-range missile of 2,000 kilometres, thus possessing a strong deterrence against Beijing.

Developing Weapons of Mass Destruction?

Related to Taiwan's development of longer-range missiles is the question of whether it has been developing weapons of mass destruction. It does not make military sense to spend huge financial resources to develop medium- and long-range missiles if these missiles are not nuclear or chemical capable, and thus a strategic deterrence. Is Taiwan secretly developing nuclear or chemical weapons?

Nuclear Weapons

Through an "appropriate channel", China once signed an agreement to put its nuclear facilities under the supervision of international atomic agencies.[129] This was one of the conditions under which China had agreed to join the International Atomic Energy Agency (IAEA). The IAEA supervision of Taiwan's nuclear development was done through an "agreed channel", commonly understood to be the United States. How conscientious are the Americans in this role is another question. Even if the United States had sabotaged Taiwan's nuclear weapons project in 1988 by taking away their blue-prints and dismantling the equipment, it could not have taken away the nuclear weapon technology that the Taiwanese have in their heads. The Chinese suspect that Taiwan may secretly start the project again.[130]

London's International Institute for Strategic Studies made the assessment in 1998 that Taiwan has the capability to develop nuclear weapons in a matter of 3–4 months.[131]

Chemical and Biological Weapons

Canada's national security and intelligence bureau has identified Taiwan as being suspected of developing chemical or biological weapons. It pointed out that Taiwan has so far developed thirty-six types of bacteria to be used for biological warfare.[132] Although it claims to abide by the United Nations Chemical Weapons Convention (CWC) rules, Taiwan is not a signatory to the CWC and has refused to allow any international chemical weapons inspections.

The U.S. Taiwan Policy: Cautious Support

The key question is the U.S. position regarding the change of Taiwan's military posture. Generally speaking, Taipei could not have changed its military posture without Washington's tacit endorsement, since the military hardware and software required for the switch would come largely from the United States. How far Washington will let, or even push, Taipei to do so is still unclear. American security planners are suggesting that the war be pushed further into the Chinese mainland. For example, a Rand report maintained

> Contemporary U.S. war-fighting strategy typically includes large-scale strikes against command, control and communications facilities, air defences, air bases and an array of other targets in the adversary's territory. The need to suppress the PLA's long-range air defences could provide the most compelling rationale for at least limited attacks on military targets in China.[133]

However, there is no evidence that Washington has officially adopted (or rejected) this suggestion. Neither is there evidence yet that it is supporting (or not supporting) Taiwan for such an attack far into the Chinese mainland.

The U.S. arms sale package, announced in April 2001, seemed to stress, at least at that point, the enhancement of Taiwan's ASW capability, without selling it *Arleigh Burke*-class destroyers, PAC-3, and *Apache* helicopters as Taiwan had requested. The eight submarines that Washington has promised to help Taiwan to obtain had been considered by the previous U.S. administrations as offensive weapons. However, it will take more than a decade for Taiwan to receive them (even if it can eventually) and commission them into service. It is possible that some offensive functions of the submarines may be removed if China can strike a deal with the United States.

The history of U.S. arms sales to Taiwan tells that the United States is not willing to sell very advanced weapons, especially advanced long-range offensive weapons, to Taiwan. This is out of its concern for the military balance over the Taiwan Strait as well as the worry that these weapons might end up in the hands of the PLA — at least their secrets, if not the hardware themselves.

In 1992, the United States sold Taiwan 150 F-16s, but only after many other countries had bought them. They were only F-16 A/B, not the advanced C/D version. They were delivered to Taiwan without a combat manual and the E-2Ts (early warning aircraft) that the United States provided Taiwan with were not connected with F-16s and Taiwan's *Perry*-class frigates.

The United States sold Taiwan two World War II-vintage *Guppy*-class submarines in the early 1970s, but without torpedoes. The Clinton Administration agreed to sell Taiwan advanced medium-range air-to-air missiles (AMRAAMs), but insisted that they be stored in Arizona, and not in Taiwan.

Defence industrial institutes in Taiwan have been repeatedly frustrated over the deliberately poor timing of U.S. arms sales to Taiwan. When a particular Taiwan-developed weapons system came close to testing, Washington would modify its earlier opposition and give the green light to sell Taiwan similar weapons. When Taiwan's IDFs were near production stage, the previous Bush Administration decided to sell Taiwan 150 F-16 A/Bs, which forced Taipei to cut down the number of its IDFs from 250 to 130. The Clinton Administration agreed in 2000 to sell the RGM-84L *Harpoon* missiles when Taiwan was near to obtaining the *Hsiung-Feng* II anti-ship missile. AMRAAMs were allowed to be sold to Taiwan because Taipei's *Sky Bow* II air-to-air missiles were nearly ready for production.[134]

According to *Taipei Times*, a pro-independence newspaper in Taiwan, the United States has installed self-destruct devices in the weapons sold to Taiwan. Washington officials said, as quoted by the newspaper, that the United States must consider stopping the sale of high-tech weapons to the island in an attempt to prevent them from falling into Beijing's hands. Taiwan would be denied high-end weapon systems, such as *Aegis*-equipped destroyers, for an indefinite period, no matter how keen the island was to have them.[135]

The American caution is well justified for their own interests. After Chen Shui-bian's election, dozens of generals in Taiwan's military forces offered to retire. Although there had never been serious doubt of the loyalty of Taiwan's military to the Constitution and their commander-in-chief, Chen is faced with an army that fundamentally opposes the pro-independence position held by the DPP. The fact is that an overwhelming majority of the officer corps did not vote for Chen.[136] They oppose communism but they may oppose Taiwan's independence even more.

Increasing Military Integration between Taiwan and the United States

The United States is thus understandably reluctant to sell very advanced weapons to Taiwan. On the other hand, it is active in pushing for military integration with Taiwan.

One essential question regarding Taiwan's arms purchase is whether it is buying these weapons as a bargaining chip for a favourable political arrangement with Beijing for future unification, as Taiwan's military claims,[137] or whether it intends to ingratiate itself into a military alliance with the United States, and hence a permanent separation from China. In the past, Taiwan's arms purchases did not alarm Beijing as much as it does today as the two armies of Taiwan and the United States are increasingly being integrated.

An intelligence report circulating within military circles revealed Taiwan's plan to build a military alliance with the United States. A *de facto* U.S.–Taiwan military alliance is actually slowly taking shape, with the United States taking the initiative most of the time. The U.S. military has volunteered to provide its Taiwan counterpart with technical assistance. A pattern of interoperability is being established between the two militaries. Both have begun to standardize military terms and rules used by the two sides as well as co-operation on combat simulation and strategic planning.[138] In April 2001, the U.S. Navy sent a delegation of officials to Taiwan to provide wireless communication codes to facilitate communication between the two militaries. The codes will enable Taiwan's fighter planes and warships to communicate with their U.S. counterparts any time in the future. The communication codes will closely link the United States to the island militarily in the absence of diplomatic ties.[139]

The United States has recently upgraded its military ties with Taiwan, by intensifying exchanges of military information, training, and high-level military visits, such as the secret visit in April 2001 by Admiral Dennis Blair, commander-in-chief of the U.S. Pacific Command. U.S. officers on active duty were not allowed to visit Taiwan until 1992. Now more than 100 visits are made every year, almost ten times the number in 1994. Hundreds of Taiwanese military officers have been trained in the United States.[140]

A U.S. think-tank, the Rand Corporation, has called for vastly stepped-up military co-operation with Taiwan. Apart from arms sales, the report has also called for direct U.S. assistance in streamlining the Taiwanese military set-up and in training personnel. What is noteworthy is that the report has recommended the integration of the command and control (C2) system of both the U.S. and Taiwanese militaries by sharing information and intelligence and by helping the Taiwanese to acquire U.S. techniques and operations in C2. Finally, it has called for an integration of troops in times of war by improving their interoperability. In doing so, it has suggested the sectorization of the air and sea space over the Taiwan Strait, with the U.S. Air Force and Navy taking over control of some parts of the Strait. For example, in coping with submarine warfare, the report recommended "quartering" the Strait, with Taiwanese submarines staying east of the traditional centre line, leaving areas west of the line (and nearer to the mainland) to the United States. If these proposals are implemented in full, it would have the effect of restoring the abrogated U.S.–Taiwan Joint Defence Pact (1953–79).[141]

The U.S. Congress has been pushing for the passage of the Taiwan Security Enhancement Act (TSEA), aimed at upgrading U.S. military co-operation and integration with the Taiwan military. In early May 2001, the U.S. House of Representatives' International Relations Committee passed a bill to give Taiwan the designation of a "major non-Nato ally" (MNNA).[142] The bill was passed in the House of Representatives in late May as one of the amendments in the Foreign Relations Authorisation Act for FY2002 and 2003 (H.R. 1646). Few countries enjoy MNNA status, and among them are Australia, Egypt, Israel, Japan, and South Korea.[143] Privileges that such allies enjoy include priority delivery of excess U.S. national defence articles and participation in joint research and development projects. In addition, countries designated as MNNA members in 1995 could take part in national defence export-loan guarantee plans.

Bush's Security Commitment to Taiwan

Four days after the April arms sales decision, President Bush, in a series of interviews on his 100th day in office, promised that the United States would do "whatever it took [*sic*] to help Taiwan defend itself." He also said, at another interview, that American military intervention was "certainly an option" if China attacked Taiwan.[144]

Hours later, however, he added more confusion in a live midday interview with the Cable News Network (CNN). He said that his statements meant only that "I'm willing to help Taiwan defend herself, and that nothing has really changed in policy, as far as I'm concerned".[145] Later, he denied that his "whatever it took" phrase represented a dramatic change in American policy.[146] "Nothing has really changed in policy as far as I'm concerned ... this is what other presidents have said and I will continue to do so. I have said that I will do what it takes to help Taiwan itself".[147]

Whatever President Bush may really have in his mind, such statements have obviously gone beyond what previous administrations had pronounced since the late 1970s. No other sitting U.S. President has gone quite as far in outlining the use of U.S. forces since the Taiwan Relations Act was forged in 1979. The Act only allows Washington to "make available to Taiwan such defence articles and defence services in such quantity as may be necessary to enable Taiwan to maintain a sufficient self-defence capability".[148] Apart from the arms sales, the Act in no way spells out, or obligates, the United States to take military action. Whatever else the United States might do to defend Taiwan has been left deliberately vague in such a sentence in the Act, which reads:

> The President and the Congress shall determine, in accordance with constitutional process, appropriate action by the United States in response to any such danger.[149]

In other words, the President alone, if he does not have the support of the Congress, cannot determine what this "appropriate action" is, other than selling weapons to Taiwan. Therefore, while noting that any mainland Chinese military adventure would be viewed with "grave concern", the previous administrations since 1979 had never explicitly spelled out military means as an "appropriate action". While the 2000 Republican Party platform strongly condemned Beijing's belligerence towards Taipei, it also stopped short of committing the United States to the military defence of Taiwan.

Challenges to the New U.S. Strategy

The reorientation of the U.S. Asia strategy has not been finalized yet. It may be revised and even aborted. Firstly, the Bush Administration has not yet reached consensus with the Congress, the military, academia, and the general public. As the new strategy is a significant turnaround and will thus greatly affect the interests of many in America, the domestic opposition will be strong. For example, the shift of security focus from Europe to East Asia and emphasis from aircraft carrier-based forward deployment to long-range weapons will greatly affect the interests of different military services and industries.

Secondly, Washington has not yet obtained support from its European and Asian allies and friends. The Europeans prefer intensive, long-term diplomatic and political engagement with potentially troublesome governments to American unilateralism and a readiness to rely on threats and the actual use of coercion. They generally do not share Washington's assessment of the security challenges. Nor are they willing to invest heavily in the European Security and Defence Program (ESDP), or in their own North Atlantic Treaty Organization (NATO). Their unwillingness adds to America's hesitancy to significantly swing its defence commitment from Europe to East Asia and to take a too confrontational approach there.

Few Asian countries like being dragged once again into a Cold-War-style two camps in Asia. The costs are more than the benefits. Previously, America was willing to position its troops in the forefront. Now, America's determination to take the casualties is very much doubted, especially when U.S. Defence Secretary Donald Rumsfeld's recommendations stress on building U.S. long-range attack capability from its home bases. Previously, the PLA shells could not reach these Asian countries to retaliate (such as Japan in the Korean War of the 1950s). Now, their nuclear- and chemical-capable missiles can. Even Taiwan President Chen Shui-bian announced, in late May 2001, a new "five no's" policy, claiming that "Taiwan will not be a pawn of any country" in their game with China.[150]

China is different from the Soviet Union. It is not expanding beyond its own borders. Neither is it exporting its ideology to threaten the governments of its neighbours. Moreover, the economies of most Asian countries are heavily involved with the Chinese economy. Their sustained development has become increasingly dependent on China's economy rather than on Japan's.

In its White Paper on trade, Japan has acknowledged that the era when Japan was far and away the strongest of the Asian economies is already over. In the future, China will play a larger role, and is likely to be the driving force spurring Asia's growth.[151] Japan's economic troubles are not cyclical, but structural, for which Tokyo's gradual approach can hardly work. Monumental transformations are needed, and Japan seems neither prepared nor willing to undertake them.

The Japanese system will not change easily and the present inertia may last longer than expected, longer than most Asian countries expect it to turn around to help boost their own economies.

Amid the U.S.-led global slowdown and Japan's economic stagnation, China, with its economic growth rate popularly predicted at around 8 per cent annually for the next one or two decades, may hold the key to Asian economic stability and development as a major driving force. Asian countries need the Chinese economy as a "buttress", should another economic crisis occur when no major Western economic powers would come to their immediate rescue. As *International Herald Tribute* points out: "If Japan and China succeed in their reforms, Asia's long-term future will be bright. The only factor that can delay it is American policies. The new U.S. Administration may be doing exactly that".[152] With such a suspicion and under such a situation, few Asian countries would support a confrontational security alliance in East Asia.

America's Achilles' Heel: Diminishing Security Surplus and Marginal Strategic Utility

Despite its overwhelming "muscles", the United States also has its own Achilles' heel. China can focus its total resources against one or a few specific targets (because it does not have security obligations outside its borders). The United States, however, has many global obligations, "hot spots", and "rogue states" to contend with. These "obligations" tap on U.S. resources steadily and *increasingly* heavily, more than on others.

Ironically, the United States will become more vulnerable as it creates more high technology that, despite giving itself some advantage, will also rapidly erode its security surplus (geostrategic protection). It used to enjoy huge security surpluses, largely because it shares borders with only two weak countries and is protected by two vast oceans; few countries could have such a strong navy and air force to threaten the U.S. continent; and none could do so without being easily located and prevented well in advance. Nowadays, with the rapid advances in military technology, more and more medium-sized and small countries, and even global terrorist groups have, or will have, more and more lethal but low-cost weapons that could threaten vital American interests in a potential asymmetrical warfare, without sending naval and air fleets across the two oceans.

Hence, instead of having just Canada and Mexico, the United States has suddenly "bordered" itself with many other countries in this more globalized world, increasingly unsure of where the threat would come from. Its surplus security has thus been massively reduced to a level much lower than even half a century ago despite having more glaringly expensive weapons at its hands. The gap between America and other major powers is fast vanishing in terms of security surplus. This trend may eventually cost America its capability for world leadership. No country in this world can become or remain the sole world leader without far greater security surplus than the next.

Together with the diminishing security surplus is the *diminishing marginal strategic utility* of America's military strength. Beyond a certain point, the marginal utility of any particular good decreases as more is consumed. Such a law exists not only in economics but also in defence studies, not only between big powers such as the U.S.–Soviet nuclear competition during the Cold War, as is commonly known but also, as rarely discussed, between the United States and more and more small powers, including international terrorists. When weapons procurement goes beyond a certain level, their marginal utility decreases as more is consumed. One reason is that there is no substantial difference between paralysing a country once and hundreds of times. Once a country has obtained credible second attack capability with mass destruction weapons, as more and more countries are likely to do, it no longer matters that the other country can paralyse it many more times, as the United States can do now. Secondly, asymmetrical warfare means to be threatened by more and more countries and terrorist groups which cannot afford to have those glaringly expensive weapons that the United States has, but can be lethal enough to threaten U.S. fundamental interests.

The rapid advance in military technology will further complicate the U.S. strategic scenario and add massively to the cost of maintaining global leadership. From this perspective, to the United States, China is not the sole or even the most serious problem in the new century. The greater challenge will be *a general and relative erosion of its power and security surplus* resulting from the massive and rapidly growing cost of maintaining leadership in a world of increasing uncertainty and volatility. In this sense, the United States will not be fighting with a specific state, but an *invisible* and, arguably, *invincible* enemy.

The NMD system being planned by the United States is an effort to enhance its security surplus as the two oceans gradually lose their strategic protection. The NMD cannot guarantee 100 per cent protection, but it can certainly raise the security surplus to a level higher than others. This is where America's long-term fundamental security interest lies.

This NMD protection is not enough, not only because smaller powers may use asymmetrical means but also because the disparate threats that the United States is likely to face in future will be fluid, multiple, and multidirectional.

One way out is, together with NMD building, to cultivate co-operation from major powers, including China, and build U.S.-led regional and global security co-operation mechanisms, so that the cost and the danger will be shared among these mechanisms, to reduce the incentive and complicate the targeting of those potential challengers. In these mechanisms, other major players should feel that they have more of a stake in co-operating with than in obstructing. Thus, the responsibility for order would devolve to other regional actors, although the United

States would keep the *de facto* veto power. If the above argument is accepted, the Bush Administration can be expected to eventually make greater effort to improve the current crisis-ridden U.S.–China relationship into a better, at least more manageable, one.

Notes

1. See China's National Conference on Taiwan in late March 2000, in Ching Chong, "It's 'One China' Principle or Nothing", *Straits Times* (Singapore), 29 March 2000.
2. Ching Chong, "Why China is going easy on Taiwan for now", *Straits Times* (Singapore), 18 August 2000.
3. Robert Burns, "China Assures U.S. on Taiwan Attack", Associated Press Newsline, 12 July 2000.
4. Ching Chong, "Why China is going easy on Taiwan for now".
5. Ibid.
6. Todd Crowell, "Now, a Beijing Peace Offensive", *Asiaweek*, 28 July 2000.
7. See China's White Paper on the Taiwan issue, in *Renmin Ribao*, 21 February 2000.
8. Crowell, op. cit. "Beijing Redefines Dogma in Overture to Taiwan", Reuters Newsline, 27 August 2000.
9. *Lianhe Zaobao*, 16 April 2000, p. 18.
10. John Pomfret, "Taiwanese Leader Voices Confidence in Face of Turmoil", *Washington Post*, 5 October 2000.
11. "Editorial: Taiwan needs its own 'united front' ", *Taipei Times*, 16 March 2001.
12. Hsieh was invited as mayor of Kaohsiung, not as chairman-elect of the DPP. Hsieh and Chen Shui-bian head two contending factions within the DPP.
13. *Chung Kuo Shih Pao*, 9 March 2001.
14. Jason Blatt, "Everything on the table, Qian tells Taipei", *South China Morning Post*, 23 January 2001.
15. See an interview with the President of the China Institute of Taiwan Studies, Xu Shiquan, in the United States, *Chung Kuo Shih Pao*, 2 March 2001.
16. *Chung Kuo Shih Pao*, 9 March 2001.
17. The rules, in 15 provisions, specify the guiding principles, ways of management and dispute settlement concerning cross-strait trade. *Renmin Ribao*, 2 January 2001.
18. "Taiwanese-Contracted China Investment Up 46%", *China Online*, 13 April 2000, quoting China's Assistant Minister for Foreign Trade and Economic Co-operation, Ma Xiuhong.
19. "China boosts trade hold on Taiwan", *Straits Times* (Singapore), 4 January 2001.
20. Charles Snyder, "Qian warns of 'flames of war' ", *Taipei Times* (Singapore), 25 March 2001. Figures are from both China's Vice Premier Qian Qichen and the Taiwan Finance Ministry. See David G. Brown, "Wooing Washington", http://www.csis.org/pacfor/cc/0101Qchina_taiwan.html
21. Ibid. See also Michael Vatikiotis and Maureen Pao, "Just a Pawn in the Superpower Game", *Far Eastern Economic Review* (Hong Kong), 26 April 2001.

22. *Renmin Ribao*, 2 Janaury 2001.
23. "Cross-strait data up 27pc as bans ease", *South China Morning Post*, 30 January 2001.
24. Ibid.
25. Ibid.
26. "Taipei's High-Tech Firms Eye China", *Straits Times* (Singapore), 29 October 2000.
27. David Brown, "Dialogue in Neutral: Private Sector in Gear", in http://www.csis.org/pacfor/cc/004Qchina_taiwan.html.
28. "China boosts trade hold on Taiwan", *Straits Times* (Singapore), 4 January 2001.
29. "Formosa Plastics to build four PVC plants in China", *Taipei Times*, 19 February 2001.
30. Mark Landler, "Taiwan's PC Makers Shift to China", *New York Times*, 29 May 2001.
31. Ibid.
32. Ibid.
33. The association surveyed 441 high-tech firms operating in Taiwan, and received 411 valid responses. "Poll: 90 Percent of Taiwan Tech Firms to Invest in PRC", *Taiwan Economic News*, 20 February 2001.
34. The Associate Press, "China attracts Taiwan's best to new hi-tech industries", *South China Morning Post*, 16 February 2001.
35. "Taiwan Unattractive to Investors: Survey", *Taiwan Economic News*, 29 October 2000. Taiwan's ranking lags behind Thailand, Vietnam, and India. The top three rankings went to mainland China, Singapore, and Hong Kong in order, while Japan and South Korea took the 8th and 9th places, respectively.
36. Ibid.
37. Ibid.
38. Mure Dickie, "Taiwan's Growth Sinks to 1%", *Financial Times*, 26 May 2001.
39. Ibid.
40. "Poll: 90 Percent of Taiwan Tech Firms to Invest in PRC", *Taiwan Economic News*, 20 February 2001.
41. Jason Blatt, "Demands grow for cross-strait contacts", *South China Morning Post*, 23 November 2000.
42. "Taiwan may ease trade and shipping ban", *South China Morning Post*, 12 September 2000.
43. Tsai Horng-Ming, "The Status of the 'Small Three Links' and Economic Security", http://www.dsis.org.tw/peaceforum/symposium/2000-07/CSR0007001e.htm.
44. John Pomfret, "China Accepts Taiwan Offer to Open Islands", *Washington Post*, 29 December 2000.
45. Mary Kwang, "China says mini-links benefit only Taiwan", *Straits Times* (Singapore), 16 December 2000.
46. Taiwan later made a concession by allowing Chinese ferries, carrying limited number of passengers, to dock at Taiwanese piers. On 6 February 2001, the ferry *Gulangyu* became the first mainland Chinese vessel to set off from Xiamen on the official trip to Kinmen, carrying 91 passengers.
47. This followed the Hong Kong model. In 1997, when Hong Kong was gearing up for the hand-over, private shipping associations representing Taiwan and the mainland finally worked out a deal under which vessels from Hong Kong and

Taiwan would remove their national flags when entering each other's ports. Instead of national flags, the vessels fly flags bearing logos representing their parent corporations.

48. "Big Three Links a Challenge", Editorial, *Taipei Times*, 12 January 2001.
49. Ibid.
50. "China Seen Warming to Direct Links", *Taipei Times*, 7 January 2001.
51. Ibid.
52. *Chung Kuo Shih Pao*, 3 June 2001.
53. "Trade and politics can be separate: Beijing", *Straits Times*, 6 January 2001.
54. "China Seen Warming to Direct Links", *Taipei Times*, 7 January 2001.
55. Francesco Sisci, "Beijing watchful as ships cross the strait", *Straits Times*, 3 January 2000.
56. Kwang, op. cit.
57. "China Seen Warming to Direct Links", *Taipei Times*, 7 January 2001.
58. "Official pans China's trade barriers", *Taipei Times*, 10 June 2001.
59. *Times* (Taipei), 22 November 2000.
60. *Chung Kuo Shih Pao,* 15 March 2001.
61. Chang Hsien-chao, "How Taiwan's Accession into the WTO Will Lead to Political, Economic and Legal Ramifications for the 'Three Links' ", http://www.dsis.org.tw/peaceforum/papers/2000-05/CSE0005001e.htm.
62. *Chung Kuo Shih Pao*, 14 March 2001.
63. *Chung Kuo Shih Pao*, 27 March 2001.
64. Chang Che-shen, "Slogans by themselves won't fix the economy", *Taipei Times*, 5 June 2001.
65. Goh Sui Noi, "Taiwan aims to be silicon island", *Straits Times*, 13 June 2000.
66. Goh Sui Noi, "Blow to Taiwan as 'father' of economy in coma", *Straits Times*, 25 May 2001.
67. "Taipei Asks U.S. to Stop China Blocking WTO Bid", Reuters Newsline, 21 September 2000.
68. For a detailed discussion, see Nancy Bernkopf Tucker, "The Taiwan Factor in the Vote on PNTR for China and its WTO Accession", *U.S. National Bureau Analysis* 11, no. 2, from http://www.nbr.org/publications/analysis/vol11no2/essay1.html.
69. Chang Hsien-chao, op. cit.
70. Ibid.
71. Ibid.
72. Ibid.
73. Tucker, op. cit.
74. The development of *Dongfeng*-31 began in the 1970s and was completed with trials in May 1995. *Jane's Defence Weekly* estimated the missile to have an 8,000-kilometre range, with a 700 kilogram nuclear warhead capability. Thus, it could target a sizeable portion of the U.S. mainland. It is equipped with an improved Global Positioning System that makes it more accurate. It also has a solid-propellant with a preparation time for launch of 10 to 15 minutes. It does not use a silo but is vehicle-mounted, vehicle-erected and vehicle-launched, and therefore highly mobile. See "Beijing Gives Details of Missile Test", *Straits Times*, 13 August 1999; *Hong Kong Business Daily*, 2 August 1999; and *Lianhe Zaobao*, 4 September 1999, p. 2.

75. "Spacecraft Launch 'a Victory for PLA'", *South China Morning Post*, 23 November 1999. See also *China Business Times,* 22 November 1999.

76. Qi Leyi, *"Chutan Zhonggong Gaokeji Qiangjun Jihua"* [A Study of China's Military High Technology], *Chung Kuo Shih Pao*, 23 March 2001.

77. MIRV stands for multiple independently-targetable re-entry vehicles. MRV stands for multiple re-entry vehicles.

78. *Sing Tao Jih Pao* quoting PLA sources, cited in *Lianhe Zaobao*, 7 January 2001, p. 25. It was also reported in the *Washington Times*, in which the 094 SSBN was said to be carrying missiles with a range of 11,906 kilometres (then, it would be *Dongfeng*-41 rather than *Dongfeng*-31). See the *Washington Times*, quoted in Greg Torode, "New Nuclear Sub Can Target 'Any US City'", *South China Morning Post*, 7 December 1999. See also Qi Leyi, op. cit.

79. Ibid. See also *Chung Kuo Shih Pao*, 5 April 2001.

80. Brian Hsu, "China builds new missile platforms to deter US forces", *Taipei Times*, 8 May 2001.

81. *Sichuan Youth Daily*, quoted in "Spy Satellites Said to Track US Warships", Agence France Press, 6 October 1999. See also Robert Burns, "China Able to Attack Taiwan by 2005", *Washington Post*, 26 February 1999.

82. *Lianhe Zaobao*, 6 January 2001, p. 33.

83. See a report by Al Santoli to the U.S. Congress, "China's New War Fighting Skills: Emerging threats to the U.S., India, Taiwan and the Asia/Pacific Region", an American Foreign Policy Council investigation in Southeast Asia, 14–26 August 2000. http://taiwansecurity.org/IS/Santoli-082600.htm.

84. Current U.S. anti-aircraft defences are cued by radar that detects and tracks incoming aircraft. However, the radar is vulnerable because its signals can be jammed or missiles can be launched to ride back down the radar beam to destroy the transmitter. China's new Passive Coherent Location (PCL) system tracks the signals of civilian radio and television broadcasts and picks up aircraft by analysing the minute turbulence their flights cause on the commercial wavelengths. Because the PCL does not transmit, its receivers cannot be detected and jammed, or destroyed. The strategic implication is significant because it can defeat current U.S. air force tactics against enemy defences. This had alarmed the United States defence community about the cost of defending Taiwan as this would make U.S. air power suddenly vulnerable. See *Newsweek,* 6 December 1999, quoted in "Anti-Plane System Causes Concern in US", *South China Morning Post*, 30 November 1999.

85. See *Science Times,* published by China Academy of Science, quoted in Christopher Bodeen, "Taiwan Blames China for Instability", Associate Press Newsline, 20 August 1999.

86. Reported in *Independence Post* in 1998, quoted in the *Straits Times* (Singapore), 2 October 1998.

87. Jasper Becker, "PLA Newspaper Details Strategies to 'Liberate' Island", *South China Morning Post*, 20 March 2000.

88. Ibid.

89. Stillman retired in 1993 after twenty-eight years at the Los Alamos National Laboratory in New Mexico where for nearly fourteen years he was leader of the

Laboratory's intelligence division. He is one of the very few foreign nuclear scientists who have visited nearly all of China's nuclear weapons facilities and bomb testing sites, and had extensive discussions with Chinese nuclear scientists and officials, and met with Chinese weapon designers. Reuters, "US nuclear weapons expert sues over book", *South China Morning Post*, 19 June 2001.

90. Ibid. The diagnostics take measurements during the nuclear test to determine the effectiveness of the weapon.

91. Ibid.

92. Zhao Yunshan, *Xiaoshi zhong de lian'an* [Bi-Coast Disappearing] (Taiwan: Xinxinwen [New News] Publishing House, 1996), Chapter 3.

93. Nadia Tsao, "Delegation Pressing for AEGIS Sale", *Taipei Times*, 18 December 2000.

94. Holmes S. Liao, "What Taiwan's Military Needs for Its Survival", *Taipei Times*, 19 April 2000. The *Hong Niao* project, believed to have started in 1977, yielded its first version or *Hong Niao*-1 in 1992. Though capable of carrying a high nuclear payload, *Hong Niao*-1 can cover only a range of 600 kilometres. *Hong Niao*-2 came off the pipeline in 1996. Now China is fitting up a third version, or *Hong Niao*-3, which covers a range of 2,500 kilometres, and can serve as a platform to yet another version that can be launched from ships, submarines, and aircraft. See "China: Quantum leaps in missile know-how", *Straits Times*, 23 January 2000. Another report put the range of the *Chang Feng*-1 cruise missile at 2,000 kilometres with the same accuracy of 5 metres. See "China studies war options, including latest space arms", *Straits Times* (Singapore), 15 August 1999.

95. "China Deploying over 400 Missiles Opposite Taiwan: Report", Central News Agency, 8 August 2000. *Chung Kuo Shih Pao*, 24 November 2000. The SA-10 is an advanced air-defence system capable of shooting down aircraft, cruise missiles, and some ballistic missiles as far as 62 miles away. The system is transportable and usually deployed in batteries of several launchers, each loaded with four missiles and tracking radar vehicles.

96. Liao, op. cit. See also "Chinese 'building missile base facing Taiwan'", *Straits Times* (Singapore), 16 January 2001.

97. *Chung Kuo Shih Pao*, 6 February 2001.

98. Liao, op. cit. See also "Chinese 'building missile base facing Taiwan'", *Straits Times* (Singapore), 16 January 2001.

99. Brian Hsu, "China builds new missile platforms to deter US forces", *Taipei Times*, 8 May 2001.

100. A photo of one PLA AWACS was published in *Lien Ho Pao*, 29 November 1993, p. 1.

101. *Chung Kuo Shih Pao*, 6 November 2000. *Lianhe Zaobao,* 12 December 2000, p. 32. John Pomfret, "Russia Moves In on Israel's Lost Jet Deal with Chinese", *International Herald Tribune*, 20 November 2000.

102. Ibid.

103. *Lianhe Zaobao*, 20 December 2000, p. 34. See also *Sing Tao Jih Pao*, 19 December 2000.

104. Anne Gruettner, "Taipei 'ready to buy US missile defence' ", *South China Morning Post*, 22 April 1999.

105. For these two launches, see the *New York Times*, 21 December 2000.
106. Brian Hsu, "Report Shows China Military Expanding", *Taipei Times*, 18 September 2000. The report is entitled "China's New Fighting Skills: Emerging Threats to the US, India, Taiwan, and the Asia–Pacific Region", see Al Santoli, op. cit.
107. See *Lianhe Zaobao,* 25 December 2000, p. 25.
108. Zbigniew Brzezinski, *The Grand Chessboard: American Primacy and Its Geostrategic Imperatives* (New York: Basic Books, 1997).
109. Stephen Hutcheon, "Chinese Critic Says US Was The Target", *The Age* (Melbourne), 9 August 1996, p. 8.
110. Charles Aldinger, "Japan: "U.S. Troop Cut Could Spark Asia Arms Race-Cohen," Reuters Newsline, 8 April 1997.
111. Kenneth Lieberthal, "U.S. Policy Toward China", Policy Brief #72 (March 2001). http://www.brookings.edu/comm/policybriefs/pb072/pb72.htm
112. For a detailed discussion of these strategic premises, see ibid.
113. Colin Powell, "U.S. Looks to Its Allies for Stability in Asia and the Pacific", *International Herald Tribune*, 27 January 2001. The *International Herald Tribune* adapted this comment from the testimony by Secretary of State Colin Powell on 17 January 2001 before the Senate Foreign Relations Committee.
114. Powell, op. cit.
115. "US Makes Suggestions for Cross-Strait Dialogue", *Chung Kuo Shih Pao*, 13 June 2001.
116. CTN TV, News Program, 25 March 2001.
117. This demand was made by Torkel Patterson, senior director of Asian affairs at the National Security Council, in June 2001. "U.S. Official Supports Cross-Strait Dialogue with No Preconditions", Central News Agency, 22 June 2001.
118. "US Makes Suggestions for Cross-Strait Dialogue", *Chung Kuo Shih Pao*, 13 June 2001.
119. The U.S. "three no's" policy towards Taiwan reads: The United States would not support Taiwanese independence, would not support a "two China" or "one China, one Taiwan" policy, and would not support Taiwan's admission to any international body based on statehood.
120. See Appendix 1 for the full list of arms sales.
121. Jim Nolt, "Assessing New U.S. Arms Sales to Taiwan", http://www.fpif.org/commentary/0104taiwanarms.html
122. It remains unclear when Taiwan will take possession of these submarines. The arms package stipulates that they will be built and delivered when Taiwan has the port facilities and operational training to support them.
123. Brian Hsu, "One Year On: National Security — Military quietly putting offshore engagement policy into practice", *Taipei Times*, 20 May 2001. Another defence strategy idea of Chen's, developing "mobile strike" capability, is also taking shape in the military.
124. Ching Chong, "Taiwan ready for war off homefront", *Straits Times* (Singapore), 4 August 2000.
125. "Taiwan to spend billions on weapons", *Straits Times* (Singapore), 6 September 2000.

126. Ibid. Refitting Boeing 767s or Airbus A-300s would enable them to do the in-flight fuelling of the Mirage 2000 jets. However, France removed the in-flight fuelling function off the jets when they were sold to Taiwan in the early 1990s.

127. Brian Hsu, "Air Force Prepares to Test AIM-120 Practice Missiles", *Taipei Times*, 5 April 2001.

128. Brian Hsu, "Missile Developed to Face Up to China", *Taipei Times*, 13 March 2001.

129. "Top Chinese Official Rules out Nuclear Attack on Taiwan", *Straits Times* (Singapore), 11 November 1998. See also Daniel Kwan, "Mainland Rules Out Nuclear Attack", *South China Morning Post*, 10 November 1998. See remarks by Sha Zukang, head of the arms-control division under China's Foreign Ministry. However, Taiwan denied such an agreement but at the same time insisted that its "official line of not developing or owning nuclear devices remained unchanged".

130. For a discussion of the Chinese suspicion, see Zheng Jian, *Gudao Chanmeng* [Lingering Dreams over the Isolated Island] (Beijing: Qunzhong Publishing House, 1997), pp. 575–76.

131. Gerald Segal's assessment was reported by Taiwan's CTN TV on 10 November 1998. At the same time, Taiwan denied having such capability.

132. "Defence Ministry Denies Developing Weapons of Mass Destruction Claim", *Taipei Times*, 17 December 2000.

133. Ching Cheong, "US think-tank tests out war scenarios", *Straits Times* (Singapore), 1 December 2000.

134. Cheng-yi Lin, "U.S. Arms Sales to Taiwan", http://www.dsis.org.tw/peaceforum/papers/2001-04/CST0104002e.htm. Brian Hsu, "Chinese military bases to be targeted by new missile", *Taipei Times*, 3 March 2001.

135. *Taipei Times*, quoted in "US arms for Taiwan can self-destruct: Fears that high-tech arms will fall into Beijing hands", *Straits Times*, 9 February 2001.

136. Alexander Chieh-cheng Huang, "Militarization of the Cross-Strait Relations: Security Challenges to the Chen Shui-bian Administration", in http://www.dsis.org.tw/peaceforum/papers/2000-05/CSM0005003e.htm.

137. For example, Taiwan's former Defence Minister, Tang Fei, justified Taiwan's arms purchases on these grounds as opposed to seeking to bolster future Taiwan independence. See Tang Fei's interview with *Chung Kuo Shih Pao*, 3 May 2001.

138. Brian Hsu, "US reluctantly seeks alliance with Taiwan", *Taipei Times*, 12 April 2001.

139. "Taiwan gets US military communication codes", *Straits Times* (Singapore), 11 April 2001. See Brian Hsu, "US reluctantly seeks alliance with Taiwan".

140. Nadia Tsao, "US Strikes a Balance with Taiwan Arms Sales", *Taipei Times*, 7 November 2000.

141. Ching Chong, "US think-tank tests out war scenarios".

142. "Taiwan may get 'ally status'", *Straits Times* (Singapore), 5 May 2001.

143. Democrat Howard Berman introduced the amendment. The Senate has yet to pass the same version of the bill before it is presented to the U.S. President to sign and take effect as law. "US House Views Taiwan as Major Ally", *Taiwan Headlines*, 18 May 2001.

144. David Stout, "Bush Says Use of Force Is 'an Option' in Defense of Taiwan", *New York Times*, 25 April 2001. "Rice: Bush Takes Taiwan Obligations Seriously",

Reuters Newsline, 26 April 2001. "Taiwan envoy says Bush sends strong message", *South China Morning Post*, 27 April 2001.

145. Stout, op. cit.
146. Ibid.
147. Greg Torode, "After 100 days in office, tact abandoned", *South China Morning Post*, 27 April 2001.
148. See Section 3(a) of the Taiwan Relations Act (U.S. Public Law 96–8).
149. See Section 3(b) of the Act.
150. This policy states: (1) weapons purchases from and stopovers in the United States are not to be considered provocative to the PRC; (2) the ROC government will not misread the cross-strait situation; (3) Taiwan will not be a pawn of any country; (4) Taipei has never abandoned its sincerity and its efforts to improve cross-strait relations; and (5) cross-strait ties are not zero-sum. "President Chen Proposes New 'Five No's' ", *United Daily News*, 28 May 2001.
151. Nan Fang Shuo, "Taiwan faces tough China choices", *Taipei Times*, 5 June 2001.
152. Ronnie C. Chan, "Watch China Move Up and Southeast Asia Down", *International Herald Tribune*, 23 May 2001.

6

Conclusion

Taiwan missed the best opportunity to cement a favourable and peaceful cross-strait arrangement in the late 1980s and the early 1990s when Beijing was most eager to make huge concessions. As discussed earlier, Lee Teng-hui misperceived and mismanaged this opportunity. Most likely, he never had the intention to negotiate for anything that would lead to reunification.

Now, Beijing is no longer in a hurry to make concessions. One reason is that their bitter experience with Lee Teng-hui tells loudly that "sweeteners" at this moment will not work out with Taipei. As Chinese President Jiang Zemin summed up in August 2000, "an important lesson to be learnt from the failure in our work towards Taiwan, which saw a deterioration from one China to two Chinas, is that only until we are fully prepared to reclaim it by force would there be a chance for peaceful reunification".[1]

Chen Shui-bian's election as President on 18 March 2000 has brought about severe political, economic and social dislocations in Taiwan. Beijing has adjusted its Taiwan policy accordingly. It resorts to both well-calculated pressure (on the DPP) and concessions (to the opposition), in the hope that the current political, economic and social disruptions in Taiwan would emasculate the DPP's will and capability for independence. By using political and economic "pincers", as discussed above, China has the confidence to solve the Taiwan problem gradually but eventually. Force mainly serves as a deterrence against potential radical moves towards Taiwan independence. The earlier discussion on the PLA's modernization demonstrates that it is now emphasizing on its strike capability rather than on its power projection capability. For example, it stresses the development of missiles rather than air and sea lift capability that is essential for a full invasion of Taiwan. This tells that China wants to deter Taiwan from any radical push for independence, but is not planning a full invasion. Such a full invasion would be China's "Vietnam". To Beijing, reunification is a means to make China stronger, but not to exhaust itself through a war.

This deterrence also serves as a catalyst, in co-operation with the political and economic "pincers", for favourable political and economic chain-reactions inside Taiwan. That is why stern warnings were issued from Beijing and exercises conducted by the PLA near the Taiwan coast (but not a war), often at a critical moment in Taiwan's internal politics. These have been very cost-effective means employed by Beijing to manipulate Taiwan's political and economic environment. One huge price Taiwan has been paying and will continue to pay is the erosion of its business environment, on which rests domestic and international investment confidence, and consequently the prospects for Taiwan's economy in future. This environment will not improve significantly as long as tension exists across the strait. If Taiwan eventually loses the economic competition with China, its current pushes for independence will be viewed by future generations as not only meaningless but also disastrous to Taiwan's long-term interests. Its current huge arms purchase would appear as a costly "white elephant" that siphoned resources that should otherwise have been used to upgrade Taiwan's economic structure.

In this perspective, the low intensity tension, short of war, serves Beijing's interests if reunification cannot be obtained now. Thus, the "uncomfortable peace", although a Cold War-style one, over the Taiwan Strait will remain for at least the near future.

A war across the strait is less likely if China believes that time is on its side. This Chinese confidence is enhanced by Taiwan's current political and economic deterioration, for which the DPP should be blamed in large part, though not all. Although the current international economic slowdown is not Taipei's fault, the ruling DPP is certainly to blame for its poor handling.

Will Taiwan bounce back? It may, but it is unlikely to be soon, because its problems, as analysed earlier, are deep-rooted, and some are simply beyond Taipei's control. Beijing is now fully exploiting the time gap before Taiwan bounces back eventually. For a long time, Taiwan's GDP per capita will remain far above that of the mainland. This factor alone, however, cannot guarantee its stability and security, especially when facing such a giant neighbour, whose lower GDP per capita does not suggest weaker national power. Even if China cannot surpass Taiwan, the fast narrowing of the economic gap between the two and the gradual depletion of Taiwan's eocnomic resources will take its toll, by and by, on its political will to push for independence.

From a long-term point of view, if Taiwan fails in its competition with Shanghai to become a regional economic centre, the chances of its economy being marginalized in the region in future and becoming dependent upon the mainland will be greater. Beijing is determined that Taiwan will never become such a centre. As long as China keeps growing steadily, it will have a greater chance to succeed in this endeavour. The only deterrent is political and economic chaos in China that would disrupt its modernization process. This scenario, however, is not within sight. The steady and massive mainland-bound investment from not only Western countries but also Taiwan clearly shows that even the Taiwanese do not foresee such a crisis in China in the near future. Otherwise, few would invest so heavily there.

Notes

1. Ching Cheong, "Why China is going easy on Taiwan for now", *Straits Times* (Singapore), 18 August 2000.

7

Postscript

This book focuses on cross-strait relations from early 2000 when Chen Shui-bian won the presidential election in Taiwan up to August 2001 when the manuscript was submitted for publication. Events after that date have further proved the major arguments in the book. For instance, the 11 September 2001 terror attacks on the World Trade Centre and the Pentagon in the United States have demonstrated the prescience in my earlier analysis in the book of the eroding U.S. security surplus and its vulnerability to asymmetrical warfare by smaller powers and global terrorists.

I said in the book that, nowadays, with the rapid advances in military technology, more and more medium and small countries, and even global terrorist groups have, or will have, more lethal but low-cost weapons that could threaten vital U.S. interests in the mainland in a potential asymmetrical warfare, without possessing and sending powerful naval and air fleets across the two oceans. Hence, instead of just with Canada and Mexico, the United States has suddenly "bordered" itself with many other countries in this increasingly globalized world, more and more unsure of where the threat would come from next. Its surplus security has thus been massively reduced to a lower level than even half a century ago despite having much more glaringly expensive weapons in its hands. The gap between America and other major powers is fast vanishing in terms of security surplus, if not in absolute terms of military weapons. This trend, if not reversed by a correct strategy, may eventually cost America its capability for world leadership.

I also pointed out that together with the diminishing security surplus is the *diminishing marginal strategic utility* of America's military strength that also contributes to the erosion of the U.S. security surplus. Therefore, to the United States, China is not the sole or even the most serious problem in the new century. The greater challenge will be *a persistent, general and relative erosion of its power and security surplus*, which will result from the massive and rapidly growing cost of maintaining leadership in a world of increasing uncertainty and volatility, as demonstrated by the 11 September 2001 attacks. In this sense, the United States will not be fighting with a clear and specific state; it will have to fight an *amorphous, invisible* and, arguably, *invincible* enemy if it does not change the way it has been conducting itself so far.

As I also said earlier in the book, the disparate threats that the United States faces in future will be fluid, multiple, and multidirectional. Therefore, the United States should enhance its moral ground, and seek political reconciliation with and closer co-operation from major powers, instead of resorting to unilateralism. It should also build regional and global security co-operation mechanisms, so that the cost and the danger will be reduced and shared among these mechanisms, and thus reduce the incentive and complicate the targeting for potential challengers, especially global terrorists. In these mechanisms, other major players should feel that they have more of a stake in co-operating than in obstructing. Thus, responsibility for order would devolve to other regional actors, although the United States would keep the de facto veto power. In this sense, the United States needs introspection and self-containment. Arrogance and unilateralism will inadvertently create festering resentment world-wide that may gang up and backfire. The Bush Administration's labelling of Iran, Iraq and North Korea as the "axis of evil" and its contingency plans of early 2002 to develop and use nuclear weapons against at least seven countries (China, Russia, Iraq, North Korea, Iran, Libya and Syria) in certain battlefield situations, despite their strategic value, could be a letter on the wall: to reign by fear and unilateralism. I believe that the war on terrorism, just like other wars in history, cannot be won by force alone. To be feared is not necessarily to be admired. To be feared and loathed, instead of being respected and admired, has led many empires into collapse in history.[1]

The December 2001 legislative election in Taiwan and post-election politics have proved my observation that Taiwan has been persistently divided along ethnic lines, one of its most severe vulnerabilities that I have mentioned in the book: the voting behaviour is less influenced by the economic performance of the ruling DPP than by the ethnic background of the candidates. Taiwan's politics and voting behaviour are often more emotional than rational, more popularistic than democratic.

One deadlock in cross-strait relations is the political implication of accepting (for Taipei) and compromising (for Beijing) the "one-China" principle. To the DPP leaders, accepting this principle constitues a denial of their long-held party ideology and is politically disastrous. Their concern is that Beijing may not be satisfied with a nominal acceptance, without raising the ante by demanding more concrete policies. If thus "trapped", they would be led by the nose by Beijing along the no-return track of "one-China". At home, accepting the principle will not increase their votes because this would only prove that the opposition (which embraces the 1992 consensus on the "one China" notion) has been correct. Instead, they would lose votes from those traditional DPP supporters who support Taiwan's independence.

On the other hand, it is also hard for Beijing not to insist on the "one-China" principle because this principle is the bedrock on which rests not only Beijing's basic design for the regional and global strategic structure, but also its legitimacy and even political survival.

Hence, there is no way out of this deadlock in the near future except to wait, with each side hoping that external and internal political and economic changes will eventually work towards the other's compromise. For Taiwan, it still hopes, as Lee Teng-hui frankly says, that the Beijing government will not last long before the democratization process topples it and China would then be divided into several autonomous regions. It also pins its hope on a renewed U.S. strategic emphasis on the island in the overall U.S global strategic reorientation.

For Beijing, it hopes that time is on its side when its momentous rising will change not only the balance of power across the strait, but also the U.S. commitment to Taiwan and, especially, the political will and social support in Taiwan for independence.

Before this change can take place, to hold back Taiwan's creeping independence, China will likely continue to marginalize and fossilize Taiwan through both global and regional strategies, such as its support for building the ASEAN Plus 3 (composed of ASEAN, China, Japan and Korea), ASEAN Plus 1 (Free Trade Area between ASEAN and China), and Northeast Asia regional economic co-operation mechanisms. It will also continue to promote cross-strait economic and cultural ties, aimed at a gradual and eventual economic integration, but short of making Taiwan a regional economic centre.

Faced with growing Chinese economic pressure and internal pressures to lift the official ban on the three links, Taipei replaced former President Lee Teng-hui's "no haste, be patient" policy with a new one called "active opening and effective management", to allow less efficient industries to move to China while Taiwan retains research and development (R&D) and high value-added manufacturing in the island, and using its geographical location to become the "Asia Pacific operations centre and a global logistics centre". To be such a centre, Taiwan extends one "arm" — its investment and trade — into the mainland, while the other "arm" pulls in international corporations to set up their headquarters in Taiwan and use Taiwan as the bridge to the mainland. For this purpose, Chen Shui-bian has appealed to the American business community to form with Taiwan a "strategic alliance of international corporations" — that is, to combine with Taiwan business and then move to China.[2] As Taiwan's *Taipei Times* pointed out: "Such a strategy intends to closely integrate Taiwanese trade interests with the national interests of other countries. When there is a change in the situation in the Taiwan Strait, it will attract international attention ..."[3]

China has reacted to this strategy. In early September 2001, it punished investment bank Credit Suisse First Boston (CSFB) for sponsoring Taiwan's Finance Minister to conferences in Hong Kong and Europe to invite foreign investment. Accusing it of "political misconduct" and warning other foreign banks and companies against any ties with the Taipei government, China removed CSFB from the list of investment banks chosen to share in underwriting multi-billion-dollar stock offerings for two Chinese companies. This move led two other big investment banks, Goldman Sachs and Merrill Lynch, to drop plans to sponsor a similar promotional tour of the United States.[4]

This "punishment" tells how Beijing will sabotage Taipei's efforts to build up the "strategic alliance of international corporations". If their ties with Taiwan will adversely affect their business prospects in China, these international corporations will be less likely to use Taiwan as a bridge into China. China is encouraging them to use Hong Kong as the bridge or set up their headquarters directly in Shanghai and other Chinese cities.

Another case is Beijing's recent withdrawal of two of its promises made in its nine-point proposal for reunification on 30 September 1981. They are: "financial aid for Taiwan from the central government when in need", and "a profitable role for Taiwanese capitalists in China's economic modernisation".[5] In sharp contrast, China is boosting Hong Kong as a regional economic centre. Since the Asian financial crisis started from the late 1990s, China has provided Hong Kong with substantial help to stabilize its currency and stock market, and to expand its exports. Now, when Hong Kong, like Taiwan, is faced with a slump in the international market, China has once again come to its help. Beijing is now urging its various local governments to boost their exports via Hong Kong to help its re-export business. It has also adopted many other measures to help revive Hong Kong's slowing economy.[6] Under central instruction, the Beijing municipal government has offered Hong Kong businessmen exclusive privileges to undertake certain large and profitable infrastructure projects for the 2008 Olympic Games which Beijing is hosting. The Chinese mainland and Hong Kong are now in talks aimed at jointly forming a Free Trade Area.

In all this, Beijing is sending out a clear message to the international business community: "Set up your headquarters in the mainland or in Hong Kong. If in Taiwan, we won't help". Under this situation, few international corporations, if they aim at the huge mainland market, would likely answer Chen Shui-bian's call to use Taiwan as the bridge. If so, Chen's envisioned "strategic alliance of international corporations" will not work, and Taiwan's "international business arm" will thus be "cut off". At this stage, it is doubtful, and there is no such evidence, that China wants to cripple Taiwan's economy. China has repeatedly said that it wants a win-win situation in economic co-operation across the strait and its economy is actually benefiting from strong Taiwanese investment. However, what it wants to see is economic integration across the strait, but not economic integration between Taiwan and the West, as Chen has designed. Since Chen's vision is politically motivated to "internationalize" Taiwan's security, Beijing will be unlikely to take it as a purely economic issue.

If the "international business arm" is cut off, Taiwan's other "arm" — opening the three links — can hardly function as it wishes. Its dilemma is apparent: in the past, the three links were its bargaining chip *vis-à-vis* the mainland. Now it is the opposite. Taipei used to disallow the three links unless the Beijing Government collapsed (as Chiang Kai-shek and Chiang Ching-kuo had insisted) or treated Taipei as a political and sovereign equal (as Lee Teng-hui had demanded). Now, Beijing is playing it back, insisting that, to open the three links, Taipei must accept the "one-China principle" and treat the three links as internal affairs within one country. China welcomes the three links, but no longer feels its urgency. First, without the three links, Taiwanese investment will still be able to find their way into the mainland. Secondly, the three links mean much more to Taiwan's economy, which is now in a bad shape, than to China, to which huge international investment keeps flowing. Taiwan's current ban on the three links, therefore, will intensify its internal strifes. Thirdly, an immediate opening of the three links will hurt Hong Kong at a time when it is facing a slowing-down of its economy, as much transhipment and re-exports will be diverted from Hong Kong.

In addition, an immediate and full opening of the three links may not serve China's own economic interest, in certain aspects. For example, at present, China does not have enough capacity to cope with the massive air and sea cargo that would follow an immediate and full opening of the three links. Much of the cargo would then have to go by Taiwan (Kaohsiung harbour). Shanghai is now fast building its deep-water Yangshan Harbour. By 2005 when the harbour is completed as scheduled, its handling capacity for containers will increase from 5.61 million 20-foot equivalent units (TEU) in 2000 to 10.6 million TEU.[7] In comparison, Taiwan's (mainly Kaohsiung harbour) handling capacity was 4.1 million TEU in 1986, and 5.23 million TEU in 1995 (for Kaohsiung).[8] As Morris Chang, the chairman of Taiwan Semiconducter Manufacturing Corporation (TSMC) said in September 2001, Kaohsiung harbour has only "a six-year niche" before new port facilities in Shanghai begin operations.[9] An immediate and full opening of the three links would jeopardize Shanghai's vision to compete with Kaohsiung as the regional transportation centre.

Taiwan's ambition to become a regional economic centre is thus faced with many difficulties. Former secretary general of China's ARATS, Tang Shubei, once said that Beijing interpreted this plan as containing the real motive for seeking Taiwan's independence. Therefore, Beijing has formulated the strategic principle of "stabilising Hong Kong and developing Shanghai" as the regional economic centre "to defeat Taiwan's plot of building the 'Asia-Pacific operation centre'".[10] Hence, China will likely make sure that Taiwan will never become such a centre. Without Chinese co-operation, Taiwan's ambition to become the centre is faced with great difficulties. China can offer Taiwan more economic "sweeteners", but not without political conditions, and short of making it the regional economic centre. If Taiwan cannot become such a centre, the chance of its economy being marginalized in the region in future or dependent upon the mainland will be greater as long as China can keep its current momentum of growth. This will tell loudly on the current stalemate in the cross-strait game of independence or reunification.

Notes

1. For details of the plans, see Paul Richter, "U.S. Works Up Plan for Using Nuclear Arms", *Los Angeles Times*, 9 March 2002; Michael R. Gordon, "U.S. Nuclear Plan Sees New Weapons and New Targets", *New York Times*, 10 March 2002.
2. Chen made the appeal when he was in New York in June 2001. See Kao Koong-lian and Lee Shin-kuan, "Cross-straight policy not the only key", *Taipei Times*, 25 August 2001.
3. Ibid.
4. Clay Chandler, "Firms Risk China's Wrath Over Taiwan Deals", *Washington Post*, 5 September 2001. See also *Chung Kuo Shih Pao*, 6 September 2001.
5. For the nine-point proposal, see *Beijing Review* 24, no. 40 (5 October 1981): 10–11. For the withdrawal, see the "seven guarantees" to Taiwan, made by Chinese Vice Premier Qian Qichen in July 2001, in which the two proposals are missing. See Jeremy Page, "China Details Taiwan Unification Offer", Reuters, 10 September 2001. "Taiwan Doubts China's 'Seven Guarantees'", *Taipei Times*, 16 July 2001.
6. *Ming Pao Daily*, quoted in "China in bid to aid HK with exports", *Straits Times* (Singapore), 11 September 2001; and *Lianhe Zaobao*, 30 September 2001, p. 23.
7. *Lianhe Zaobao*, 28 August 2001, p. 1.
8. Li Jian, "Lian'an Tonghang Dui Lian'an Guanxi Fazhan Zhi Yingxiang" [The Impact of Direct Shipping on Cross-Strait Relations] (Paper presented at the Symposium on Cross-Strait Relations, Beijing, July 1996), p. 5.
9. Robert Keatley, "Taipei Moguls Eye Mainland", *South China Morning Post*, 8 September 2001.
10. "Cross-Strait Relations Official — New Guiding Principle towards Taiwan Proved Correct", *Ming Pao Daily* (Hong Kong), 20 January 1996, p. A2; quoted in Reuters, 7 February 1996. Taiwan began to talk about this plan as early as 1996.

Appendix 1

The April 2001 U.S. Arms Sales to Taiwan

(Unless specified, it is unclear how many of each item Taiwan will receive.)

- Four *Kidd*-class destroyers.
- Twelve P-3C *Orion* aircraft.
- Eight diesel submarines
- *Paladin* self-propelled artillery system.
- MH-53E mine-sweeping helicopters.
- AAV7A1 Amphibious Assault Vehicles.
- Mk 48 torpedoes without advanced capabilities.
- *Avenger* surface-to-air missile system.
- Submarine-launched and surface-launched torpedoes.
- Aircraft survivability equipment.
- The United States will also give Taiwan a technical briefing on the *Patriot* anti-missile system.

Source: "Weapons the U.S. Will Sell Taiwan", Associated Press, 23 April 2001.

Appendix 2

The One-China Principle and the Taiwan Issue

Statement issued by the Taiwan Affairs Office and the Information Office of the State Council, 21 February 2000.

Foreword

On October 1, 1949, the Chinese people won a great victory in the new democratic revolution and founded the People's Republic of China (PRC). The Kuomintang (KMT) ruling clique retreated from the mainland to entrench in China's Taiwan Province in confrontation with the Central Government with the support of foreign forces. This is the origin of the Taiwan issue.

Settlement of the Taiwan issue and realization of the complete reunification of China embodies the fundamental interests of the Chinese nation. The Chinese government has worked persistently toward this goal in the past 50 years. From 1979, the Chinese government has striven for the peaceful reunification of China in the form of "one country, two systems" with the greatest sincerity and the utmost effort. Economic and cultural exchanges and people-to-people contacts between the two sides of the Taiwan Straits have made rapid progress since the end of 1987. Unfortunately, from the 1990s, Lee Teng-hui, the leader of the Taiwan authorities, has progressively betrayed the One-China Principle, striving to promote a separatist policy with "two Chinas" at the core, going so far as to openly describe the cross-Straits relations as "state to state relations, or at least special state to state relations". This action has seriously damaged the basis for peaceful reunification of the two sides, harmed the fundamental interests of the entire Chinese nation including the Taiwan compatriots, and jeopardized peace and stability in the Asia–Pacific region. The Chinese government has consistently adhered to the One-China Principle and resolutely opposed any attempt to separate Taiwan from China. The struggle between the Chinese government and the separatist forces headed by Lee Teng-hui finds its concentrated expression in the question of whether to persevere in the One-China Principle or to create "two Chinas" or "one China, one Taiwan".

In August 1993, we issued a White Paper entitled "The Taiwan Question and Reunification of China", which systematically expounds the fact concerning Taiwan as an inalienable part of China, the origin of the Taiwan issue, and the Chinese government's basic principles and related policies regarding resolution of the Taiwan question. We deem it necessary here to further explain to the international community the Chinese government's position and policy on the One-China Principle.

I. The Basis for One China, *De Facto* and *De Jure*

The One-China Principle has been evolved in the course of the Chinese people's just struggle to safeguard China's sovereignty and territorial integrity, and its basis, both *de facto* and *de jure*, is unshakeable.

Taiwan is an inalienable part of China. All the facts and laws about Taiwan prove that Taiwan is an inalienable part of Chinese territory. In April 1895, through a war of aggression against China, Japan forced the Qing government to sign the unequal Treaty of Shimonoseki, and forcibly occupied Taiwan. In July 1937, Japan launched an all-out war of aggression against China. In December 1941, the Chinese government issued the Proclamation of China's Declaration of War Against Japan, announcing to the world that all treaties, agreements and contracts concerning Sino–Japanese relations, including the Treaty of Shimonoseki, had been abrogated, and that China would recover Taiwan. In December 1943, the Cairo Declaration was issued by the Chinese, U.S. and British governments, stipulating that Japan should return to China all the territories it had stolen from the Chinese, including Northeast China, Taiwan and the Penghu Archipelago. The Potsdam Proclamation signed by China, the United States and Britain in 1945 (later adhered to by the Soviet Union) stipulated that "The terms of the Cairo Declaration shall be carried out". In August of that year, Japan declared surrender and promised in its instrument of surrender that it would faithfully fulfill the obligations laid down in the Potsdam Proclamation. On October 25, 1945, the Chinese government recovered Taiwan and the Penghu Archipelago, resuming the exercise of sovereignty over Taiwan. On October 1, 1949, the Central People's Government of the PRC was proclaimed, replacing the government of the Republic of China to become the only legal government of the whole of China and its sole legal representative in the international arena, thereby bringing the historical status of the Republic of China to an end.

This is a replacement of the old regime by a new one in a situation where the main bodies of the same international laws have not changed and China's sovereignty and inherent territory have not changed therefrom, and so the government of the PRC naturally should fully enjoy and exercise China's sovereignty, including its sovereignty over Taiwan.

Since the KMT ruling clique retreated to Taiwan, although its regime has continued to use the designations "Republic of China" and "government of the Republic of China", it has long since completely forfeited its right to exercise state sovereignty on behalf of China and, in reality, has always remained only a local authority in Chinese territory.

The formulation of the One-China Principle and its basic meaning

On the day of its founding, the Central People's Government of the PRC declared to governments of all countries in the world, "This government is the sole legitimate government representing the entire people of the People's Republic of China".

It is ready to establish diplomatic relations with all foreign governments that are willing to abide by the principles of equality, mutual benefit and mutual respect for each other's territorial integrity and sovereignty". Shortly afterwards, the Central People's Government telegraphed the United Nations, announcing that the KMT authorities had "lost all basis, both de jure and de facto, to represent the Chinese people", and therefore had no right to represent China at all. One principle governing New China's establishment of diplomatic relations with a foreign country is that it recognizes the government of the PRC as the sole legitimate government representing the whole of China, and severs or refrains from establishing diplomatic relations with the Taiwan authorities.

These propositions of the Chinese government met with obstruction by the U.S. government. On January 5, 1950, the U.S. President Truman issued a statement, saying that the U.S. and other Allied countries recognized China's exercise of sovereignty over Taiwan Island in the four years since 1945. However, after the start of the Korean War in June 1950, to isolate and contain China the U.S. government not only sent troops to occupy Taiwan, but it also dished out such fallacies as "the status of Taiwan has yet to be determined" and later, step by step, lobbied for "dual recognition" among the international community in order to create "two Chinas". Naturally, the Chinese government resolutely opposed this, insisting that there is only one China in the world, Taiwan is a part of China and the government of the PRC is the sole legal government representing the whole of China. China has evolved the One-China Principle precisely in the course of the endeavour to develop normal diplomatic relations with other countries and the struggle to safeguard state sovereignty and territorial integrity.

The above propositions constitute the basic meaning of the One-China Principle, the crucial point being to safeguard China's sovereignty and territorial integrity.

During the 30 or 40 years after 1949, although the Taiwan authorities did not recognize the legitimate status of the government of the PRC as the representative of the whole of China, they did insist that Taiwan is a part of China and that there is only one China, and opposed "two Chinas" and "Taiwan independence".

"This shows that for a long time there has been a common understanding among the Chinese on both sides of the Taiwan Straits on the fundamental question that there is only one China and Taiwan is a part of Chinese territory. As far back as October 1958, when the People's Liberation Army (PLA) was engaged in the battle to bombard Jinmen, Chairman Mao Zedong declared to the Taiwan authorities, "There is only one China, not two, in the world. You agree with us on this point, as indicated in your leaders' proclamations". In January 1979, the Standing Committee of the National People's Congress (NPC) issued a Message to Taiwan Compatriots, pointing out that "the Taiwan authorities have always stood firm on the one China position and opposed the independence of Taiwan. This is our common stand and our basis for cooperation".

The Chinese government's solemn and reasonable stand for the One-China Principle has gained the understanding and support of more and more countries and international organizations, and the One-China Principle has been gradually accepted by the international community at large. In October 1971, the United Nations General Assembly adopted, at its 26th session, Resolution 2758, which expelled the representatives of the Taiwan authorities and restored the seat and all the lawful rights of the government of the PRC in the United Nations. In September 1972, China and Japan signed a Joint Statement, announcing establishment of diplomatic relations between the two countries, and that Japan recognizes the government of the PRC as the only legitimate government of China, fully understands and respects the Chinese government's position that Taiwan is an inalienable part of the territory of the PRC, and promises to adhere to the position as prescribed in Article 8 of the Potsdam Proclamation. In December 1978, China and the U.S. issued the Joint Communique on the establishment of diplomatic relations, in which the U.S. "recognizes the government of the People's Republic of China as the sole legal government of China" and "acknowledges the Chinese position that there is but one China and Taiwan is a part of China".

Up to now, 161 countries have established diplomatic relations with the PRC; they all acknowledge the One-China Principle and promise to handle their relations with Taiwan within the one-China framework.

II. The One-China Principle — the Basis and Prerequisite for Achieving Peaceful Reunification

The One-China Principle is the foundation stone for the Chinese government's policy on Taiwan. On Comrade Deng Xiaoping's initiative, the Chinese government has, since 1979, adopted the policy of peaceful reunification and gradually evolved the scientific concept of "one country, two systems". On this basis, China established the basic principle of "peaceful reunification, and one country, two systems". The key points of this basic principle and the relevant policies are: China will do its best to achieve peaceful reunification, but will not commit itself to rule out the use of force; will actively promote people-to-people contacts and economic and cultural exchanges between the two sides of the Taiwan Straits, and start direct trade, postal, air and shipping services as soon as possible; achieve reunification through peaceful negotiations and, on the premise of the One-China Principle, any matter can be negotiated. After reunification, the policy of "one country, two systems" will be practised, with the main body of China (Chinese mainland) continuing with its socialist system, and Taiwan maintaining its capitalist system for a long period of time to come. After reunification, Taiwan will enjoy a high degree of autonomy, and the Central Government will not send troops or administrative personnel to be stationed in Taiwan. Resolution of the Taiwan issue is an internal affair of China, which should be achieved by the Chinese themselves, and there is no call for aid by foreign forces. The afore-mentioned principles and policies embody the basic stand and spirit of adhering to the One-China Principle, and fully respect Taiwan compatriots' wish to govern and administer Taiwan by themselves.

On May 1, 1995, President Jiang Zemin put forward eight propositions on the development of relations between the two sides of the Taiwan Straits and the promotion of peaceful reunification of China, explicitly pointing out: "Adhering to the One-China Principle is the basis and prerequisite for peaceful reunification".

Only by adhering to the One-China Principle can peaceful reunification be achieved. The Taiwan issue is one left over by the Chinese civil war. As yet, the state of hostility between the two sides of the Straits has not formally ended. To safeguard China's sovereignty and territorial integrity and realize the reunification of the two sides of the Straits, the Chinese government has the right to resort to any necessary means.

Peaceful means would be favourable to the common development of the societies on both sides of the Straits, and to the harmony and unity of the compatriots across the Straits. Peaceful means is therefore the best means. The Chinese government's declaration in 1979 on implementing the principle of peaceful reunification was based on the premise that the Taiwan authorities at that time upheld the principle that there is only one China in the world and Taiwan is a part of China. Meanwhile, the Chinese government took into account the fact that the U.S. government, which for many years had supported the Taiwan authorities, had accepted that there is only one China in the world, Taiwan is a part of China and the government of the PRC is the only legitimate government of China, and saw this acknowledgement as being beneficial to the peaceful resolution of the Taiwan issue. While carrying out the policy of peaceful reunification, the Chinese government always makes it clear that the means used to solve the Taiwan issue is a matter of China's internal affairs, and China is under no obligation to commit itself to rule out the use of force. This is by no means directed against Taiwan compatriots, but against the scheme to create an "independent Taiwan" and against the foreign forces interfering with the reunification of China, and is intended as a necessary safeguard for the striving for peaceful reunification. Resort to force would only be the last choice made under compelling circumstances.

As for Taiwan, upholding the principle of one China indicates that it acknowledges that China's sovereignty and territory are inalienable. In this way, both sides of the Taiwan Straits will have a common basis and premise and may find ways to solve their political differences and realize peaceful reunification through consultation on an equal footing. If Taiwan denies the One-China Principle and tries to separate Taiwan from the territory of China, the premise and basis for peaceful reunification will cease to exist.

As for the United States, if it promises to follow a one-China policy, it should earnestly implement the three communiques between the Chinese and U.S. governments and fulfill the series of promises it has made. It should maintain only cultural, commercial and other non-governmental relations with Taiwan; oppose "Taiwan independence", "two Chinas" or "one China, one Taiwan" and not to stand in the way of the reunification of China. Acting otherwise will destroy the external conditions necessary for the Chinese government to strive for peaceful reunification.

As for countries in the Asia-Pacific region and other regions in the world, the situation across the Taiwan Straits has always been closely linked with the stability of the Asia–Pacific region. Adherence to the policy of one China by countries concerned will be beneficial to peace and stability in the Asia–Pacific region and favourable for China to develop friendly relations with other countries, and therefore conforms to the interests of the Asia–Pacific region and other countries in the world.

The Chinese government is actively and sincerely striving for peaceful reunification. To achieve peaceful reunification, the Chinese government has appealed time and again for cross-Strait negotiations on the basis of equality and the One-China Principle.

Taking Taiwan's political reality into full account and out of consideration for the Taiwan authorities' request for the negotiations to be held on an equal footing, we have put forward one proposal after another, such as that the negotiations should be held between the Communist Party of China (CPC) and the Chinese KMT on a reciprocal basis and that the talks between the two parties may include representatives from all parties and mass organizations of Taiwan, and we have never spoken of negotiations between the "central and local authorities". The Chinese government has also proposed that dialogues may start first, including political dialogues, which may gradually move on to procedural consultations for political talks to solve the name, the topics for discussion and the forms of official talks before political talks are held. Political talks may be carried out step by step. First, negotiations should be held and an agreement reached on an official end to the state of hostility between the two sides under the principle of one China so as to jointly safeguard China's sovereignty and territorial integrity and work out plans for the development of future inter-Strait relations. In January 1998, to seek and expand the political basis for relations between the two sides, the Chinese government explicitly proposed to the Taiwan side that before the realization of reunification and in handling affairs concerning inter-Strait relations, especially during the talks between the two sides, the One-China Principle should be upheld, namely, that there is only one China in the world, Taiwan is a part of China and China's sovereignty and territorial integrity is not to be separated. The Chinese government hopes that on the basis of the One-China Principle, the two sides will hold consultations on an equal footing and discuss national reunification together.

To strive for peaceful reunification, the Chinese government has adopted a series of positive policies and measures to promote the comprehensive development of cross-Strait relations. From the end of 1987, when the state of isolation between the two sides was terminated, to the end of 1999, the number of Taiwan compatriots coming to the mainland of China for visiting their relatives, sightseeing or exchanges reached 16 million by turnstile count.

The total indirect trade volume between the two sides of the Straits has exceeded US$160 billion; the agreed capital to be invested by Taiwan business people in the mainland has exceeded US$44 billion, of which US$24 billion has been actually used. Great progress has been made in the exchange of mail and telecommunications across the Straits; and some progress has been made in the exchange of air and shipping services too. The NPC and its Standing Committee, the State Council, and local governments have worked out a sequence of laws and regulations to safeguard the legitimate rights and interests of Taiwan compatriots. To properly solve the concrete issues arising from the people-to-people contacts between the two sides through consultations, in November 1992 the mainland's Association for Relations Across the Taiwan Straits and Taiwan's Straits Exchange Foundation reached the common understanding during talks on routine affairs that each of the two organizations should express verbally that "both sides of the Taiwan Straits adhere to the One-China Principle". On this basis, the leaders of these two organizations successfully held the "Wang Daohan-Koo Chen-fu talks" and signed several agreements on protecting the legitimate rights and interests of the compatriots on both sides of the Taiwan Straits in April 1993. In October 1998, the leaders of the two organizations met in Shanghai, starting political dialogue across the Straits. The talks between the two organizations were carried out on an equal footing.

Practice has proved that on the basis of the One-China Principle, it is entirely possible to find a proper way for holding talks, based on equality, between the two sides. Since Hong Kong and Macao's return to China, people-to-people contacts and exchanges between Hong Kong and Taiwan and between Macao and Taiwan have continued and developed on the basis of the One-China Principle.

III.   The Chinese Government — Staunch Champion for the One-China Principle

Separatist forces in Taiwan are bent on violating the One-China Principle. In 1988, after Lee Teng-hui became the leader of the Taiwan authorities, he publicly stated time and again that the basic policy of the Taiwan authorities was that "there is only one China, not two", and "we have always maintained that China should be reunited, and we adhere to the principle of 'one China'".

However, since the early 1990s, Lee Teng-hui has gradually deviated from the One-China Principle, trumpeting "two governments", "two reciprocal political entities", "Taiwan is already a state with independent sovereignty", and "At the present stage the Republic of China is on Taiwan and the People's Republic of China is on the mainland". Moreover, he went back on his words, saying that "I have never said that there is only one China". In addition, he has connived at and provided support for the separatists who advocate "Taiwan independence" and their activities, thus helping the rapid development of the "Taiwan independence" forces and the spread of the "Taiwan independence" ideology. Under the direction of Lee Teng-hui, the Taiwan authorities have adopted a series of measures towards actual separation. In matters of Taiwan's form of government, the Taiwan authorities are seeking to transform Taiwan into an "independent political entity" through a "constitutional reform", so as to suit the needs of creating "two Chinas". In foreign relations, the Taiwan authorities have spared no effort to carry out the activities for "expanding the international space of survival", with the aim of creating "two Chinas". Since 1993, for seven years running, the Taiwan authorities have manoeuvred for participation in the United Nations. In military affairs, the Taiwan authorities have bought large quantities of advanced weapons from foreign countries and sought to join the Theater Missile Defence System (TMDS), in an attempt to establish a military alliance in a disguised form with the United States and Japan.

In ideology and culture, the Taiwan authorities have endeavoured to obliterate the Chinese awareness of Taiwan compatriots, especially young people, and their identification with the motherland, in order to create misunderstanding of the motherland among Taiwan compatriots and estrange them from her, thus cutting off the ideological and cultural ties between the compatriots on both sides of the Taiwan Straits.

Since 1999, Lee Teng-hui has stepped up his separatist activities. In May, he published the book "The Road to Democracy", which advocates the division of China into seven regions, each enjoying "full autonomy". On July 9, he went so far as to publicly distort inter-Strait relations as "state to state relations, or at least special state to state relations", in an attempt to fundamentally change the status of Taiwan as a part of China, sabotage the relations between both sides of the Taiwan Strait, especially the basis for cross-Strait political dialogues and negotiations, and wreck the foundation for peaceful reunification. Lee Teng-hui has become the general representative of Taiwan's separatist forces, a saboteur of the stability of the Taiwan Straits, a stumbling block preventing the development of relations between China and the United States, and a trouble-maker for the peace and stability in the Asia–Pacific region.

The Chinese government firmly defends the One-China Principle. The Chinese government and people have always maintained sharp vigilance and fought resolutely against the secessionist activities of the Taiwan separatists, represented by Lee Teng-hui.

After Lee Teng-hui's "private" visit to the United States in June 1995, the Chinese government has waged a resolute struggle against separation and against "Taiwan independence", and made strong protests and representations to the U.S. government for openly allowing Lee Teng-hui to visit the United States, violating its promises made in the three Sino–U.S. joint communiques, and seriously prejudicing China's sovereignty. This struggle has shown the Chinese government's and people's firm resolve and ability to safeguard state sovereignty and territorial integrity, and exerted an important and far-reaching influence. Compatriots in Taiwan have further realized the serious harm "Taiwan independence" can cause. Lee Teng-hui has received a heavy blow for his separatist activities in the international community, so that some of the "Taiwan independence" protagonists have had to abandon certain extremist propositions aimed at division. The international community has further realized the necessity of upholding the one-China policy. The U.S. Government has explicitly undertaken not to support "Taiwan independence", not to support "two Chinas" or "one China, one Taiwan", and not to support Taiwan joining any international organization whose membership is restricted to sovereign states.

The Chinese government and people have fought more unremittingly after Lee Teng-hui cooked up his "two states" theory. The relevant department of the Chinese government has clearly stated that the attempt of the Taiwan separatists to implement the "two states" theory in "legal" form was an even more serious and dangerous step towards division and a grave provocation against peaceful reunification. Were the attempt to succeed, it would be impossible for China to achieve peaceful reunification. The struggle against this attempt has grown in momentum with Chinese both at home and abroad condemning the "two states" theory with one voice. Most countries in the world have reaffirmed their position of upholding the One-China Policy. The U.S. Government has also reasserted its adherence to the One-China Policy and its commitment to the "Three Non-supports" for Taiwan. Finally, the Taiwan authorities have been compelled to announce that they will not amend their "constitution" and "laws" according to the "two states" theory.

Nevertheless, separatists in Taiwan are still attempting to detach Taiwan "*de jure*" from China in the name of the "Republic of China" by various forms, including "formulating a new constitution", "amending the constitution", and "explaining the constitution" or through "legislation". Special vigilance should be maintained to the fact that the Taiwan separatists are continually scheming to disrupt Sino–U.S. relations and provoke conflicts and confrontation between the two nations to achieve their aim of dividing China.

Facts prove that a serious crisis still exists in the situation of the Taiwan Straits. To safeguard the interests of the entire Chinese people, including compatriots in Taiwan and maintain the peace and development of the Asia–Pacific region, the Chinese government remains firm in adhering to "peaceful reunification" and "one country, two systems"; upholding the eight propositions put forward by President Jiang Zemin for the development of cross-Strait relations and the acceleration of the peaceful reunification of China; and doing its utmost to achieve the objective of peaceful reunification. However, if a grave turn of events occurs leading to the separation of Taiwan from China in any name, or if Taiwan is invaded and occupied by foreign countries, or if the Taiwan authorities refuse, *sine die*, the peaceful settlement of cross-Strait reunification through negotiations, then the Chinese government will only be forced to adopt all drastic measures possible, including the use of force, to safeguard China's sovereignty and territorial integrity and fulfill the great cause of reunification. The Chinese government and people absolutely have the determination and ability to safeguard China's sovereignty and territorial integrity, and will never tolerate, condone or remain indifferent to the realization of any scheme to divide China. Any such scheme is doomed to failure.

IV. Several Questions Involving the One-China Principle in Cross-Strait Relations

Chinese territory and sovereignty have not been split, and the two sides of the Straits are not two states. The Taiwan authorities support their position on "two Chinas", including the "two states" theory proposed by Lee Teng-hui, with the following arguments:

— Since 1949, the territories on either side of the Straits have been divided and governed separately, with neither side having jurisdiction over the other;

— the government of the PRC has never ruled Taiwan; and
— since 1991 Taiwan has witnessed a form of government that has nothing to do with that of the Chinese mainland.

These arguments are absolutely untenable, and can never lead to the conclusion that Taiwan may declare itself a state under the name of the "Republic of China", or that the two sides of the Straits have been divided into two states. Firstly, state sovereignty is inseparable. The territory is the space in which a state exercises its sovereignty. In the territory of a country there can only be a central government exercising sovereignty on behalf of the state. As we have already said, Taiwan is an inalienable part of Chinese territory and, after replacing the government of the Republic of China in 1949, the government of the PRC has become the sole legal government of China, enjoying and exercising sovereignty over the whole of China, including Taiwan.

Although the two sides of the Straits have not been reunified, Taiwan's status as a part of Chinese territory has never changed, neither, therefore, has China's sovereignty over Taiwan ever changed. Secondly, the international community recognizes that there is only one China, that Taiwan is a part of China, and that the government of the PRC is the sole legitimate government of China. Thirdly, the reason that the Taiwan question has not been settled for such a long period of time is mainly due to the intervention of foreign forces and the obstruction of the separatist forces in Taiwan.

Although the two sides of the Straits remain to be reunified, the long-term existence of this abnormal situation has not imbued Taiwan with a status and rights in international law, nor can it change the legal status of Taiwan as a part of China. The problem now is that the separatists in Taiwan and some foreign anti-China forces seek to change this state of affairs, and it is this that the Chinese government and people are firmly against.

We firmly oppose changing Taiwan's status as a part of China by referendum. The Taiwan separatists' attempt to change Taiwan's status as a part of China by referendum on the pretext that "sovereignty belongs to the people" is futile. Firstly, under both domestic and international laws Taiwan's legal status as a part of Chinese territory is unequivocal, and there can be no premise for using referendum to decide any matter of self-determination. Secondly, the phrase "sovereignty belongs to the people" refers to all the people of a state, and not certain people or the people of a certain area. The sovereignty over Taiwan belongs to all the Chinese people, including Taiwan compatriots, and not to some of the people in Taiwan. Thirdly, at no time in history has Taiwan been a state in its own right, and since 1945 Taiwan has not been a foreign colony, nor has it been under foreign occupation. The issue of national self-determination, therefore, does not exist. In short, from the time that China recovered Taiwan in 1945, there has been no question at all of changing Taiwan's status as a part of China by holding a referendum. The only future for Taiwan is reunification with the China mainland, and certainly not separation. Any attempt to separate Taiwan from China through so-called referendum would only lead the Taiwan people to disaster.

The "two German states formula" cannot be applied to the settlement of the Taiwan issue. Some people in Taiwan have suggested that cross-Strait relations should be dealt with according to the "two German states formula", since Germany was divided into two states after World War II, and was later reunified. This proposal shows a misunderstanding of history and reality. The division of Germany after the war and the temporary division between the two sides of the Strait are questions of a different nature, the difference lying mainly in three aspects. The first is the reasons for, and the nature of, the division. After its defeat in World War II in 1945, Germany was divided into zones occupied separately by the four victorious nations of the United States, Britain, France, and the Soviet Union according to a declaration on the defeat of Germany and the assumption of supreme authority and the subsequent Potsdam Agreement. The reunification of Germany became a focus of the confrontation in Europe between the United States and the Soviet Union during the Cold War. The Federal Republic of Germany and the German Democratic Republic were established in the zones occupied by the United States, Britain and France, and that occupied by the Soviet Union. Thus, Germany was divided into two states. Obviously, the German question arose entirely from external factors, while the Taiwan issue, left over by China's civil war, is a matter of China's internal affairs. The second aspect is the difference in status between the two under international law. Germany was divided according to a series of international treaties during and after World War II, while the Taiwan question involves provisions of the Cairo Declaration, the Potsdam Proclamation and other international treaties, stating that Japan must return Taiwan, which it had stolen from China, to the Chinese. The third is the difference between the two in their actual conditions of existence.

Against the backdrop of the confrontation between the United States and the Soviet Union, the two German states had foreign troops stationed in their territories and so were compelled to recognize each other and co-exist in the international community. The Chinese government has always persisted in the principle of one China. Before Lee Teng-hui assumed power, and during his early days in office, the Taiwan authorities recognized only one China and opposed "two Chinas", and the One-China Principle has also been widely accepted by the international community. For these reasons, the Taiwan issue and the German issue cannot be placed in the same category, nor can the "two German states formula" be copied to settle the Taiwan question.

Any question can be discussed under the One-China Principle. The Chinese government advocates that the final purpose of cross-Strait negotiations is to achieve peaceful reunification; and that to achieve this purpose, talks should be held based on the principle of one China. However, the proposals for "Taiwan independence", "two Chinas" and "two states", aiming for separation instead of reunification, violate the One-China Principle, and are naturally unacceptable to the Chinese government. Provided that it is within the framework of one China, any question can be discussed, including the various issues that are of concern to the Taiwan side. The Chinese government believes that Taiwan's international space for economic, cultural and social activities compatible with its status, the political status of the Taiwan authorities, and other questions can be finally settled in the process of peaceful reunification through political negotiations within this framework.

The so-called controversy about democracy and system is an excuse for obstructing the reunification of China. In recent years, the Taiwan authorities have repeatedly declared that "democratization on the China mainland is the key to the reunification of China" and that "the real essence of the cross-Strait issue is a contest between systems". This is an excuse for postponing and resisting reunification, as well as a scheme to deceive compatriots in Taiwan and world opinion. The CPC and the Chinese government have consistently striven to achieve socialist democracy. To achieve peaceful reunification in the form of "one country, two systems," and to allow the two different social systems on both sides of the Straits to coexist without imposing them on one or the other: this is best able to embody the wishes of compatriots on both sides of the Straits and is itself democratic. The different social systems across the Straits, therefore, should not constitute a barrier to peaceful reunification. Moreover, the Chinese government acknowledges the differences between Taiwan, on the one hand, and Hong Kong and Macao, on the other and, after peaceful reunification, is prepared to apply a looser form of the "one country, two systems" policy in Taiwan than in Hong Kong and Macao. It is totally unreasonable and undemocratic for the Taiwan authorities to seek to obstruct reunification on the pretext of the "controversy about democracy and system" and to force the more than 1.2 billion people living on the Chinese mainland to practise the political and economic systems in Taiwan. The demand for democracy should not be used as a reason for refusing reunification. The essence of the difference between the two sides of the Strait on this question lies by no means in the controversy over whether to practise democracy or in the controversy over what system to practise, but rather a controversy over the choice between reunification and separation.

V. Several Questions Involving Adherence to the One-China Principle in the International Community

The Chinese government has expressed its appreciation to the international community for widely pursuing a one-China policy. In August 1993, we published the White Paper, *The Taiwan Question and Reunification of China*. In Chapter V of this document, "Several Questions Involving Taiwan in International Relations", we explained our position and policy on a number of issues, including relations between Taiwan and countries maintaining diplomatic ties with China, relations between international organizations and Taiwan, aviation services between Taiwan and countries having diplomatic relations with China, and arms sales to Taiwan by countries having diplomatic relations with China. Here, we would like to reaffirm our related position and policy.

Taiwan is ineligible for membership in the United Nations and other international organizations whose membership is confined to sovereign states. The United Nations is an intergovernmental international organization composed of sovereign states. After the restoration of the lawful rights of the PRC in the United Nations, the issue of China's representation in the U.N. was resolved once and for all, and Taiwan's re-entry became totally out of the question. The Taiwan authorities have asserted that Resolution 2758 of the U.N. resolved only "the problem of China's representation", but not "the problem of Taiwan's representation", and demanded participation in the U.N. We will never permit such a separatist act of creating "two Chinas" or "one China, one Taiwan".

All members of the U.N. should adhere to the purpose and principles of the Charter of the United Nations and related U.N. resolutions, abide by norms governing international relations, including mutual respect for sovereignty and territorial integrity and non-interference in each other's internal affairs, and never, in any form, support Taiwan's joining the U.N. or other international organizations whose membership is confined to sovereign states.

On the basis of the principle of one China, the Chinese Government has made arrangements for Taiwan's participation in some intergovernmental international organizations which accept regional membership in an agreeable and acceptable way according to the nature, regulations, and actual conditions of these international organizations. As a region of China, Taiwan has participated in the Asian Development Bank (ADB) and the Asia–Pacific Economic Co-operation (APEC), respectively, under the names "Taipei, China" and "Chinese Taipei". In September 1992, the chairman of the council of the predecessor of the World Trade Organization (WTO), the General Agreement on Tariffs and Trade (GATT), stated that Taiwan may participate in this organization as "a separate Taiwan–Penghu–Jinmen–Mazu tariff zone" (abbreviated as Chinese Taipei) after the PRC's entry into GATT. The WTO should persist in the principle defined in the aforesaid statement when examining the acceptance of Taiwan's entry into the organization. This is only an ad hoc arrangement and cannot constitute a model applicable to other intergovernmental international organizations or international gatherings.

No country maintaining diplomatic relations with China should provide arms to Taiwan or enter into military alliance of any form with Taiwan. All countries maintaining diplomatic relations with China should abide by the principles of mutual respect for sovereignty and territorial integrity and non-interference in each other's internal affairs, and refrain from providing arms to Taiwan or helping Taiwan produce arms in any form or under any pretext.

The Taiwan question is the most crucial and most sensitive issue in the relations between China and the United States. The three Sino–U.S. joint communiques are the basis for the healthy and steady development of relations between the two countries. For over 20 years, the United States has promised to adhere to a one-China policy, which has brought to itself benefits such as the establishment of diplomatic relations with China, the development of Sino–U.S. relations, and the relative stability of the Taiwan situation. Regrettably, the United States has repeatedly contravened its solemn understandings with China made in the August 17 Communique and continued its sale of advanced arms and military equipment to Taiwan. Recently, some people in the U.S. Congress have cooked up the so-called Taiwan Security Enhancement Act and are attempting to include Taiwan in the TMDS. This is gross interference in China's internal affairs and a grave threat to China's security, obstructing the peaceful reunification of China and jeopardizing the peace and stability of the Asia-Pacific region and the world at large. The Chinese government is firmly against such actions.

The Chinese government adheres to the One-China Principle in dealing with Taiwan's contacts with the outside world. The Taiwan authorities have spared no effort to promote "pragmatic diplomacy" in the international arena and enlarge their "international space of survival", the essence of these being to create "two Chinas" or "one China, one Taiwan". It is only natural that the Chinese government should firmly oppose these moves. Meanwhile, considering the needs of Taiwan's socio-economic development and the actual benefits of compatriots in Taiwan, the Chinese government has no objection to Taiwan's non-governmental economic and cultural contacts with foreign countries; in fact, on the premise of one China, it has adopted many flexible measures to make Taiwan's economic, trade, and cultural contacts with foreign countries more convenient. For example, Taiwan may stay on the International Olympic Committee in the name of "Chinese Taipei". As a matter of fact, Taiwan has maintained extensive economic, trade, and cultural relations with many countries and regions in the world. Every year, a million Taiwan compatriots go abroad for travel, business or study, as well as for academic, cultural or sports exchanges, and Taiwan's annual import and export trade volume has exceeded the US$200-billion mark. This has demonstrated that adhering to the One-China Principle has not prevented Taiwan compatriots from engaging in non-governmental international exchanges or affected the needs of Taiwan's normal economic, trade, and cultural activities.

The Chinese government safeguards all the justified and lawful rights and interests of Taiwan compatriots abroad. The people of Taiwan are of the same flesh and blood with us. The Chinese government has always worked for safeguarding their justified and lawful rights and interests abroad. Chinese embassies and consulates stationed abroad have always considered it their duties to strengthen their ties with Taiwan compatriots, listen to their suggestions and requests and safeguard their interests, and do everything they can to help them overcome their difficulties. During the Gulf War, the Chinese Embassy helped Taiwanese labour service personnel stranded in Kuwait pull out of dangerous places safely. After the big earthquakes in Osaka and Kobe, Japan, the Chinese Embassy and consulate there promptly extended their sympathies to stricken Taiwan compatriots. When the civil war in Cambodia broke out, the Chinese Embassy lost no time in helping Taiwanese business people and tourists, whose lives and property were seriously imperiled by the war, move to safe places. All the above-mentioned facts reflect the Chinese government's care for Taiwan compatriots. When both sides of the Taiwan Straits are reunified, Taiwan compatriots will, together with people of all ethnic groups in the country, have more possibilities to fully enjoy the dignity and honour of the PRC in the world.

Conclusion

China has a long history of 5,000 years. The Chinese people have lived and multiplied on this land where all ethnic groups have mixed together, in the course of which they have developed a powerful cohesiveness, and the values of cherishing and safeguarding unity. Over the long course of history, the Chinese nation has witnessed changes of dynasties, transfers of governments, local separatist regimes, and foreign invasions, especially the untold invasions and dismemberment by foreign powers in modern history. However, unity has always been the main trend in the development of Chinese history. After every separation, the country was invariably reunified, only to be followed in its wake by rapid political, economic, cultural, scientific, and technological development. Our compatriots in Taiwan have a glorious tradition of patriotism, and have performed brilliant exploits in the struggles against foreign invasions of Taiwan. Since the founding of the PRC, the Chinese people have particularly valued their hard-earned national independence, firmly upheld state sovereignty and territorial integrity, and struggled unswervingly for reunification of the motherland. The 5,000-year history and culture have been implanted deeply in the minds of the Chinese people, sprouting the strong national consciousness of the need for national unification.

The Chinese government hopes that the international community will follow the principle of one China now and always, and that the U.S. government will earnestly fulfil all the principles concerning the Taiwan issue in the three Sino–

U.S. joint communiques, and its solemn promise to uphold the One-China Principle.

As the Chinese government has successively resumed the exercise of sovereignty over Hong Kong and Macao, the people of the whole of China are eager to resolve the Taiwan issue as early as possible and realize the total reunification of the country. They cannot allow the resolution of the Taiwan issue to be postponed indefinitely. We firmly believe that the total reunification of China will be achieved through the joint efforts of the entire Chinese people, including compatriots on both sides of the Taiwan Straits and those living overseas.

Source: Taiwan Affairs Office and the Information Office of the State Council, 21 February 2000.

Appendix 3

Chen Shui-bian's Victory
Speech after the 10th Republic of China
Presidential and Vice-Presidential Election

Victorius Chen Shui-bian and Annette Lu. The election results for the 10th ROC Presidential and Vice-Presidential election have been declared. The Democratic Progressive Party candidates, Chen Shui-bian and Annette Lu, have been elected President and Vice-President in Taiwan's second democratic presidential election.

First, we want to thank the people of Taiwan with our most solemn and modest hearts. We would like to thank the DPP comrades. We want to thank the Academia Sinica President Lee Yuan-tseh and the national policy advisers for boldly pledging their support. We furthermore would like to thank all those who have contributed to the campaign process.

This moment is a dignified and sacred one in the history of Taiwan — because the courageous people of Taiwan, with love and hope, have conquered fear and darkness.

They have used their sacred ballots to express their determination to uphold the democracy of Taiwan.

That A-bian and Annette Lu are elected does not mean a personal victory or a victory for the DPP. This is a victory for democracy and a victory for the people. This glorious moment also marks the beginning of our responsibility.

We want to thank all the countries of the world who have over the years shown concern and support for Taiwan. This has facilitated the smooth completion of Taiwan's presidential election. Today, Taiwan has written a new chapter in our road to democracy, and has given birth to a renewed opportunity for democracy and peace in the Asia–Pacific region. It has also concretely acted as a demonstration of the third wave of global democratization.

From now on, Taiwan will continue to enhance the exchange and interaction between the government and people of the Western Pacific regions. We will dedicate ourselves toward preserving the peace and stability of the Taiwan Strait and Asia–Pacific regions.

A-bian and Annette Lu's government for the people will take advantage of Taiwan's developmental experience to assist the promotion of democracy and preservation of human rights in international societies. With our economic strength, we will assist Third World countries in reforms and developments, and fulfill our responsibility as a member of the international society.

This election is not only the pride of the people of Taiwan, but it is also the pride of Chinese all over the world. We share the same bloodlines and culture. We hope that through more intimate exchange and interaction, with patience and respect, we can collectively create a harmonized and joyous new era.

Peace and stability in the Taiwan Strait is the common hope of people on both sides. In the future, we are willing to conduct extensive, constructive communication and dialogue with the utmost sincerity and determination.

Under the priority of ensuring national security and social benefits, we are willing to negotiate in various issues, including direct transportation links, business links, investments, peace agreement and a confidence-building mechanism for military affairs.

We will also, with sincerity, invite Mr. Jiang Zemin, Mr. Zhu Rongji and Mr. Wang Daohan to visit Taiwan. A-bian and Annette Lu are also willing to embark on a trip of negotiation and communication to Mainland China before our inauguration.

We believe that the leaders of both parties are willing to exercise our wisdom and courage to initiate positive development for future relations, so as to launch an everlasting objective of "goodwill reconciliation, active cooperation and permanent peace".

The results of the election may mean a momentary triumph or failure, but we believe the end of the election is the beginning of reconciliation. The people in Taiwan will need to collaborate on building a grand vision for the future and not dissipate our power by one moment's emotions.

When tomorrow's sunlight shines on the top of the Yushan Mountains, it will be another dawn for Taiwan's progress to peace, democracy and reform. The people in Taiwan need to convene and face the engineering of future reform.

"The dream has come true and the sunlight is seen". We believe Taiwan can transcend its historical burdens and prejudices if we only truly respect and understand each other.

By doing so, we can conquer the anxiety and aversion in our hearts. The people in Taiwan should use their noblest souls and their most benevolent hearts to ratify the advancement of our country and society successfully.

Therefore, let us use our humblest hearts to embrace anyone who disagrees with us. We must use the most passionate love to mend divisions.

We will invite representatives from every political party, from the Kuomintang, the New Party, the Taiwan Independence Party, and non-affiliated persons, to assemble a "non-partisan team". The group will employ the utmost tolerance and respect to heal the wounds that arose during the election.

Furthermore, we will present our respect and appreciation to the other four groups of presidential and vice-presidential candidates. The candidates have taught A-bian and Lu a great deal and given us a fair chance to compete in the election. The future "non-partisan team" will stand on its broad-minded party and ethnic spirit to sustain other candidates and be a reference for our future new government.

"Party rotation, cessation of 'black gold' politics; clear-steam governance, all-citizen government; cross-strait peace, persistent development" are the promises A-bian made to the people of Taiwan, and they are what the people had hoped for. A-bian and Annette Lu will be rational and responsible in their efforts to maintain peace and stability in the Taiwan Straits. A-bian and Lu will improve the lives of the people and create better prospects for Taiwan.

From today, A-bian and Annette Lu and the Democratic Progressive Party will take on the mission mandated by the people and by history to serve Taiwan's 23 million citizens.

May the heavens bless the people and may the heavens bless Taiwan — our motherland forever.

Source: Government Information Office, 18 March 2000.

Appendix 4

Taiwan Stands Up: Advancing to an Uplifting Era
Inaugural Address by Chen Shui-bian

Leaders of our friendly nations, honored guests and compatriots from Taiwan and abroad.

This is a glorious moment; it is also a moment of dignity and hope.

I thank our distinguished guests, who have come here from afar, as well as those friends from around the world who love democracy and care about Taiwan, for sharing this glorious moment with us.

We are here today, not just to celebrate an inauguration, but to witness the flowering of hard-won democratic values and the dawn of a new era.

On the eve of the 21st century, the people of Taiwan have completed a historic alternation of political parties in power. This is not only the first of its kind in the history of the Republic of China, but also an epochal landmark for Chinese communities around the world. Taiwan has not only set a new model for the Asian experience of democracy, but has also added an inspiring example to the third wave of democracy the world over.

The election for the 10th-term President of the Republic of China has clearly shown the world that the fruits of freedom and democracy are not easy to come by. Twenty-three million people, through the power of determined will, have dispelled enmity with love, overcome intimidation with hope, and conquered fear with faith.

With our sacred votes, we have proved to the world that freedom and democracy are indisputable universal values, and that peace is humanity's highest goal.

The outcome of Taiwan's Year 2000 presidential election is not the victory of an individual or a political party. It is a victory of the people, a victory for democracy, because we have, while at the focus of global attention, transcended fear, threats and oppression and bravely risen to our feet together.

Taiwan stands up, demonstrating a firm insistence on reason and a sturdy faith in democracy.

Taiwan stands up, representing the self-confidence of the people and the dignity of the country.

Taiwan stands up, symbolizing the quest for hope and the realization of dreams.

Dear compatriots, let's always remember this moment; let's always remember to value and feel gratitude for it, because the fruits of democracy did not come out of the blue. We reaped the fruits only after we had been subjected to many perils and countless hardships. If not for the fearless sacrifice of our democratic forebears, if not for the unswerving faith of the tens of millions of Taiwanese people in freedom and democracy, we could not possibly be standing on our beloved land today and celebrating a glorious occasion that belongs to all the people.

Today, it is as if we are standing before a fresh new gate in history. In the process of democratization, the Taiwanese people have created a brand-new key to our shared destiny. The new century's gates of hope are soon to open. We are humble but not submissive. We are full of self-confidence but do not have the slightest bit of complacence.

Since that moment on March 18 when the election results came to light, I have accepted the mandate of all Taiwanese people in a most earnest and humble frame of mind, and have vowed to devote all my heart, knowledge and courage to assuming the heavy responsibility of our country's future.

I personally understand that the significance of the alternation of political parties and of the peaceful transition of power lies not in that it is a change of personnel or political parties. Nor in that it is a dynastic change. Rather, it is the return of state and government power to the people through a democratic procedure. The country belongs to the people, rather than to any individual or political party. The government and its officials, from the head of state down to the rank-and-file employees, exist for the service of the people.

The alternation of political parties does not mean an across-the-board negation of the past. We should be fair in evaluating the contributions made by those in power throughout the ages. Mr. Lee Teng-hui deserves our highest tribute and heartfelt gratitude for his promotion of democratic reforms and for his excellent performance during his twelve years of leadership.

Taiwan society has rallied and participated energetically in the election. Despite the diverse views and stances, all individuals share the same commitment — to come forward for the sake of their political ideas and the country's future. We believe that the end of an election is the beginning of reconciliation. After the curtain falls on emotional campaigns, rationality should prevail. Under the supreme principles of national interests and the welfare of the people, those in power and in opposition should both fulfill their mandates given by the people and realize the ideals of fair competition in multiparty politics, as well as the checks and balances of democratic politics.

A democratic society with fair competition, tolerance and trust is the strongest impetus for a nation's development. Placing national interests above those of political parties, we should solidify the will of the people and seek consensus among the ruling and opposition parties, to promote the country's development and reforms.

"A government for all people" and "rule by the clean and upright" are promises I made to the people during the campaign period. They are also Taiwan's key to stepping over its fault lines and rising to a higher level in the future.

The spirit of a "government for all people" lies in the fact that "the government exists for the people". The people are the masters and shareholders of the state. The government should rule on the basis of majority public opinion. The interests of the people should reign supreme over those of any political party or individual.

I have always taken pride in being a member of the Democratic Progressive Party, but from the moment I take my oath and assume the presidency, I will put all my efforts into fulfilling my role as a "president for all people". As in the formation of the new government, we recruit people according to their talents and do not discriminate on the basis of ethnicity, gender or party affiliation. The welfare of the populace shall be our primary goal in the future.

"Rule by the clean and upright" has as its topmost priority the elimination of "black gold" — the involvement of organized crime and moneyed interests in politics — and the eradication of vote-buying. For a long time, the Taiwanese people have been deeply repelled by money politics and the interference of organized crime. Vote-buying in grassroots elections has also robbed the people of their right to elect the wise and the able, and tainted the development of Taiwan's democracy.

Today, I am willing to promise hereby that the new government will eliminate vote-buying and crack down on "black gold" politics, so that Taiwan can rise above such downward sinking forces. We must give the people a clean political environment.

In the area of government reforms, we need to establish a government that is clean, efficient, far-sighted, dynamic, highly flexible and responsive, in order to ensure Taiwan's competitiveness in the face of increasingly fierce global competition. The age of "large and capable" governments has now passed, replaced by one of "small and effective" governments, which have established partnership relations with the people. We should accelerate the streamlining of government functions and organization and actively expand the role of public participation.

This will not only allow the public to fully utilize its energy but also significantly reduce the government's burdens.

Similar partnership relations should also be set up between the central and local governments. We want to break the authoritarian and centralized control over both power and money. We want to realize the spirit of local autonomy, where the local and central governments share resources and responsibilities, where "the central government will not do what the local governments can". Whether in the east, west, north or south, or whether on Taiwan Proper or on offshore islands, all will enjoy balanced, pluralistic development, and the gap between urban and rural areas will be reduced.

We should understand that the government is no panacea for all ills. The driving force for economic development and societal progress is the people. Over the past half-century, the Taiwanese people have toiled hard to create an economic miracle that has won global applause, and to lay the foundation for the survival and development of the Republic of China. Today, facing the impact of the fast-changing information technologies and trade liberalization, Taiwan must move toward a knowledge-based economy. High-tech industries need to be constantly innovative, while traditional ones have to undergo transformation and upgrading.

In the future, the government should not necessarily play the role of a "leader" or "manager". On the contrary, it should be the "supporter" and "service-provider", as expected by private enterprises. The responsibility of a modern government is to raise administrative efficiency, improve the domestic investment environment, and maintain financial order and stock market stability, so as to allow the economy to move toward full liberalization and globalization through fair competition. Based on these principles, the vitality of the public will naturally bloom and create a new phase in Taiwan's economic miracle.

Apart from consolidating democratic achievements, promoting government reforms, and raising economic competitiveness, the new government should, as its foremost objective, closely watch the public opinion and implement reforms accordingly, so that the people on this land can live with more dignity, greater self-confidence and a better quality of life.

Let our society not only be safe, harmonious and prosperous, but also follow the principles of fairness and justice. As we cultivate the ever-growing abilities of our citizens, we will let our next generation learn in an environment filled with happiness and hope.

The 21st century will be a time when "the right to a quality life" and "a refined way of life" are much emphasized. The government will find solutions for issues relating to the people's lives, such as law and order, social welfare, environmental protection, land-use planning, waste treatment, river cleaning, transportation and community renewal. It will also have to implement these solutions thoroughly.

At present, we need to immediately improve law and order and environmental protection, two important indicators of the quality of life. We will build a new social order so that the people may live in peace without fear. A balance must be ensured between nature conservation and economic development so that Taiwan may develop into a sustainable green silicon island.

Judiciary integrity is the bulwark of political democracy and social justice. An impartial, independent judicial system is a protector of social order and a defender of the people's rights. At present, we still have a long way to go in our judicial reforms. Our compatriots must continue to keep close watch over the judiciary and voice their expectations. At the same time, we should also restrain our administrative power and give the judiciary room to operate independently and without interference.

Humans are Taiwan's most important resources. Talented people hold the key to the country's competitiveness, while education is a long-term cause for "accumulating wealth among the people". We will soon seek a consensus among the ruling and opposition parties, academia and the public so as to carry on with educational reforms and build a healthy, proactive, lively and innovative education system, which will allow Taiwan to cultivate an uninterrupted stream of top-notch talents amid the fierce international competition. We will let Taiwan move gradually toward a "learning organism" and a "knowledge-based society". We will also encourage people to take up lifetime learning to fully develop their potential and creativity.

Grassroots community organizations are now developing around the country, working to explore and preserve the history, culture, geography and ecology of their localities. These are all part of Taiwan culture, whether they are local cultures, mass cultures or high cultures. Due to special historical and geographical factors, Taiwan possesses a wealth of diversified cultural elements. But cultural development is not something that can bring immediate success. Rather, it has to be accumulated bit by bit. We must open our hearts with tolerance and respect, so that our diverse ethnic groups and different regional cultures may communicate with each other, and so that Taiwan's local cultures may connect with the cultures of Chinese-speaking communities and other world cultures, and create a new milieu of "a cultural Taiwan in a modern century".

The September 21 earthquake that struck last year brought to our land and our compatriots an unprecedented catastrophe, the pain of which is yet to heal. The new government will brook no delay in the reconstruction of disaster areas, including industrial and spiritual recovery. We will not cease until the last victim is taken care of and the last destroyed place is rebuilt. Here, we would like to express our highest respect again for all individuals and non-governmental organizations that have selflessly lent a hand to the rescue and reconstruction work after the disaster. Amid the fierce power of Nature, we have seen Taiwan's most beautiful compassion, strongest faith and greatest trust. Our compatriots have been injured by the September 21 earthquake, but with the spirit of a "volunteer Taiwan", Taiwan's new family will stand up resolutely on its feet once again.

Dear compatriots, 400 years ago, Taiwan was called "Ilha Formosa" — the beautiful island — for its lustrous landscape. Today, Taiwan is manifesting the elegance of a democratic island, once again attracting global attention, as the people on this land create a new page in our history.

We believe that the Republic of China, with its democratic achievements and technological and economic prowess, can certainly continue to play an indispensable role in the international community. In addition to strengthening the existing relations with friendly nations, we want to actively participate in all types of international non-governmental organizations. Through humanitarian care, economic cooperation, cultural exchanges and various other ways, we will actively participate in international affairs, expand Taiwan's room for survival in the international arena, and contribute to the welfare of the international community.

Besides, we are also willing to commit a more active contribution in safeguarding international human rights. The Republic of China cannot and will not remain outside global human rights trends. We will abide by the Universal Declaration of Human Rights, the International Convention for Civil and Political Rights, and the Vienna Declaration and Program of Action. We will bring the Republic of China back into the international human rights system.

The new government will urge the Legislative Yuan to ratify the International Bill of Rights as a domestic law of Taiwan, so that it will formally become the "Taiwan Bill of Rights". We hope to set up an independent national human rights commission in Taiwan, thereby realizing an action long advocated by the United Nations. We will also invite two outstanding non-governmental organizations, the International Commission of Jurists and Amnesty International, to assist us in our measures to protect human rights and make the Republic of China into a new indicator for human rights in the 21st century.

We firmly believe that at no time, or in any corner of the world, can the meaning and values of freedom, democracy and human rights be ignored or changed.

The 20th century left us with a major lesson — that war is a failure of humanity. Waged for whatever lofty purposes or high-sounding reasons, war is the greatest harm to freedom, democracy and human rights.

Over the past one hundred plus years, China has suffered imperialist aggression, which left indelible wounds. Taiwan has had an even sadder fate, tormented by brute force and colonial rule. These similar historical experiences should bring mutual understanding between the people on the two sides of the Taiwan Strait, setting a solid foundation for pursuing freedom, democracy and human rights together. However, due to the long period of separation, the two sides have developed vastly different political systems and ways of life, obstructing empathy and friendship between the people on the two sides, and even creating a wall of divisiveness and confrontation.

Today, as the Cold War has ended, it is time for the two sides to cast aside the hostilities left from the old era. We do not need to wait further because now is a new opportunity for the two sides to create an era of reconciliation together.

The people on the two sides of the Taiwan Strait share the same ancestral, cultural, and historical background. While upholding the principles of democracy and parity, building upon the existing foundations, and constructing conditions for cooperation through goodwill, we believe that the leaders on both sides possess enough wisdom and creativity to jointly deal with the question of a future "one China".

I fully understand that as the popularly elected 10th-term President of the Republic of China, I must abide by the Constitution, maintain the sovereignty, dignity and security of our country, and ensure the well-being of all citizens. Therefore, as long as the CCP regime has no intention to use military force against Taiwan, I pledge that during my term in office, I will not declare independence, I will not change the national title, I will not push forth the inclusion of the so-called "state-to-state" description in the Constitution, and I will not promote a referendum to change the status quo in regard to the question of independence or unification. Furthermore, there is no question of abolishing the Guidelines for National Unification and the National Unification Council.

History has proved that war will lead to more hatred and enmity, without the least help to the development of mutual relations. Chinese people emphasize the difference between statesmanship and hegemony, believing in the philosophy that a government which employs benevolence "will please those near and appeal to those from afar", and "when those from afar will not submit, then one must practice kindness and virtue to attract them". Such Chinese wisdom will remain universal value.

Under the leadership of Mr. Deng Xiaoping and Mr. Jiang Zemin, the mainland has created a miracle of economic openness. In Taiwan, over a half century, not only have we created a miracle economy, we have also created the political marvel of democracy. On such a basis, as long as the governments and people on both sides of the Taiwan Strait can interact more, following the principles of "goodwill reconciliation, active cooperation, and permanent peace", while at the same time respecting the free choice of the people and excluding unnecessary obstacles, both sides of the Strait can make great contributions to the prosperity and stability of the Asia–Pacific region. Both sides will also create a glorious civilization for humanity.

Dear compatriots, we hope so much to share the moving scene of this moment with all Chinese-speaking people around the world. The wide Ketagelan Boulevard before us was bristling with security guards only a few years ago.

The building behind me used to be the Governor General's Mansion during the colonial era. Today, we gather here to extol the glory and joy of democracy with songs of the earth and the voice of the people.

With a little reflection, our compatriots should be able to appreciate the deep and far-reaching meaning of this moment:

Authoritarianism and force can only bring surrender for one time, while democracy and freedom are values that will endure forever.

Only by adhering to the will of the people can we pioneer the paths of history and build enduring architecture.

Today, as a son of a tenant farmer with a poor family background, I have struggled and grown on this land and, after experiencing defeat and tribulation, I have finally won the trust of the people to take up the great responsibility of leading the country. My individual achievements are minor, but the message is valuable because each citizen of Formosa is a "child of Taiwan" just like me. In whatever difficult environment, Taiwan will be like a selfless, loving mother, who never stops giving her children opportunities and who helps us realize beautiful dreams.

The spirit of the "child of Taiwan" reveals to us that even though Taiwan, Penghu, Kinmen and Matsu are tiny islands on the rim of the Pacific, the map of our dreams knows no limits. The map extends all the way to the horizon as long as our 23 million compatriots fear no hardship and move forward hand in hand.

Dear compatriots, this magnificent moment belongs to all the people. All grace and glory belongs to Taiwan — our eternal Mother. Together, let's extend our gratitude to the earth and respect to the people.

Long live freedom and democracy!

Long live the people of Taiwan!

We pray for the prosperity of the Republic of China, and for the health and happiness of all compatriots and all our distinguished guests!

Source: Information Division, Taipei Economic and Cultural Office, New York, 20 May 2000.

Glossary

AMRAAM	Advanced Medium Range Air-to-Air Missiles
APEC	Asia-Pacific Economic Co-operation
ARATS	Association for Relations Across the Taiwan Strait
ASAT	anti-satellite (warfare)
ASEAN	Association of Southeast Asia Nations
AWACS	airborne warning and control system
CASS	China Academy of Social Sciences
CBM	confidence-building measures
CCP	Chinese Communist Party
CIA	Central Intelligence Agency
CNN	Cable News Network
CWC	Chemical Weapons Convention
DPP	Democratic Progressive Party
E.U.	European Union
EMP	electronic magnetic pulse
ESDP	European Security and Defence Programme
GATT	General Agreement on Tariffs and Trade
GDP	gross domestic product
GPS	global positioning system
IAEA	International Atomic Energy Agency
IDF	indigenous defence fighter
JCP	joint counter-offensive platform
KMT	Kuomintang
LACM	land-attack cruise missiles
MAC	Mainland Affairs Council (Taipei)
MFN	most-favoured-nation
MIRV	Multiple Independent Re-entry Vehicle
MRV	Multiple Re-entry Vehicle
NP	New Party

NAFTA	North American Free Trade Agreement
NATO	North Atlantic Treaty Organization
NMD	National Missile Defence
NPC	National People's Congress
NUC	National Unification Council
PCL	Passive Coherent Location (system)
PFP	People's First Party
PLA	People's Liberation Army
PLAN	PLA Navy
PNTR	permanent normal trade relations
PRC	People's Republic of China
ROC	Republic of China
ROT	Republic of Taiwan
SEF	Strait Exchange Foundation
SSBN	ballistic missile nuclear submarine
SSM	surface-to-surface missiles
TMD	Theatre Missile Defence
WTO	World Trade Organization

Index

About the Author

Sheng Lijun is a Senior Fellow at the Institute of Southeast Asia Studies, Singapore. He received his Master's degree from the Australian National University (ANU) and his Ph.D. from the University of Queensland, Australia. His research focus has been on China's foreign relations, both when he was at the ANU and the Australian Defence Force Academy, and since he joined ISEAS in 1995. He has written extensively on this subject, with articles published in the *Washington Quarterly*, the *Journal of Strategic Studies, Cambridge Review of International Affairs, Security Dialogue, Asian Perspective*, the *Journal of Northeast Asian Studies, Far Eastern Economic Review* (The 5th Column), *Contemporary Southeast Asia, Issues and Studies, Pacific Focus*, and others. He is also the author of *China's Dilemma: The Taiwan Issue* (Singapore: ISEAS/ London & New York: I.B. Tauris Academic Studies, 2001).